MUSEUMS, THEIR HISTORY AND THEIR USE : WITH A BIBLIOGRAPHY AND LIST OF MUSEUMS IN THE UNITED KINGDOM (VOLUME 1)

MUSEUMS, THEIR HISTORY AND THEIR USE : WITH A BIBLIOGRAPHY AND LIST OF MUSEUMS IN THE UNITED KINGDOM (VOLUME 1)

David Murray

General Books

www.General-Books.net

Publication Data:

Title: Museums, Their History and Their Use : With a Bibliography and List of Museums in the United Kingdom
Volume: 1
Author: Murray, David, 1842-1928
Reprinted: 2010, General Books, Memphis, Tennessee, USA
Publisher: Glasgow J. MacLehose
Publication date: 1904
Subjects: Museums
Museums – Bibliography

1

MUSEUMS, THEIR HISTORY AND THEIR USE : WITH A BIBLIOGRAPHY AND LIST OF...

PREFACE.

I Having at various times, during the last thirty years, visited the principal museums of the United Kingdom, of Denmark, Norway and Sweden, Finland and Russia, Austria, Hungary, Germany, Italy, Switzerland, France, Belgium and Holland, the United States and Canada, I was anxious to learn something of the history and development of museums as scientific institutions. Strange to say, however, there is little or nothing bearing upon the subject in the ordinary books of reference. There are only twenty-three lines upon it in the last edition of Chambers' Cyclopatdia; there is no article upon Museums in the last edition of the Encyclopaedia Britannica, but there is a short notice, principally relating to art museums, in the recent supplement to this work. ' Museum" does not appear as a title in Leon Vallee's Bibliographie des bibliographies or Petzholdt's Bibliotheca bibliographic a. " Museums" is not an independent subject in Mr. Fortescue's exhaustive Subject-index of the modern works in the British inIuseum, but is included under "Exhibitions" and "Natural History" and such headings as "Anatomy," "Art," "Ceramics" and the like. The title only casually occurs in Mr. Sonnenschein's valuable Reader s Guide and The Best Books.

I had beside me several of the catalogues of the older collections; amongst others those of Ole Worm's museum and of the Copenhagen museum, Grew's Catalogue of the Rarities belonging to the Royal Society, Sibbald's Auctarinm Musei Balfouriani, Mercati's Metallotheca, the Museo Cospiano, and Aldrovandi's Mtiseum Metallicum. I often consulted them and found both amusement and instruction in turning over their pages, and it seemed to me that from such sources one could learn something of the idea of what a museum ought to be, which the old collectors had, their schemes of classification and the science on which these were based. Working upon these lines, with 1 the help of other catalogues, old and new, and of sundry volumes of travels and general works, I prepared a paper which I read as a Presidential Address to the Glasgow Archaeological Society in the winter of 1897. As I pursued the subject I gradually ascertained that it possessed a considerable literature and my paper grew into the following volume. Substantially, however, it is the same as the original Address, and this explains the local allusions and the prominence given to museums of archaeology. Had I known, when I took up the subject, that so much had already been written upon it, my paper would no doubt have taken a different shape, or, what is more probable, it would not have been written. Previous writers have followed much the same method as I have done. Museum catalogues have supplied their material; the actual catalogues used varying in each case. Each writer, however, seems to have been unaware that he had a predecessor in the same field. After the greater part of this volume had been printed off I therefore thought that it would be useful to future inquirers if I were to add a list of the works cited and of those which I had consulted, so as to provide a tentative bibliography of museums. This list was prepared and printed, but was not satisfactory. Some museums were fully dealt with; others were merely referred to; many were omitted. With this draft to work upon I endeavoured to fill up the blanks, and the work gradually increased from some fifty pages to two volumes. These do not by any means exhaust the subject. It was not my aim to provide a complete bibliography, or to include all the works relating to the general subject or to particular museums, and I have excluded books in the Russian and other less generally known languages. What I have attempted is, in the first place, to give a short list of the books bearing on the bibliography of museums, which I had found useful, that is a bibliography of bibliographies. The list could easily be enlarged, but is probably sufifi-cient for the purpose. The next subject, Museography, is dealt w th more fully, but not exhaustively, and many books have no doubt escaped me. This section is followed by a selection of books on the practical work of museums the collection, preparation, and preservation of specimens, their registration and exhibition. This is a wide field, and I have kept my selection within moderate limits, but have prefixed to the section a short subject-bibliography. The greater part of the second and third volumes is devoted to Catalogues and other works relatino- to particular museums and special collections. The

VIll PREFACE museums and collections dealt with, it should be explained, are those of which there are printed catalogues or descriptions. Museums of which there are no catalogues, or which are not otherwise described in other works, consequently do not appear. Many museums therefore, and some of great importance, are not to be found in the list.

The difficulty there is in getting information regarding museum catalogues will scarcely be credited. As a rule, I ask in every museum I visit whether there is a catalogue or handbook. In very many cases the answer is in the negative. I have been so told repeatedly when I was already in possession of the catalogue. The explanation I found to be that if the catalogue or handbook is out of print it is treated not only as non-existent, but as if it had never existed. Having been unable to get information regarding a certain catalogue I wrote to the Museum for a copy of the title page. I had no reply. In answer to a further application I received this: " We certainly have a small Museum, but have lost all trace of our catalogue since the death of Mr. in., who then was the Curator." Librarians again seem to take little interest in catalogues of museums, except in the case of Art collections, and do not collect them systematically. I have not found in any library, at home or abroad, anything like a complete collection of the published works relating to the museums in the same town. The British Museum possesses far more works on museums in general than any other library with which I am acquainted, but it has not a complete collection of the works relating to itself. I asked in a University museum whether there was a catalogue. I was told that there was not and that there never had been a catalogue. I then went to the University library and examined the catalogue of the library, which is on the card system and is kept up-to-date. The library did not contain a single volume relating to the museum. A printed catalogue of the museum nevertheless exists. In another University Library I went over the catalogue to ascertain what had been published in reference to the museums in the town, and found several entries. The University possesses an excellent museum; but the library had nothinof relating to it; and the librarian told me that he did not think that the museum had issued a catalogue. I walked over to the museum, purchased the catalogue, and brought it back to the library. The librarian promised to make a note of it. In a third library, presided over by one of the leading exponents of the art of cataloguingr, I found that the title " Museum " did not exist in his own catalogue, and that the library did not possess a copy of a "Visitors' Guide" to a well-known museum in the neighbourhood, of which there had been at least two editions.

In the Bibliography the museums are arranged under the towns or places where they are situated, and in the case of private collections under the name of the collector, or of his residence when it is well known. Names of authors are given separately as cross-references.

The term " museum " I have taken in its ordinary English acceptation, and have excluded galleries of painting and sculpture from my lists. Collections of coins are, as a rule, likewise excluded. Numismatics is a specialised subject with an extensive literature and it would have served no good purpose to incorporate catalogues of coin collections in a work dealing with museums generally. When coins or works of ancient art form part of a University or similar collection, I have, however, given shortly the principal works relating to them.

Where there are a number of museums in one town I have endeavoured to keep them distinct and to give separately the works relating to each museum. This, however, is not always possible. One volume often treats of several museums. Museums again change their names or are split up or are absorbed by others. One edition of a book refers to a collection when it was an independent institution: another treats it as part of a larger collection. I have done the best I could to meet these and other difficulties, not altogether successfully I fear, as local knowledge is often necessary to unravel the history of particular museums and collections. In many cases I have spent both time and trouble in identifying under a new name the collection to which some book refers. I have searched numbers of local histories for information of this kind, generally without reward. Few historians concern themselves with details about museums.

Following the bibliography of particular museums and collections, I have given a list of travels and books of a general nature which are cited in the text or which I have consulted. It would have been easy to increase this list, as many books of travel and most guide-books refer, more or less fully, to museums, but a mere enumeration of collections or the repetition of what has been already said by some previous writer is of little use to one who desires special information. As it is, several of the books included are of this character, and are mentioned only because I had passed them through my hands. A considerable number of Travels are referred to in Part IV. as authorities on particular museums. These, as a rule, are not again given in Part V. I have also omitted from this Part the most of the old scientific and oreneral works referred to in Volume I., as not bearing directly upon museums.

The references to the transactions of learned bodies, to journals and other periodical publications have mostly been made ciirrente calamo and generally when I was engraoed in searchino- for other infor-mation. Had I been able to go systematically through several journals of different countries and relating to different branches of science for a series of years, a great deal of additional information would have been obtained, but this would have required an amount of time and opportunity for research far beyond what I could command.

I have endeavoured to give the names of authors in full, a point which involves more trouble than is apparent. I have also, in the majority of cases, given the date of their births and if dead of their deaths, with an indication of their profession or position. This has added much to my labour. Even in the case of names to be found in the

XII PREFACE ordinary biographical dictionaries, it takes some little time to extract the information; but a very large number of those who ficrure in the literature of museums do not appear in such dictionaries and the work of running them to earth is often very tedious, but I ought to add, very fascinating. In some cases I have failed. With plenty of time and with the British Museum behind me I would have been more successful, but to a large extent I have had to depend upon my own library, and in addition time was scant. Engaged all day in an exacting profession and with many of the duties of citizenship to perform, I have never had more than a few hours of the evening- to give to this work; I have had many interruptions, and continuous labour has been impossible.

More errors have crept in than I could have wished. In some cases, in deference to some accepted authority, I have altered names and dates and other particulars which I had in my notes, and have found when too late that my original note was right and that my trusted guide was wrong. In other cases the mistakes are slips or oversights. In dealing with such a multitude of particulars, and with entries in many languages, it is difficult to avoid inaccuracy. The bibliography has been written on the margins and backs of a long series of proof sheets, so that occasionally some things have got out of joint and transcription has been at fault. What has been done I have done myself without assistance of any kind.

Now that the work is finished it is easy to see

PREFACE XIII where it fails and how it could have been improved, but this is incident to most undertakings of the kind and few things would be attempted if one could see at the commencement the difficulties that were to be surmounted and the labour to be encountered. I have written for my own amusement, but I hope not altogether without profit to others. Be this as it may the preparation of the book has given me much pleasure during several years. I have read a great deal of out-of-the-way literature, and have m. ade the acquaintance of a large number of men who were prominent in their day, and with whom I have found it pleasant to hold converse through their books. Some of them have waited long for a reader. I have cut the leaves of, I should say, a score of volumes which have stood unopened on the shelves of various libraries, some for two, some for three hundred years.

Not being a librarian or a bibliographer by profession, I have not felt myself bound by any of the ingenious rules laid down for cataloguing. All such rules are apt to be embarrassing when carried out rigidly, and with long experience of catalogues I have found that they are generally more useful when not too systematic. I have not always been consistent, and there is a satisfaction in not being subject to any formal rule. The French De is a disturbing element. Sometimes I have followed the practice of the British Museum and in other cases I have not. In taking an entry from a catalogue or bibliography one naturally accepts it as given, and as each cataloguer treats the particle as it pleases him it is difficult for a third person to alter J the entries uniformly. I have endeavoured to adopt the form that I thought would be most readily-recognised.

The list of Museums in the United Kingdom is based upon that prepared by the British Museum Association in 1887, which the Association has been CTood enough to allow me to use. I have omitted some of the particulars furnished by them, as being unnecessary for my purpose, and have inserted at the beo; inninor a list of museums in London. A number of museums will be found in the Bibliography which do not occur in the list.

At the end of volume three there is a list of some corrections and of some books accidentally omitted or published since the bibliography was printed.

In conclusion may I be allowed, without undue assumption, to adopt the words of Aldo Manuzio, "Etsi opere in magno fas est obrepere somnum (non enim unius diei labor hie noster, sed multorum annorum, atque interim nee mora nee requies,) sic tamen doleo, ut si possem mutarem singula errata nummo aureo."

DAVID MURRAY.

169 West George Street,

Glasgow, 27th September, 1904.

A Museum, as now understood, is a collection of the monuments of antiquity or of other objects interesting to the scholar and the man of science, arranged and displayed in accordance with scientific method. In its original sense it meant a spot dedicated to the Muses, and secondarily, a place for study and for the intercourse of learned men, or, in other words, a place appropriated to literature and philosophy. By far the most important museum of antiquity was the great institution at Alexandria founded by Ptolem. y Philadelphus in the third century before Christ for the promotion of learning and the support of students. It formed part of the palace and contained cloisters, a public lecture-room and a common hall with botanical and zoological gardens attached. It was supported by a grant from the treasury and was under the superintendence of a priest nominated by the king,

As to the Alexandrine Museum, see Strabo, Geographica xvii. i, 8; Gronovius and Neocorus, De Museo Alexandrino, in Gronovii, Thesaurus Graecariim Antiquitatum, viii. 2741-78; Parthey, Das alexandrinische Museum, Berlin, 1838; Klippel, Ueber das alexandrinische Museum, Gottingen, 1838; Weniger, Das alexandrinische Museum, Berlin, 1875.

and, after Egypt became a Roman province, by the emperor. In the language of modern times it would be called an Academy or perhaps a College or University. After Alexandria passed under Roman rule its prosperity began to decline; its public buildings were allowed to fall into disrepair, its works of art were removed to Italy; and by the end of the fourth century of our era it had well nigh been ruined and the museum closed.

Those authors who undertake to treat of museums in a thorough and exhaustive manner find in Noah's Ark the most complete Museum of Natural History that the world has ever seen. Coming to later times they make sure that King Solomon had a collection of curiosities; and when King Hezekiah in a boastful mood showed the envoys of the King of Babylon all the house of his precious things, the silver and the gold and the spices and the precious oil and all that was found in his treasures, they are certain that he took them round his museum. Some of these objects of interest were thought to have come down to our times, all duly catalogued by Collin de Plancy.- The Cathedral of

Neickelius, i. e. Caspar Friedrich Einckel, "Von dem Ursprung der Kunst- und Naturalien-Kammern," in Muscographia, p. 8, Leipzig, 1727, 4to; Johann Daniel Major, Unvorgreiffliches Bede7icken von Kunst- und Naturalien-Kamvierti itisgemein, Kiel, 1674, 8vo, reprinted by Valentin! in his Museum Museorum, vol. i.; and Valentini himself, in his Museum Museorum, Introduction, vol. i., Franckfurt-a.-M., 1704, fol.; Daniel Wil-helm Moeller, Cotmnentatio de Techtiophysiotameis., p. 199, in Koehler, Sylloge aliquot Scriptorum de bene ordinanda et ornanda Bibliotheca, Francof., 1728, 4to; Koehler, Aitiueisung fiir Reisende gelehrte, p. 217, Frankf., 1762, 8vo; p. 728, Magd., 1810, 8vo.

Dictionnaire critique des Reliques et des Images miraculeuses. Paris, 1821, 8vo, 3 vols.

Milan, says Addison, " is very rich in relics, which run up as high as Daniel, Jonas, and Abraham": and in the ninth century hair from the beard of Noah was shown at Corbie.- The great Abbey of St. Denis possessed a large and curious goblet of rock cr) stal which was formerly in Solomon's temple, a gold and jewelled cup which belonged to King Solomon himself, and a gamahe of white agate on which was impressed the likeness of the Queen of Sheba; and on a column in the nave of San Ambrogio, Milan, travellers are still shown the brazen serpent which was raised by Moses in the wilderness. These learned writers come to firmer ground when they refer to the great collection of animals, drawn from all parts of the world, which Alexander the Great is said to have provided for

"Remarks on Italy," 1701-1703, lvorks, u., p. 13. London, 1811, 8vo.

In the Treasury of Durham was "a piece of the tree under which were the three angels with Abraham," and "a part of the rod of Moses." Raine, Saint Cjithbert, pp. 122, 124. Durham, 1828, 4to.

A wonderful series of the relics of his cloister is catalogued by Angilbert, Abbot of St. Riquier (Abbas Centulensis). Ada SS. O. S. Betiedicti, ed. Mabillon, iv. i. 108.

Abrege de rinventaire dti Trhesor de St. Denys, pp. 12, 14, Paris, 1668, 8vo; Evelyn, Diary., i., p. 45, London, 1879 Valentini, Museum Museorum, ii. Appendix ii., p. 7.

A foot of King Solomon and an arm of the Queen of Sheba were extant until recently, but seem now to have disappeared. VInicrniediaire des Chercjieurs et Curieux, xxii. (1889), 291.

The engraved figures on Gamahes were supposed to be produced directly by nature, and were considered to have peculiar virtues. See post, p. 237. Another theory was that they were made by the children of Israel during their forty years' wanderings in the wilderness. The words gamahe and cameo are the same. The art of cameo cutting was practised by the Egyptians, Greeks, and Romans, but was lost in the Middle Ages. Labarte, Arts of the Middle Ages, p. 52, London, 1855.

Aristotle to enable him to write his natural history, but even if the tradition be well founded this was a zoological garden rather than a museum, which does not admit live specimens.

While the Romans were industrious collectors of statues and paintings they sought after them merely as decorative objects and not for the purpose of cultivating taste, or as instruments for the study and teaching of the arts of design. At first they were employed exclusively for the decoration of temples and places of public resort; but private collections began to be formed and by the close of the Republic it had become fashionable for wealthy citizens to have a room in their houses for the reception and display of works of art. Vitruvius, writing in the time of Augustus, includes the pinacotheca amongst the apartments of a great house and gives directions as to its form and aspect.-

A collection of precious stones was known as a " dactyliotheca"; and according to Pliny, the first person who possessed one at Rome was Scaurus, the stepson of Sulla. For a long time there was no other, until Pompey the Great, amongst other donations, dedicated in the Capitol one which had belonged to King Mithridates. Following his example, Julius Caesar consecrated six collections in the temple of Venus Genetrix, and Marcellus the nephew of Augustus presented one to the temple of the Palatine Apollo.

See Curtius, Kunsttnuseeiij ihre Geschichte und ihre Besti?? iinufig, p. 15, Berlin, 1870, 8vo; Friedlander, Sittetigeschichte Roms, ii., p. 154 sqq., Leipzig, 1881, 5th ed.; Evelyn, Numistnata, p. 69, London, 1697, fol.

"De Architectura, i. 2; vi. 5, 7; cf. Pliny, Hisioria Naiuralis, xxxv. 4; Dezobry, Rofne an Steele ctAugusie, i., p. 92, Paris, 1875, Svo.

Pliny, Hisioria Naturalis, xxxvii. 5; Dezobry, Op. laud., i., p. 289.

Natural objects, such as we call curiosities, had long been preserved in temples, both in Greek and Roman times, not as scientifically interesting but because of their rarity or peculiarity, and Pliny incidentally mentions numerous examples; many of them, it is to be feared, of a very fanciful description, e. g. the bones of the monster to which Andromeda had been exposed, and which had been brought to Rome from Joppa, where the remains of the chains by which she had been fastened to the rock were still to be seen. Suetonius tells us that the villa of Augustus was remarkable not so much for statues and pictures as for things notable by their age and rarity res vettistate ac raiitate iwtabiies), such as the huge members of wild beasts known as the bones of giants, and the weapons of heroes; and there seems

E. g. Historia Naturalis, v. lo; vi. 36 (31); viii. 14; xi. 36 (31); xii. 42 (19); xxviii. 6. Sachse de Lewenheimb, Gammarologia., p. 49. Franc of., 1665, 8vo.

2. N., ix. 4; V. 14.

Vita Augusti, c. 72. See Reinach, "Le Musee de rempereur Auguste," in Revue danthropologie, 1889, p. 28 sqq.

Pliny mentions Historia Natiiralis, vii. 16) that the bones of two very tall men over nine feet in height were kept as curiosities in the gardens of the Sallust family. These gardens belonged to the Emperor Augustus, and the bones in question may have been part of those referred to by Suetonius.

Pliny says they were preserved iti coiditorio, from which it might be assumed that conditorium' was the appropriate term for a cabinet of curiosities. Leibnitz refers to museums as " conditoria renan pere-grinarumr Protogaea, 35, Goetting., 1749, 4to.

5 The latter were objects which the Greeks had been accustomed to display in their temples. The spear of Achilles was preserved in the sanctuary of Athena at Phaselis, and the sword of Memnon in the temple of Esculapius at Xicomedia. Pausanias, iii. 3. 8. The blade and the spike at the butt-end of the spear and the whole of the sword were of bronze, which Pausanias adduces as showing that in the Heroic Age some ground for believino- that Tiberius also had a museum.

In the Middle Ages many monasteries had collections of curiosities, most of them the gifts of travellers on their return from distant lands." Princes and ecclesiastics had collections of the relics of saints which they carried about from place to place in a reliquary, chest or cabinet capelld), and these had a most important bearing on the life of the time in peace as well as in war. "The reliquary was the most precious ornament in the Lady's chamber, in the Knight's armoury, in the King's hall of state, as well as in that of the Bishop or the Pope." It was to relics that men, of a faith altogether material, gave the greatest credence, and they were employed in all solemn acts of justice and administration. The shift of the Virgin, which Charles the Bald had brought with other relics from Constantinople, when displayed upon weapons were all of bronze. Pausanias, Description of Greece, by Frazer, i., p. 136; iii., p. 314.

The expression "arma heroum" has been thought to refer to palaeolithic weapons of stone or weapons of bronze of the prehistoric period. See Reinach, in Revue ctAnthropologic, 1889, p. 28; Reinach, Antiquites natiotiales, i., p. 83; Evans, Ancient Stone Weapons, p. 4 (2nd ed.).

Reinach, Antiquites nationales, i., p. 28, Paris, 1889.

- Lacroix, Science et Lettres au moyen age, pp. 124, 137, Paris, 1877; English translation, pp. no, 114. London, 1878, 8vo.

See Smith, Dictionary of Christian Antiquities, s. v. Relics and Reliquary; Milman, History of Latin Christianity,.,. 153, 154; ix., pp. 84-88. London, 1864, 8vo.

Milman, Op. la7id., x., Y- 84; Lacroix, 6 .a., p. 363 j. London, 1878. De Coulanges, La Monarchic Franque, p. 149, Paris, 1888, 8vo; Du

Cange, Glossarium, s. v. Capella; Spelman, Glossariuin Archaiologicuin, s. v. Capella. Smith, Dictionary of Christian Antiquities, s. vv. Relics, Reliquary, Wonders.

the ramparts of Chartres, brought defeat upon the hitherto all-conquering Rollo. An Eastern king inserted the thumb of St. Sergius in his own right arm, and, as a reward for his faith, was able to conquer his enemies by the raising of that arm." Amongst the relics of Croyland, Abbot Turketul set especial value on the thumb of St. Bartholomew the Apostle, so much so that he always carried it about him, and in all times of danger, tempest, and lightning crossed himself therewith. As Gregory of Tours was travelling from Burgundy to Auvergne a thunderstorm came on; when, plucking some relics from his bosom, he held them up towards the threatening cloud. It at once parted in twain, and the traveller passed on in safety. Every church had its treasury, and most treasuries contained relics many possessed illuminated manuscripts and works of art, often of very early date and of great historic interest, and some of them curiosities

Gulielmus Malmesburiensis, Degestis regjivi Anglorutn, ii. 5.

Gregorius Turonensis, Historia Fraticorum, vii. 31, Opera 355, Lutet., 1699, fol-Ingulphus, Historia Croylandensis, in Gale et Fell, Rerutn Angli-carum Scriptores, i., p. 51, Oxon., 1684, fol.

De Gloria Mariyrum, i. 84, Opera 817. Numerous examples of the same thing are recorded by the hagiographers, e. g. Acta SS. O. S. Bene-diciti, ed. Mabillon, iii. 2, 438.

See the very interesting Inventory of Relics which belonged to the Cathedral of Durham in 1383. Raine, Saitit Cuthbert., pp. 120-130. Durham, 1828, 4to. The relics of Durham were, in the Middle Ages, one of its most striking features. See poem in Hickes, Thesaurus, i., p. 179. Oxon., 1705, fol.

The older authorities are conveniently collected in Von Schlosser, Quellenbuch zur Kunstgeschichte des abetidliindischen Mittelalters. Wien, 1896, 8vo. As a later example see Ingulph's description of the treasury of Croyland, supra.

and rarities brought home by pilgrims or travellers. In some churches," says Durandus, "two eggs of ostriches and other things of the like kind, which cause admiration and which are rarely seen, are accustomed to be suspended, that by their means the people may be drawn to church and have their minds the more affected." This practice was more common in the East than in the West, and is still continued in both Christian churches and Mohammedan mosques. There are, however, examples of it in the West. An ostrich Qgg, for instance, used to hang in the old Dom of Goslar in the Harz; while the griffin's eggs, which appear in many church inventories of the Middle Ages,

Otte, Handbuch der kirchlidien Kitnst-Archdologie, p. 48, Leipzig, 1854, 8vo; i., p. 213, Leipzig, 1883, 8vo. Klemm, Geschicjite der Satnnlungen fur IVissetisciaft und Kttnst in Deutscjiland, p. 142, Zerbst, 1837, 8vo. Milman, Op. laud., iv., p. 171; ix., p. 86.

2 Rationale divi7ioriim Officiorutn, i. 3, 42.

Durandus is not altogether satisfied with this explanation, and 43 suggests another: " Again some say that the ostrich, as being a forgetful bird, leaveth her eggs in the dust Job xxxix. 14, and at length when she beholdeth a certain star returneth unto them, and cheereth them by her presence. Therefore the eggs of ostriches are hung in churches to signify that man, being left by God on account of his sins, if at length he be illumined by the Divine Light, remembereth his faults and returneth to Him, who by looking on him His mercy cherisheth him."

A. and Q., 3rd S. iv. 470; 5th S. xii. 46; 8th S. v. 434; vi. 57. Tozer, Visit to Mount Athosj Vacation Tourists, p. 103; Burnaby, On Horseback through Asia Minor, i., p. 310; Valentini, Museum Museoru7n, vol. ii., Appendix xxi., p. 87. Franckfurt-a.-M., 1714, fol.

R.2i nq, Sai7it Cuthbert, p. 122; Meyers, Konversations-Lexikon, s. v. Greif. Amongst the relics belonging to the Cathedral of Durham were several griffin's eggs. Raine, Saint Cuthbert, pp. 123, 125, 127, 128.

An ostrich egg was often used as a stand for a reliquary. The egg, clasped in a metal ring, rested on a metal foot, and the reliquary stood on the top attached to the ring. There are two in the Welfen Museum, Hanover; one in the treasury of Quedlinburg; two at Hildesheim, one of them dating from the eleventh century; and there are many elsewhere.

are believed to have been ostrich eggs. But other rarities were to be found, and their use goes to strengthen the suggestion of Durandus that they were kept as attractions. Thus, in the porch of the Cathedral of Merseburg, on the Saale, there is a large carapace of a tortoise. There are "antediluvian" (vorsilnd-fluthliche) bones in the church of St. Kilian, at Heilbronn, in Wurtemberg, and in the old Romanesque church of Alpirsbach, in the Black Forest. One hangs in the western entrance of the Cathedral of Halberstadt, and used to be passed off as one of the bones of Jonah's whale; while on the wall opposite it hangs a thunderbolt, or as we would now say, a stone axe, which was kept as a protection against drought and lightning. In the sacristy of the Cathedral of Brunswick there is the horn of an antelope, which Duke Henry the Lion (1129-1195) brought back from Palestine as being the claw of a griffin. In the church of St. Michael, in Hildesheim, another griffin's claw was exhibited, which was in reality a goat's horn, and two others were to be seen in a church near Helmstadt. In the Schloss-Kirche of Witten-

Briickmann, Epistola Itineraria, 53, Cent. i. There was also preserved in this church the hand which Rudolph of Suabia lost in battle with the Emperor Henry IV. Briickmann, Op. laud., 49, Cent. i.

- Otte, Op. laud.

Hermes, Der Dom zii Halberstadt, p. 50, Halberstadt, 1896, 8vo. It is mentioned in the Catalogue of Davila's Museum, iii., p. 15.

A large axe of jade was found in 1884 on one of the tie-beams in the roof of a granary belonging to the old Cistercian nunnery, known as Martha's Hof, in Bonn. Bonnerjahrbucher, xx. (1884), p. 216; Ixxix. (1885), p. 280.

Oi. e, utsupra. See Tylor, Early History 0Mankind, p. 319, 3rd ed.; Y. vzx s, Ani7nal Synbolismin Ecclesiastical Architecture,". 106. Lond., 1896. There is an interesting note on the griffin in Frazer's Pausanias, ii., p. 318.

Bartholin, Epistolae niedicinales. Cent, ii., Ep. 11, p. 339.

lo RARITIES IN CHURCHES here on whose doors Luther affixed his famous theses two whale ribs were suspended, when Faber wrote in 1717, which were said to have been brought from the Holy Land, but which in fact belonged to a whale thrown up on the shores of the Baltic. Above them hung a hunting horn reputed to be made of a griffin's claw also brought from the Holy Land The treasury of Durham Cathedral possessed two such claws." In the church of St. Nicholas at Juterbog, in Brandenburg, there is the rib of a whale, In the choir of the parish church of Ensisheim, in Upper Alsace, there is a portion of a meteorite, which fell in 1492 and weighed 260 pounds." In the parish

Matthaeus Faber, Kurtzgefasste historische Nachricht von der Schloss-Kirche in Wittenberg, pp. 140-142. Wittenberg, 1717, 8vo.

At p. 191 sqq. he gives a curious list of the Relics preserved in the Treasury.

2 Raine, Saint Cuthbert, p. 122.

Otte, ut supra.

There is also preserved in this church one of the Indulgence boxes of Friar Tetzel, "der Ablasskramer." He was waylaid in a wood near the convent of Zinna by a robber Knight, Hans von Hacke, as he was carrying it home filled with gold, the produce of the pardons he had sold.

There is another such bo. x in the cathedral of Magdeburg.

Gesner, De reriim fossilitim, lafidiun et gemtnaricm Liber, f. 66, Tiguri, 1565, 8vo; Chladni, Ueber Feuer-Meteore, pp. xvi., 90, 205, 427, Wien, 1819, 8vo; Leonhard, Geologic, iv., p. 177. Stuttgart, 1841, 8vo.

The Emperor Maximilian, arriving at Ensisheim shortly after the fall, presented a fragment to the Archduke Sigismund, retained another for himself, and deposited the remainder in the parish church.

During the Revolution the stone was taken from the church and placed in the public library of Colmar. Fragments were broken off and presented to various persons and institutions. Fourcroy obtained a piece of 9 kilos, for the Museum of Natural History, Paris. The remainder was afterwards returned to Ensisheim. Chladni, supra. Meunir, "Notice historique sur la collection de Meteorites du musdum dhistoire naturelle," in Centenaire de la fondation du Museum dhistoire nalurelle, p. 403, Paris, 1893, 4to.

church of Petty, on the Moray Frith, the bones of a iant, known as " Httle John," were still preserved in the sixteenth century. Giants' bones were preserved in the Cathedral of Vienna. Boccaccio records that, in his day, in the church of the Annunciation in Trapani, in Sicily, three teeth weighing a hundred ounces, of an enormous giant of 200 cubits in height, were hung up on wire. Certain elephants' tusks, found in 1605, were suspended in the church at Halle In the church of St. Vulfran, in Abbeville, a cayman is suspended on the wall near the north-west door. The drinking horn and fork of Charlemagne are still shown in the treasury of Hildesheim. In the treasury of St. Denis there were the horn of a unicorn, the claw of a griffin presented to Charlemagne in the year 807 by King Aaron of Persia, and two tusks of a walrus or hippopotamus

The Historic of Scotland by Leslie. Translated in Scottish by Dal-rymple, i., p. 46. Edinburgh, 1888, 8vo.

2 Briickmann, Epistolae liinerariae, 5 and 12, Cent, i., Wolfenb., 1729, 4to. Also in the Kreuz Kirche of Breslau, Kundmann, Promtuariujn, p. 12, Vratislav., 1726, 4to; but no longer to be seen there.

De Genealogia Deorufn, Lib. iv., c. 68, p. 115, Basil., 1532, fol. Boccaccio gives a most graphic account of the finding of the giant sitting in a cave, and of his resolving into dust when touched. Nothing was left but these teeth and part of the skull.

As to other giants' teeth, see Briickmann, Op. laud.

Hoffmann, Dissertatio itiauguralis physico-medica de ebore fossili Suevico Halensi, p. 8. Hal. Magd., 1734, 4to.

A. and Q., 8th S. vi. 512; Joanne, Itin raire gmeralde la France Le Nord, p. 35. Paris, 1892.

This was a famous specimen duly described and commented on by writers on the unicorn. See Bartholinus, De Unicornu, p. 250, Amstel., 1678, i2mo; Historiariim anatomicariim Rariora, Cent, iv., 4, p. 217.

There were two similar horns in the Treasury of St. Mark, Venice. Bartholinus, De Ufticornu, p. 253.

presented to the Abbey by David, King of Scotland, probably indicating that there had been a find of fossil ivory in this country at the time. In the treasury of St. Mark in Venice " they shew you likewise a lilly, offerd by Henry III, of France to the most Serene Republic, and a surprizing pearl, calld mother-pearl, and several things of that nature."- The acquisition of articles prompted by piety or superstition was no doubt on a different footing from collecting for purposes of instruction or study, but it stimulated the taste for collecting, and secured the preservation of numerous interesting objects. The treasuries of many foreign churches still contain some of the finest existing examples of ancient art, and many of those beautiful and valuable objects which now adorn our great museums at one time belonged to churches.

"Abrege de PInventaire du Trhesor de St. Deiiys, p. 25, Paris, 1668, 8vo; Valentini, Museum Museoriim, ii., Appendix ii., p. 7. " Deux dents dun cheval marin de grandeur prodigieuse," according to the official Inventory. " Zwei tiberaus grosse dentes Hippopotami," in Valentini's version.

Montfaucon, The Antiquities of Italy, translated by Henley, p. 40. London, 1725, fol.

The revival of learning in the fifteenth century led to a passionate admiration for the monuments of classical antiquity, and to an eager desire for their acquisition and preservation. Cosmo, and afterwards Lorenzo de Medici, stood forward as the patrons of the new learning, assisted and encouraged the numerous scholars who made Florence famous. Popes, princes and magistrates promoted and carried on vast excavations on ancient sites. Between the years 1450 and 1550, an immense number of antiquities were unearthed in Rome and its neighbourhood, and many palaces were filled with them. Coins and medals were especially attractive to men filled with the new enthusiasm for art and antiquity. Petrarch was a coin collector; Politian used coins as vouchers of ancient orthography and customs, Benedetto Dandolo is said to have been the first to

Fiorillo, Geschichte der zeichietiden Kiiiiste, i. 125 sqq.; ii. 48 sqg., Gottingen, 1798, 8vo; Gregorovius, Rovie in the Middle Ages vii., p. 588 sqq., London, 1900, 8vo; Miintz, Des Antiquites de la Ville de Rome, p. 53 sqq., Paris, 1886, 8vo. The estimates of the number of statues found at Rome vary from 6o, cxx) to 170,000. Miiller, Attcietit Alt and its Remains, 261, London, 1852, 8vo.

form a cabinet of coins. Cardinal Pietro Barbo, afterwards Pope Paul II., was a specialist in this branch of antiquity, which was pursued by Pietro Tommasi, Ciambatista Egnazio, and Cardinal Domenico Grimani (1460-1523). The museum collected by the latter and added to by his nephew Giovanni, was so extensive that when Alfonso, Duke of Ferrara, and Henry III. of France visited Venice in 1574, it took them a whole day to look over it. Gian Vincenzo Pinelli (i535-1601) is best known as a book collector, and his magnificent library was long celebrated, but he had also a museum of crlobes, mathematical and philosophical instruments, fossils, natural objects, and coins, which was acquired after his death by Cardinal Federigfo Borromeo. The formation of cabinets of coins and medals grew apace, and by the middle of the sixteenth century, there were 200 in the Low Countries, 175 in Germany, more than 380 in Italy,

The catalogue of part of his collections has been printed by Eugene Mlintz in Revue Archeologique, xxxvi., N. S., p. 87, Paris, 1878, 8vo; Zeitschrift fiir Museologie, 1878, No. 16.

- Fiorillo, Geschichte der zeichnenden Kiinste, ii. 56; Tiraboschi, Storia delta Letteratura Italiana, wu., t. 342. Milano, 1824. Pflaumern, il r-curius Italicus, Partii., p. 58. August. Vindel., 1650, i2mo. Montfaucon, The Antiquities of Italy translated by Henley, p. 29. London, 1725, fol.

An account of the collection was published at Venice in 1497; and again Courte description dcs choses plus remarquables du Palais Grimani a Sainte Marie Formosa, Svo, n. p., n. d.

The Pinelli library, formed by another member of the family, purchased in 1788 by James Robson, was sold by auction in London in 1789. Nichols, Literary Anecdotes of the Eighteenth Century, v., p. 324; iii., pp. 438, 735; The Gentleman's Magazine, lix., Part L (1789), p. 69.

Tiraboschi, Storia delta letteratura Jtaliana, vii., p. 356.

Hubert Goltz in his C. Ivtivs Caesar sive Historiae hnperatorvm Caesarvmque Romanortim ex antiqvis numismatibvs restitvtae, Brug., 1563, fol., enumerates the collectors to whom he was indebted for information and assistance.

and about 200 in France. Engraved gems were specially coveted and many collections were made. The first English collector was Thomas Howard, Earl of Arundel (1586-1646). whom Horace Walpole calls the Father of Vertu in Eno-land." It was he who brought together the magnificent collection of intaglios and cameos long known as "The Marlborough Gems"; the Arundel MSS., now in the British Museum; and the "Marmora Arundeliana," one of the ornaments of Oxford.

The value of inscriptions had long been recognised, and from the seventh century onwards, pilgrims to Rome had been in the habit of noting such as they met with and carrying home their transcripts for preservation.- The scholars of the Renaissance, 1 Evelyn, writing in 1689, laments that there was no collection of coins in England, Diary, iii., p. 442, London, 1879; and Zedler, when enumerating, in 1739, the principal cabinets of Europe does not mention one in this country. Universal Lexicon, s. v. Aliintz-Kabinet.

In 1719-20, however, Nicolas Haym, an Italian musician, published at London (4to, 2 vols.) his Tesoro Britannico, in which he proposed to describe all coins, gems, statues and other works of art to be found in the cabinets of England and not hitherto described. The work was intended to extend to about 12 quarto volumes. In 1746 the Catalogue of the Collection Cinielinin) of Thomas, Earl of Pembroke, appeared in 4 vols. 4to infra, p. 137), and in 1750 that of the Bodley Collection at Oxford. In 1780 the Marlborough gems were described, Choix de pierres antiques gravccs dii Cabinet du Due de Marlborough, 1780-91, fol., 2 vols.

The earliest collection, of this description, is one made in the eighth or ninth century which is preserved in the monastery of Einsiedeln and was published by Mabillon, Analecta, p. 358 sqq., Paris, 1723, fol., but which first appeared at Paris, 1675-85, in 4 vols. 8vo. The collection was subsequently edited by Haenel, in Seebode und Jahn, Archiv fiir Philologie und Paedagogik, v., idisic. i., p. 116. See C. I. L., vi., pt. i., p. viii.; De Rossi, Inscriptioties Christianae Urbis Romae, ii., pt. i., p. 9 sqq., and pp. 15, 47, 159; Jordan, Topographie der Stadt Rom im Alterthicm, ii., pp. 330 sqq., 6 6 sqq. Berlin, 1871.

Pastrengo, Poggio, and Signorili, devoted themselves to the systematic search for and transcription of epigraphic monuments in Italy, while Cyriaco of Ancona, the earliest of scientific travellers, travelled abroad under the patronage of Pope Nicholas V., for the purpose of making collections in foreign lands. Criticism, no doubt imperfect but at all events earnest, followed upon collection. Flavio Biondo (1388-1463), the Secretary of Eugenius IV., described the monuments of ancient Rome in various works commencing in 1449. He was followed by Andrea Fulvio, the contemporary of Raphael, and somewhat later by Bartolomeo Marliani. The accomplished Venetian humanist, Ermolao Barbaro, Patriarch of Aquileia (1454-1495), "unus ex reliquiis aurei saeculi," turned inscriptions to account in interpreting the classics and amending texts." The celebrated Cardinal Bembo (1470-1547) formed a museum in which were several fragments of bronze tables on which certain ancient laws were engfraved which have been of great service to jurists and

Fiorillo, Op. laud., i. 126. Tiraboschi, Storia della Letterauira Italiana, vi., p. 178 sqq. His family name was Pizzicoui.

Romae Topographia, Romae, 1534, 8vo; and 1544, folio, with wood cuts; Basileae, 1550, fol., and Venetiis, 1588, fol. It has found a place in the great Thesmirus of Graevius, vol. iii., p. 54 sqq.

"Voxxtx-AW, Epistolae., Lib. ii., Epist. 9, p. 59, Amstelod., 1542, i2mo; cf. Lib. i., Epist. 6; Lib. ix., Epist. 4; Lib. v., Epist. i.

His Castigationes Plinianae were printed at Rome, 1492, fol., and often subsequently. He was a good Grecian and translated several portions of the works of Aristotle. The story goes that, being puzzled by the word evt 4x La, he consulted the devil as to the meaning, and received as answer, " perfectihabia." Leibnitz, however, defends his rendering Theo-dicee, par. i., 87), and says that he owed it to good scholarship and not to an evil spirit.

philologists. The first comprehensive printed Corpus of Inscriptions' was the work of two professors of Ineolstadt, the mathematician Peter Apianus and the poet Bartholomew Amantius, and was published in 1534 at the expense of Raimund von Fugger, baron of Kirchberg. The study of coins was placed upon a scientific basis, and the foundations of numismatics were laid by the writings of two learned Venetians, Enea Vico and Sebastian

Tiraboschi, Op. land., vii., pp. 344, 369; Fiorillo, Op. laud., ii., p. 53. On the Cardinal's death they were sold and dispersed. One has disappeared, two are at Vienna, and the remainder in the Museo Borbonico at Naples. See C. I. L., i. 49-54.

2 The first printed collection of Inscriptions was that of Desiderio Spreti for Ravenna (Venet., 1489, 4to). Then followed those of Konrad Peutinger, the proprietor of the MS. of the famous Roman Itinerary known as the Tabula Peuti7igcria7ia, for Augsburg (Augsb., 1505, fol.), of which a second edition appeared in 1520 (Mainz, 1520, fol.), and in the same year the collection of Johann Huttich in his work on the Antiquities of Mainz (1520, fol.). Francesco Albertini collected those for Rome in his Mirabilia Romac, 1520, 4to, of which earlier editions had been published in 1508, 1510, 1515, and 1519. It was re-edited by Schmarsow, Heilbronn, 1886, 8vo.

Originally Bienewitz which he rendered Apianus, after the fashion of the time. He was one of the earliest writers on the methods of arithmetic by means of the Arabic numerals.

Augustus de Morgan doubts whether Apianus was the author or only the printer of the Inscriptiones. The Biographical Dictionary of the Society for the diffusiott of useful Knowledge, iii., s. v. Apianus. But there seems no foundation for the doubt. The name of Apianus appears on the title page as author as well as printer. Both sign the dedication. See also Dr. Siegmund Giinther, Peter and Philipp Apia? t, p. 13, Prag, 1882, 4to, in the Abhandlungen der Konigl. bohmischen Gesellschaft der IVissen-schaften, vol. xi., 6th series, 1882; and note by David Clement in his Bibliotheque curieuse, i., p. 402, Gottingen, 1750, 4to.

Fiorillo, Geschichte der zeichnenden Kilnste, ii. 57; Tiraboschi, Storia delta Letteratura Italiana., vii., pp. 1248, 1249.

The cabinet of Erizzo was preserved in the family of Capello. Spon, Voyage dltalie, de Dahnatie, c., i., p. 74. Lyon, 1678.

Echinus or Erizzo, which they gave to the world in 1555 and 1559. In 1601 Abraham Gorlee of Delft published his Dactyliotheca which for upwards of a century remained the standard authority upon rings, seals, and gems. Nearly every subject of classical antiquity was treated more or less exhaustively by various scholars during the sixteenth and seventeenth centuries, and their monographs were subsequently brought together and methodically arranged in the portly volumes of Graevius and Gronovius, Sallengre and Polenus, which still remain cyclopean monuments of industry and learning, and indispensable aids in any exhaustive antiquarian inquiry.

The vast treasures of art which had been recovered in Italy were gradually absorbed into special collections and formed the foundation of the museums of the Vatican and the Lateran at Rome, of the museum of Florence and of those of Vienna, Dresden, Munich, Paris, St. Petersburg, and London.

Some copies bear date 1605, and others 1609. James Gronovius prepared a new edition which appeared in 1695 (2 vols. 4to), and again in 1707. The plates without the text were published at Paris in 1778.

2 It has been said that the learned preface to the Dactyliotheca was written by Aelius Everhard Vorst, and that Gorlee was ignorant of the Latin language. Bayle, Dictionnaire, vii., p. 158 (ed. 1820). His knowledge of Latin was limited, but he had a thorough knowledge of his subject. Gassendi, Vita Peirescii, p. 55, Hag. Com., 1655, 4to; Stark, Hatidbuch der Archdologie der Kunsf, p. 122. There seems to be no sufficient foundation for depriving him of his own preface.

Dr. John Bargrave who visited Rome on four occasions between 1646 and 1660 mentions that statues of marble or bronze were constantly being unearthed, and that " the Pope's, and every Cardinal's and Prince's pallaces are nobly adorned with them." He himself made a small collection which he bequeathed to the Cathedral library, Canterbury. Pope Alexander the Seventh. by John Bargrave, D. D., with a Catalogue of Dr. Bargrav s Museum, p. 115. The Camden Society, 1867, No. xcii.

While humanism was spreading in every land and literature was becoming a profession, the objects of animated nature and the phenomena of the material world were beoinninof to be regarded with scientific interest. Aristotle and Theophrastus, Pliny and Dioscorides still reigned as masters in natural history, but more exact observation was correcting and expanding their statements and creating a new science. "It is not to be esteemed a small matter," says Bacon, "that by the voyages and travels of these later times, so much more of nature has been dis-

Gitnther Christoph Schelhanimer (1649-1716), professor of the practice of medicine at Kiel, a prodigy of learning, vigorously defended, in the early part of the eighteenth century, Aristotle's opinion that all metals are the products of exhalations. C. S. Scheffel, Via Schelhammeri, p. 37, in G. C. Schelhammerum Epistolae Selectiores, W sm2ir, 1727,8vo. Aristotle's opinion will be found, Meteorologica, iii. 7; iv. 8. Exhalations are of two kinds, fuliginous and vaporous; from the former are generated fossils opvkTo.) which are of a stony nature, such as ochre, sulphur, vermilion, and the like. From vaporous exhalations metals are generated.

In medicine, Schelhammer followed the system of the peripatetics and opposed Van Helmont, Descartes, Sylvius, and Stahl, covered than was known at any former period. It would, indeed, be disgraceful to mankind, if, after such tracts of the material world have been laid open which were unknown in former times so many-seas traversed so many countries explored so many stars discovered philosophy, or the intelligible world, should be circumscribed by the same boundaries as J before."

The opening up of the sea route to India, the discovery of the New World, the founding of factories and trading stations in the East and West Indies and on the American continent, and the establishment of missions by the Church amongst heathen nations brought Europeans into touch with many remote lands, and enabled them to become acquainted with their natural productions, with the manufactures, the dresses, the tools and weapons of their people, and a traffic in the rarities and curiosities of Eastern Asia soon sprang up.

The naturalists of the sixteenth and seventeenth centuries were as unwearied in their search after rocks and minerals, flowers and plants, as were scholars in digging up antiques. Collections of natural objects became as common as collections of works of art and the two were often included in the one repository. Maistre Pierre Borel of Castres (1614-1671), the biographer of Descartes, who had himself a considerable museum, published in 1649 a roll of the principal cabinets of curiosities in the chief towns of Europe in alphabetical order.- Fol-

The dates are taken from the Notice of Maistre Pierre Borel by Ch. Pradel in his edition of Les Atitiquitez de Castres.

"Rooue des Principaux Cabinets curieux, et autres choses remarqu- lowing his example Dr. Jacob Spon of Lyons (1647-1685), who too was a collector gives similar and somewhat extended lists. Philipp Jakob Sachse von Lowenheim of Breslau (1627-1672), another collector, in his very curious Tajufxapoxoyia, shortly describes all the more important collections of his day, largely from personal inspection and apparently without any knowledge of Borel's list. This was added to by Johann Daniel Major of Kiel (1634-1693), writing in 1670; Everhard Werner ables qui se voyent ez principales Villes de lEurope. Redige par ordre Alphabetique" in Les Antiqnitez, Raretez. de la Ville et Co? nte de Castres dalbtgeois, pp. 124-131, Castres, 1649, 8vo; ed. Pradel, pp. 137-145. Paris, 1868, i2mo.

Discours sur une piece antiqtie et curieuse du Cabinet de Jacob Spon. Lyon, 1674, i2mo. Reference is made to other objects belonging to himself in his Recherches curieuses dantiquite. Lyon, 1683, 4to. Post, p. 125.

2 In his Recherche des Antiqtiites et Curiosites de la Ville de Lyon, Lyon, 1673, i2mo, reprinted 1676 and 1857, he gives lists of (i) Collectors in Lyons, (2) Collectors in Paris, and (3) Collectors and Antiquaries in other towns of Europe. The Paris portion was reprinted at Paris in 1866. In his Voyage ditalic, de Dahiiatie, c., he gives a list of the principal collections in Rome, i., pp. 39 sqq., 388 sqq. Lyon, 1678, i2mo.

Responsoria Dissertatio de miranda Lapidum Natura, p. 59, in Johann Daniel Major's Dissertatio Epistolica de cancris et serpentibus petrefactis, Jenae, 1664, 8vo, which is a long epistle to Sachse von Lowenheim.

TAMMAPOAOria sine Gaimnaroriini, viilgo Cancroricm consideratio, pp. 46-53. Francof. et Lipsiae, 1665, 8vo. Some correspondence passed between Sachse von Lowenheim and Thomas Bartholin. See Bartholin, Epistolae medicinales, Cent, iv., Epist. 15, 16, 35, 36, 62, 63. Hag. Com., 1740, i2mo.

See-Farth 7iach derneuen Welt ohtie Schiff- und Segel, p. 86, Hamburg, 1683. i2mo. The first edition (Kiel, 1670, 4to) is very inconvenient for reference from want of pagination. See also the list in his Unvorgreif-fliches Bedencken von Kunst- und Aaturalien-Kamjnern insgemein, Kiel, 1674, fol., reprinted by Valentini in his Museum Museorum, vol. i., Francof., 1704, fol.

As to Major, see Renauldin, Les medicins numistnatistes, p. 302 sqq. Paris 1852, 8vo.

Happel (1647-90) about the same time gives a detailed description of a considerable number; Sir Robert Sibbald (1641-1722) gives a short account of those known to him.- Daniel Wilhelm Moeller (1642-17 12) mentions the principal museums of his time; Caspar Friedrich Einckel, a merchant of Hamburg, (who wrote under the pseudonym

Neickelius,) a few years afterwards, gives another long list which is added to by his editor. Johann Kanold (1679-1729); and Michael Bernhard Valentini of Giessen enumerates many others. Professor Beckmann of Gottingen (1739-1811) treats of " Collections of Natural Curiosities " in his History of Inventions y Discoveries, and Origins, and gives many

Grosseste Denkwurdigkeitefi der Welt, oder sogenarmte Relationes Curiosae, part iii., 117-139, Hamburg, 1687, 4to.

Auctarium Musaei Balfouriaiii e Musaeo Sibbaldiano, pp. i., vii., Edinburgh, 1697, i2mo.

Conwientatio de Technophysiotafueis, p. 228 (1704), in Koehler, Sylloge aliquot Scriptorutn de bene ordinanda et ornanda Bibliotheca, Francof., 1728, 4to.

The Cotmnentatio as originally published appeared as a Thesis to be defended, under the presidency of Moeller, by Friedrich Sigismund Wurffbain (whose name appears on other theses at Altdorf in 1702, and Basle in 1707), Dissertatio de Technophysiotajneis. quani. defenders annitetur. Fridericus Sigismundus Wurffbain. Altdorf, 1704, 4to.

Museographia,. 18 sqq.,". 138 sqq.,-. 181 sqq., Leipzig, 1727, 4to. As to Neickelius, see Lesser in Hamburgisches Magazin, iii. (1748), p. 560.

In the Musetim Museorujti, Appendices to vol. ii., Franckfurt, 1714, fol. Several of Valentini's lists are taken from Edward Brown, M. D., Durch Niederland, Teiitschland, Hungaren. Reiseti (Niirnberg, 1686, 4to), the German version of Dr. Edward Brown's Travels in Divers Parts of Europe (London, 1673, 1679, 4to; 1685, fol.); and, as mentioned above, he has reprinted in his first volume, p. 19, J. D. Major's list of 1674.

Beytrdge zur Geschichte der Erfindungen, Leipzig, 1780-1805,8vo, 5 vols.; curious particulars regarding them; while, so far as concerns German museums, Hirsching (i762-1800) Meusel (1743-1820), Klemm (1802-1867), and the Berlin Handbook of Museums' bring down our information to the present time. Johann Craft Hiegel of Mainz, physician to the Elector of Treves, was amongst the first to give a bibliography of museums.

Bd. ii., 3 Stiick, p. 364 sqq., Leipzig, 1786, 8vo; English translation, i., p. 282 sqq. i London, 1846, 8vo. The translation has not been made from the latest German edition, and lacks some of the author's notes.

Friedrich Karl Gottlob Hirsching, Nachrichten vofi sehenswiirdigen Gemalde- und Kiipferstichsammlhnge? i, Afiinz-, Gemtnen-, Kuttst- und Naturalienkabineten, Sammlungen von Modellen, Maschinen, physikal-ischen und matliejnatischen Instrutnenten, anatoniischen Prdparaten und botanischen Garten in Teutschland nach alphabetischer Ordnung der Stddte. Erlangen, 1786-92, 6 vols., 8vo.

Johann Georg Meusel, "Verzeichniss sehenswlirdiger Bibliotheken, Kunst-, Miinz-, und Naturalienkabinette in Teutschland und in der Schweiz," in the third volume of his Tciitscjies Kunstlerlexicoti 2nd edition, Lemgo, 1808-14, 8vo, 3 vols.

Gustav Klemm, Ztir Geschichte der Sammlungen fiir IVissenschaft und Kunst in Deutsckland, Zerbst, 1837, 8vo.

Kunsthandbuch fiir Detitschland, Berlin, 1897, 8vo, fifth edition by Dr. Ferdinand Laban, librarian of the Royal Museums, Berlin.

In his Museii7n Hiegelianum, Confluent, 1714 4to. This is a short account of part of his museum which, besides paintings, engravings, statues, and other works of art, contained costumes and utensils of various peoples, physical and mathematical instruments, and specimens of Natural History. There is prefixed a selected list of books in his library, bearing on the subject of the Catalogue, which includes a large number of the books then published relating to museums. In an earlier work, Collectaneoru7H tiaturae artis et afitiquitatis Specitneti priynuni, Mogunt., 1687, 4to,. with 5 plates, he dealt with the sepulchral urns found in the neighbourhood of Mainz.

Hiegel is mentioned by Baier, Sciagraphia Musei sui, p. 21; and James Petiver infra, p. 135) was indebted to him for various fossils.

Neickelius in his Mtiseographia also gives a short bibliography of Museums. Tiraboschi Storia delta Letteratura Jtaliana, vii., p. 901; Spon, Voyage dltalie, de Daltnatie, Qrc., p. i., p. 68, Lyon, 1678, i2mo.

Lists of works relating to Museums, particularly those of Natural

Amongst the early naturalists who had collections of specimens of natural history and other objects, were Henry Cornelius Agrippa von Nettesheym (1486-1535), best known as the author of Three Books of Occuli Philosophy and of The Vanity of Sciences and Arts; Nicolas Monardes of Seville (d. 1578); Paracelsus (1493-1541); Georg Agricola (properly Bauer, 1494-1555), the father of mineralogy, and whose writings induced the Elector

History, will be found in Boehmer, Bibliotheca Scriptorum historiae naturalis i., p. 369 sqq. Lipsiae, 1785, 8vo; Dryander, Catalogus Bibliothecae Historico-Naturalis Josephi Banks, i. 217, and in various parts of the other volumes, London, 1796-1800, 8vo, 5 vols.; Engelmann, Bibliotheca Historico-Naturalis, p. 4 sqq., Leipzig, 1846; Bibliotheca Zoologica, i., p. 3 sqq., Leipzig, 1861.

For the literature of anatomical and pathological museums, see Index Catalogue of the Library of the Surgeon Generavs Office United States Army, vol. ix., pp. 581-589, Washington, 1888; Catalogue of the Library of the Royal Medical and Chirurgical Society, London, vol. ii., s. v. Museums, London, 1879.

He was the author of various works; amongst others, Simplicitim Medicainentortim ex Novo Orbe delatorum, quorum in Medicina usus est, Historia (Antwerp 1579, and in 1574), originally published in Spanish in 1565; translated into Latin by Clusius, and into English from the Spanish by John Frampton, a Spanish merchant, and published in 1577 with woodcuts; Pulteney, Sketches of the Progress of Botany, i., p. 114.

The date of his birth is usually but erroneously stated to be 1490, and his family name Ackermann or Landmann. See Herzog in Afitthcilungen des Freiberger Alterthumsvereiiis, 1865, p. 365, Freiberg, 1866, 8vo.

"What Conrad Gesner," says Cuvier, "was to zoology, Agricola was to mineralogy." Schelhammer styles him " Decus universae Germaniae, deque re metallica optime meritus," Note on Conringii, In universam artein medicam Introductio, p. 287, Spirae, 1688, 4to. As to his scientific position, see G. H. Jacobi, Der Mineralog Georgius Agricola, und sein Verhdltnis zur Wissenschaft seiner Zeit, Werdau, 1889. A new edition of his works, edited by Lehmann, appeared at Freyberg as recently as 1806-1813, in 4 vols., 8vo. The De re metallica was published at Basle, in 1546, 1556,

1558, 1561, and 1657, in folio; and there were numerous other editions and German translations (1557 and 1621).

Augustus of Saxony (1552-1586) to form a collection (Kunst und Naturalien Kammer), which has since developed into the various museums at Dresden; Valerius Cordus (1515-1544), the botanist, "felicissimus indagator herbarum antea ignotarum"; Pier Andrea Mattioli of Sienna (i501-1577), the commentator on Dioscorides; Jerome Cardan (1501-1576) of Milan, mathematician and physician, still remembered in Scotland by his visit in 1552 to the unfortunate John Hamilton, abbot of Paisley, then Archbishop of St. Andrews; Julius Caesar Scaliger (1484-1558), the antagonist of Cardan; Conrad Gesner of Zurich (1516-1565), the German Pliny, to whom archaeologists are indebted for an account illustrated with drawings of the various forms of stone axes and stone hammers which had come under his observation; Joachim Camerarius (in German books Kammermeister) of Nuremberg (i534-1597), who acquired the botanical portion of Gesner's collection.

Guide to the Royal Collections of Dresden translated by C. S. Fox, pp. 71, 119, Dresden, 1897, 8vo.

He refers to his museum as " In nostris musarum thesauris," De Subtilitate, Exercitatio 112, p. 422, Francof., 1612, 8vo. See also Gassendi, Vita Peirescii, p. 42, Hag. Com., 1656, 4to.

His collection comprised animals, plants, gems, metals, and fossils, and was open to all his friends. Adam, Vitae Ger7nanoriijn Medicorum p. 160, Heidelb., 1620, 8vo; see post, p. 97; Sachse von Lowenheim, ut supra, p. 53; and Zedler, Universal Lexicon, s. v. Gesnerus.

De reriim fossiliinn, lapidiun et etntnarum Liber, p. 62 sqq., Tiguri, 1565, 8vo. The book is somewhat rare. Clement, Bibliotheque curieuse, ix., p. 169; Denis, Die Merkwiirdigkeiten der garellischen Bibliothek, p. 509, Wien, 1780, 4to.

Adam, Op. laud., p. 340. The curious history of Gesner's woodblocks is given by Pulteney, Sketches of the Progress of Botany, i., p. 160, London, 1790, 8vo.

Pierre B61on (15 17-1564), professor at the College of France, a busy traveller in Palestine and Egypt, Greece and Arabia, and the translator of Theo-phrastus into French; Guillaume Rondelet (1507-1566), professor of medicine at Montpellier, an accurate ichthyologist; Leonhardt Thurneisser (1530-1596), traveller, chemist, mineralogist and botanist; Dr. James Cargill (d. 1616) of Aberdeen; Abraham Ortel (i527-1598), the eminent geographer and antiquary, who assembled in his house a collection of busts, statues, coins, shells, marbles, and carapaces of tortoises great and small. Andrea Cesalpini (1519-1603) formed an herbarium which is still preserved at Florence. Anselm de Boodt (Latinised Boetius, d. circa 1634) of Bruges, physician to the Emperor Rudolph the Second, collected rocks, minerals, and fossils, and wrote a work on gems and stones which was for long a standard authority on the subject. Dissatisfied with the classification

De historia Piscium Libri xviii., Lugd., 1554, fol., 2 vols., with illustrations. Translated into French, Lyon, 1558, fol. The authorship has been attributed to Guillaume Pelicier, bishop of Montpellier, but without foundation.

Thurneisser was the first person in Brandenburg who formed a collection of natural curiosities, plants and seeds, shells, rocks and minerals. Moehsen (J. C. W.), Beit7dge ziir Geschichte der Wissenschaften itt der Mark Brandenburg, p. 142, Berlin, 1783, 4to.

Pulteney, Op. laud., ii., p. 2. Scottish N. and Q., viii., p. 164.

Melchior Adam, Vitae Germanorum Philosophorum, p. 431, Heidelb., 1615, 8vo.

Gemmarum et lapidtim Historia, ii., c. 168. Lugd. Bat., 1647, 8vo, originally published, Hanov., 1609, 4to.

There is a French translation of de Boodt's work by Jean Bachou, Le parfaict loaillier on Histore des Pierreries, Lyon, 1644, 8vo. John de Laet's treatise, De gemtnis et lapidibus, p. 103, Lugd. Bat., 1647, 8vo, Hanov., 1609, 4to, is a kind of supplement to De Boodt.

of Gesner he proposed another, which he sets out in two elaborate tables. But although he was learned in the predicables and could accurately distinguish between genius and species, differentia and accidens, this did not enable him to devise a logical system of mineralogy. The science of the time was altogether inadequate for the purpose. It proceeded mainly on the external shapes of stones, and form was made a determining element in classification.

One of the earliest printed catalogues of a collection is said to have been by Samuel von Quiccheberg, Quiccelberg, or Quichelberg, a physician of Antwerp, who resided at Ingolstadt in the middle part of the sixteenth century. John Kentmann (Latinised Chent-mannus, 1518-1574), a physician of Torgau, formed, at very considerable expense, a cabinet of rocks and minerals of 1600 specimens, a catalogue of which, based on the system of Agricola, he sent to Gesner by whom it was published in 1565. Another physician, Michele Mercati of San Miniato (i 541-1593), appointed keeper of the botanic garden of Pope Pius v., was an industrious collector and formed

His work is entitled Inscriptiones vel tituli Theatri amplisswii cofri-plectentis rerian universitatis siiigulas materias et imagines eximias, Munich, 1565, 4to; but it was rather a scheme for a general antiquarian and ethnographical collection than a catalogue of a particular museum. See Stark, Systematik nnd Geschichte der Archiiologie der Kuiist, p. 151, Leipzig, 1880, 8vo; Beckmann, Beytrdge zur Geschichte der Erfindungen ii., pt. 3, p. 388, Leipzig, 1786; English translation, i., p. 291, London, 1846, Svo. Klemm, Geschichte der Sammlungen fiir Wissenschaft und Kunst in Deutschland, p. 196, Zerbst, 1837, 8vo. The book is a scarce one. There is a copy in the Breslau University library.

It is the first piece in Gesner's collection, De omni rerum fossilium genere, Tiguri, 1565, Svo.

a museum at the Vatican. He prepared an account of its most interesting objects, which, although well known to scientific men and often quoted, remained in manuscript until 1719, when it was edited by Monsignor Lancisi, with notes by Pietro Assalti, and published at the expense of Pope Clement XI.

The first collections for the great museum of Dresden were made by the Elector Augustus of Saxony (1553-1586), and the year after his death his son and successor, the Elector Christian, caused an elaborate inventory of the collection to be prepared, which is still preserved in manuscript at Dresden.

One of the first printed catalogues in English, if we were to rely upon title pages, is that " of all the cheifest Rarities in the Publick Theater and Ana-tomie-Hall of the

University of Leyden " which bears to have been published at Leyden in 1591, and is so entered in the British Museum Catalogue but the date seems to be a mistake for 1691. It is written in Roman letters and apparently a C has accidentally dropped out. The catalogue was prepared by Jakob Voorn, the keeper of the collection, for the use of visitors, and is certainly curious reading. The

Tiraboschi, Storia delta Letteratiira Italiana xn.,). 899, Milano, 1824.

-Metallotheca, Romae, 1717, fol.; Appendix, lb., 1719, fol., with plates and portraits, and a life of Mercati by Monsignor Majelli.

Koehler thought that the MS. was lost, Aniueisung fiir Reisende gelehrte, p. 228, Frankf, 1762.

Klemm, Geschichte der Sammlimgen fiir Wissenschaft und Kiinst in Deutschland, p. 166 sqq., Zerbst, 1837, 8vo. Zeitschrift fiir Museologie, 1879, Nos. 2, 3, and 4.

Catalogue of the Books in the Library of the British Museum. to the year 1640, i., p. 343, London, 1884, 8vo.

Other editions of this Catalogue in English were published at Leyden exhibits were not confined to anatomical subjects but were very general in their character. Here are a few of them: A Norway house, built of beams without mortar or stone; shoes and sandals from Russia, Siam, and Eg-ypt; the skin of a man dressed as parchment; a drinking cup of the skull of a Moor killed in the beleaguering of Haerlem; warlike arms used in China; Chinese songs, Chinese paper, Chinese books, and a great many other articles from China; Egyptian mummies and Egyptian idols; several Roman coins; a Roman lamp which burns always under ground and another which burned eternally; an hand of a Meermaide presented by in 1683 and 1687. In 1695, I7ci) 7 3, 1707, 1716 the name of Gerard Blancken, who was the next keeper, appeared on the title-page. He was succeeded by Francis Schuyl, who was the editor of an edition pubushed in 1719; and in the edition of 1753 John Eysendrach was the editor. All these editions are the same, except that the later ones contain a few more exhibits. See also A Cotnpleat Volume of tite Memoirs for the 1 Curious i., pp. 189, 217, London, 1710, 4to, a reprint of volumes i. and ii. j of the Monthly Miscellany, London, 1707-09, 4to.

The same Catalogue was also published in Latin, Catalogus anti-quaruin et novariitn reriim ex longe dissitis terrarum oris, quarum visendarum copia Ljigduni iti Batavis in Anatomia publica. Quae ita disposita et digesta omnia ut suis ordine locis facile invenianfur, at Leyden in 1681 and 1690, 4to, edited by Voorn; and in 1703 and 1709 edited by Blancken. The latter published a French edition in 1713.

In 1726 Francis Schuyl, who was then keeper, issued it with a new title-page, Catalogus rerum tnemorabilium quae in Theatre Anatomico Academiae qui Lugduni Batavorum floret demonstrantur, Ludg. Bat., 1726, 4to. Schuyl also issued a French edition, Catalogue de ce quon voit de plus remarquable dans la cha7nbre de Fanatomie publiqu6, de runiversite de la ville de Leide. Leyden. 1718, 1721, 1735, 4to. A Dutch version published at Leyden in 1669, 1690 and 1710, 4to; and a German one is given in Valentini, Museum Museorum, vol. ii. Appendix xv., p. 53.

The belief that there were such lamps was common in the sixteenth and seventeenth centuries, and many of them were reported to have been found. See Peacham, Valley of Varietie, p. 49 sqq., London, 1638,

Prince Mauritz; a mushroom above loO years old, which grew on the banks of the Haerlemer river; a petrified toad-stool;- a box of very large amber presented by Daniel Beckler; a thunderbolt given by Melchior de Moncheson and a mallet or hammer that the savages in New Yorke kill with, presented by Herman Broem.

i2mo. Deusing, Vindiciae foetus extra uterttm geniti, p. 98, Groning., 1664, i2mo. Fortunio Liceto (1577-1657), an Italian physician, a man of vast learning but somewhat credulous, in his book, De lucernis anti-quorum rcconditis Libri zv., Van., 1621, 4to, Utini, 1653, fol., Patav., 1662, fol., while remarking upon the extraordinary nature of the phenomenon, accepts it and deals with it at length. (See pp. 7, 104, 190 of edition of 1662.) Montfaucon has doubts on the matter. Antiquity Explained, translated by Humphreys, v., p. 140, London, 1722, fol. They are referred to in Hudibras:

Love in your heart as idly burns
As fire in antique Roman urns,
To warm the dead, and vainly light
Those only that see nothing by't. Part ii. Canto i., 309.

Dr. Plot explained how lamps might burn perpetually, or at least for a very long period, by leading a spring of petroleum into a suitable position and burning it in a wick of asbestos or gold wire. The Philosophical Transactio? is, xiv., p. 106; Kirchmaier, Noctiluca consta? is, Wittenb., 1676, 4to; Parkinson, Orgajiic Remains of a former World, i., p. 149, London, 1804, 4to.

In the museum of the Royal Society of London there was " a bone said to be taken out of a Maremaid's head." Grew, Mzisaeufn Regalis Societatis, p. 81, London, 1681, fol.

Canon Bargrave had in his museum " a fair large toadstool or mushroom, very weighty, which is not a mushroom petrified, but grew always a stone, in this shape and figure." Catalogue of Dr. Bargrave's Museum, No. 35. Pope Alexander the Seventh and the College of Cardinals, p. 126, 1867, 4to. Camden Society, No. xcii.

As to the Leyden museum, see post, p. 190; Journal des voyages de Monsieur De Monconys, Pt. ii., p. 151, Lyon, 1666; Hegenitius, Itiner-arium Frisio-Hollandicum, p. 61, Lugd. Bat., 1667, i2mo; Northleigh, Topographical Descriptions, p. 37, London, 1702, 8vo; Ray, Travels through the Low Countries, i., p. 32, London, 1738, 8vo; Skippon,

There was a separate collection of " curiosities and rarities to be seen in the Gallery of the Garden of the Academie of Leyden," and in the Indian Cabinet to which the gallery led. The collection in the Gallery consisted of natural history specimens and ethnographical objects; birds, fish and other animals of various kinds, amongst them " Barnacles a sorte of Geese sayd to grow in Scotland on trees "; " cups made of gourds, and pots out of which the negroes in Africa drink palm wine"; "an almanack used by the Laplanders"; "an hunting pouch used by the Moores on Guinea"; " bows and arrows used by the negroes"; "a Brasilian weapon used in war"; "stockings and shoes worn by the Japonners "; " the foot of the Bird Cassuaris"; "the skin of a mermaid"; "a modell of Muscoviter's palace"; "paper money of the siege of Leyden." This consisted of pieces of card issued when the town was besieged by the Spaniards in 1574,

Journey, in Churchill, Collection of Voyages, vi., p. 414, London, 1752, fol.; Neickelius, Museographia, p. 62, Leipzig, 1727, 4to; Brown, Travels, p. 93, London, 1685, fol.; Misson, A New Voyage to Italy,., p. 14, London, 1699, 8vo; Wright, Travels in Fraiice, Italy, Src., ii.,. p. 512, London, 1764, 4to; Memoirs of Sir John Clerk of Pennicuik, p. 14, Edinburgh, 1892.

1 Curiosities ajid Rarities, to be seen in the Gallery of the Garden of the Academie of Leyden, n. p., n. d., bound up with Blancken's Catalogue of the Rarities in the Anatomie Hall, Leyden, 1695, 4to (Advocates' Library, Edinburgh).

There is another copy, circa 1700, in the Rylands Library, Manchester, and an edition of 1737. A Latin edition appeared as early as 1659, Res curiosae 2 exoticae quae in Ambiilacro Horii Acculemiae Leydensis curiositatem amantibus offeruntur Anno 1659, fol.; often reprinted with a slightly different title-page, n. p., n. d., 4to; and in Valentini, Museum Museorum, vol. ii. Appendix ix., p. 21.

A? t Index to the Indian Closset, which contains several foreign creatures,.

bearing on the one side Haec libertatis ergo, and on the other side Pugno pro patria An Enghsh catalogue of this collection appeared as early as 1665.

The museum at Leyden is now one of the great institutions of the world, remarkable for its Egyptian and Etruscan antiquities and its fine ethnographical and natural history departments, which were enriched a generation ago by the remarkable collections of the ethnologist Philipp Franz von Siebold (1796-1866), an officer of the Dutch Embassy to Japan.

and plants swimming in Balsamick liqiiours as if now alive. To be seen in the Garden of the Academy of Leyden. Leyden 1688, 4to.

Register van't Indiaanse Cabinet. zijnde te sien i7i de Thiiyn van de Academie tot Leyden, n. p., n. d., 4to.

Musaei Indici Index, n. p., n. d., 4to, several editions.

Misson, A new Voyage to Italy, i., p. 15, London, 1699, O- This money is more fully described, Museum Wormianum, p. 361.

A Catalogue of the Rarities that are shown to the Curious, i7t the University-garden at Leyden in Holland. Translated out of Latin. No doubt that of 1659, supra. This forms part (pp. 72-76) of Hubert's Catalogue of tnany Natural Rarities, London, 1665, i2mo. It is not in the edition of 1664. Post, pp. 127, 128.

Leemans, Het Rijks Museum van Oudheden en het Rijks Ethno-graphisch Museum te Leiden, Leiden, 1870 and again 1877, 8vo; Ver-slag van den Directeur van s Rijks Museum van Oudheden te Leiden, Leiden, 1888, 8vo.

The anatomical museum was described by Sandifort, Musaeum ana-tomicum Academiae Lugduno-Batavae descriptum, Lugd. Bat., 1793-1835, fol., 4 vols.

Kentmann terms his collection thesaurus fossilium, and the cabinet in which it was contained area rerum fossiliunt. Gazophylacium Cimeliarehium or its English equivalent "Repository," eimelium,

This was a common and appropriate name for a cabinet of coins and gems. It was originally used of the Treasury of a church; and is rendered in German, " die Schatzkammer."

Thus Lorenz Beger uses it of the cabinets of the Elector Palatine of the Rhine and of the Elector of Brandenburg. Thesaurus Branden-burgicus selectus, sive gemmarum et numistnatum Graecorutn in cim-eliarchio Electorali Brandendurgico, elegantiorutn Series, commetitario illustratae. Coin. a. d. Spree, 1696-1701, fol. 3 vols, with engravings. The Catalogue of the Cimeliarehium of the Elector Palatine was published at Heidelberg in 1685. We have also Cimeliarehium seu Thesaurus num-niorum. Friderici Augjisti, D2icis Wurtembergiae, Stuttg., 1710, fol.

The museum of the Royal Society was generally spoken of in its earlier days as "the Repository." Weld, History of the Royal Society, i., pp. 186, 189, 224, 280, London, 1848, 8vo. In the Act 26 Geo. II., c. 22, establishing the British Museum, the term "Repository" is used. The Museum is referred to as a "Repository" in 1776, and objects are said to be " reposited" in it. Archaeologia, ii., p. 121.

Evelyn speaks of " the Ceimeliarcha or Repository" in the Palazzo Vecchio, Florence, Diary, i., pp. 106, 224, London, 1879; see also his Numismata, p. 244, London, 1697. Cimeliarcha, however, means the keeper, not the repository. Thus Edward Lhuyd, in his Lithophylacii Britannici Ichnographia, London, 1699, 8vo, styles himself, "Apud Oxonienses Cimeliarcha Ashmoleanus."

Robert Ainsworth, the Lexicographer, who prepared the account of John Kemp's museum (London, 1720, 8vo), terms it "cimelium."

Keifxiixiou, cimeliotheca rarotheca and other terms were sometimes used, but gradually the word 7nuseum came to be adopted as the technical term for a collection of objects of art, of monuments of antiquity or

Praef., p. iii., and title-page of part ii. Nathaniel Sendel in his work on amber describes the examples as " ex regiis Augustorum Cimeliis Dresdae." Historia Succinoriim Lipsiae, 1742, fol. On the other hand, Christian Gottlieb Ludwig, when describing the earths in the same collection, styles it " Museum." Terrae Musei Regit Dresdensts, Lipsiae, 1749, fol.

E. g. Powell, Humane Industry, p. 51, London, 1661, i2mo; Worm, Monumenta Danica, pp. 48, 49.

Sachse a Lewenheimb, Responsoria dissertatio de miranda Lapidum nafura, p. 53, with Major, Dissertatio epistolica de Cancris et Serpentibus petrefactis, Jenae, 1664, 8vo.

Schelhammer, note on Conringii In universam artem medicam Intro-ductio, p. 294, Spirae, 1688, 4to; Briickmann, Epistola Itineraria, Cent. i., p. 12, Wolfenb., 1728, 4to.

Gotfried Hegenitius of Leyden uses TexfvJ-o-roipvxdkLov or Pinacotheca, Itinerarium Frisio-Hollandicum, p. 30, Lugd. Bat., 1667, originally published 1630. Olaf Bromel of Gothenburg styles his collection a Pinacotheca. Catalogus generalis. rerum curiosarum tarn arti-ficialium quam 7iaturaliutn in Pinacotheca Olai Bromelii, M. D., Goth., 1694, 4to. Thomas Bartholin refers in 1652 to the Copenhagen museum as " Technicotheca Regia." Historiarum anatoniicarutn Rariora, Cent, ii., Hist. 61, Amstel., 1654, i2mo. J0rgen Hahn, who pronounced a funeral oration over Bartholin, had a collection which he styled " Phy-s'xcothcdl," Physicotkeca beati Doct. Georgii Hannaei. Hafniae, 1699,410.

Daniel Wilhelm Moeller proposed the term "Technophysiotameium" as the equivalent of the German " Eine Kunst- und Naturalien-Kammer, Zimmer oder Gemach," and wrote of Museums under the title Com-fnentatio de Technophysiotameis, Altorf, 1704; reprinted by Koehler in his Sylloge aliquot Scriptorutn de bene ordinanda et ornanda biblio-theca, Francof., 1727, 4to. Friedrich Christian Lesser uses " Physiotech-notameum" in his Epistola de praecipuis tiaturae et artis curiosis specimenibus Musei vel potius Piysiotechnotamei Friderici Hofftnanni, Nordhusae, 1736, 4to. Sachse von Lowenheim suggested "Litho-phyto-therophylacia" and invented the word E utikooavxatovpyrjfjlatOTajldov, under which title he describes the collection at Dresden. Gammarologia, p. 50.

Johann David Major makes merry over this ten yards word, as he calls 't, and explains that with all its length it is not sufficiently of specimens of natural history, mineralogy, and the like, and generally of what were known as "rarities" and "curiosities." In the lano-uaq e of Dr. Johnson a museum was "a repository of learned curiosities." Occasionally the Latin musaeiifn was rendered into English and "study" is used as the equivalent. Later the French word cabinet came into use with the same meaninof and was adopted into English or translated by " closet " and descriptive, as it omits artificial objects, and that it should have been Yi wnkOT voba. vu-o. Tovpy iw. rota. tov. See his Bedenckett von Kunst- und Nahiralien-Kamtnern p. 5, in Valentini, Museum Museorum, vol. i., Francof., 1704, Neickelius, Museographia, p. 408 (Leipzig, 1827), and Moeller, Op. laud., p. 194.

Major's own See-Farth nach der fteuen Welt ohne Schiff U7id Segel, is about the last title that one would consult on the subject of museums; and the title of Sachse's Gammarologia, i. e. a Treatise on Crabs, is not more instructive.

Nathan Bailey, English Dictionary 17 j), defined "Museum" as "a study or library; also a college or publick place for the resort of learned men." "The Museum, a neat building in the city of Oxford, founded by Elias Ashmole." Defoe, speaking of the same museum, calls it "the museum or chamber of rarities." A Tour thro' the whole of Great Britaitt by a Gentleinafi, ii., p. 227, London, 1753, 8vo, originally published in 1725.

Thus Evelyn, when at Rome in 1644, visited " Signor Angeloni's study; where with greater leysure we surveyd the rarities, as his cabinets and medaills especially." Diary, i., p. 128, London, 1879. See also Sibbald, Auctariutn Musaei Balfouriani, Praef, Edinb., 1697.

E. g. the king's " cabinet of curiosities," Ward, Lives of the Professors of Gresham College, p. 100, London, 1740, fol.; "a cabinet of shells," Evelyn, Diary, ii., p. 23, London, 1879; "a paradise and cabinet of rarities," lb., ii., p. 270; cf. ii., p. 119; " cabinets or collections of medals," Evelyn, Numisviata, p. 199, London, 1697, fol. " Nothing can be pleasanter than to see a circle of these virtuosos about a cabinet of medals, descanting upon the value, rarity, and authenticalness of the several pieces that lie before them." Addison, "Dialogues on Medals," Works, i., p. 340, London, 1811.

Thus by Henley in his translation of The Antiquities of Italy, by De Montfaucon, pp. 16, 17, London, 1725, fol.; Ashmole Diary, y. 126, the terms 'galerie " chambre," 'chambre des raretes," Raritat en-cabinet, Curiositdten-Cabinet are also found."-

London, 1774) refers to Tradescant's museum as his "Closet of Curiosities." "After dinner, his highness was pleased to call us into his closet, and show us many curiosities." Ray 1663, Travels through the Low Countries ii., p. 71, London, 1738, 8vo.

All are exemplified in the works of the antiquary, Nicholas Chevalier, a Huguenot refugee in Holland: (rt) Catalogue des Medailles doubles qui sont dans le Cabinet de Nicholas

Chevalier a Amsterdam. Amsterdam, 1696, 4to. b) Catalogue de toutes les Raretez qui se montrent dans la Chambre de la Ville dutrecht. Utrecht, 1707, 4to. ( ) Remarques sur une piece antique de Bronze trouvee. aux environs de Rome,. avec une description de la Chambre des Raretez de IAuteur. Amsterdam, 1694, i2mo, with 12 plates by Schoonebecks. d) Catalogue de toutes les Raretez qui se montrent dans la Gallerie dantiquitez au dessus de la Bourse a Amsterdam. Amsterdam, i2mo. n. d., circa 1700. e) Description de la piece dambre gris que la chambre damsterdam a recue des Indes Orientales, pesant 182 livres; avec un petit traite de son origine et de sa vertu. Amsterdam, 1700, 4to. () Recherches curieuses des Antiquitez venues ditalic, de la Grece, degypte et trouvees k Nimegue, k Santen,. que Ton, void dans la gallerie de Raretez de Iauteur. Utrecht, 1712, fol. The greater part of Chevalier's own collection was purchased by the Elector Augustus of Saxony and transferred to Dresden.

Sir Andrew Balfour uses Gallery as synonymous with Museum; e. g. " Septalie's Galerie"; 'His Galerie of Curiosities." Letters., p. 245. It was the word in common use in Italy.

Bacon says. New Atlantis., "we have two very long galleries; in one of these we place patterns and samples of all manner of the more rare and excellent inventions." Works., ed. Spedding, iii., p. 165.

The Germans used the terms "Raritaten-Cabinet," " Raritaten- Kammer," and " Kunst-Kammer," while a particular collection was styled " Natural-ien-Cabinet," " Miinz-Cabinet," " Mineralien-Cabinet," and so on. Speaking of the Elector of Saxony and his museum at Dresden, Dr. Edward Brown says: " But that which affords greatest delight is his Kunst-Kammer, Art Chamber of Collection of Rareties, both of Art and Nature." Travels., p. 166, London, 1685, fol. There is a corresponding definition in Zedler, Universal Lexicon, s. v. " Kunst-Kammer," where "museum" and "cabinet" are given as equivalents.

Brown mentions the " Chamber of Rareties" of the Burgomaster

Museum was used not only for the collection but also for the place where it was kept conclave redtcs rarioribus et pretiosoribtis sive nature sive arte elaboratis servandis destinatum). From the closing years of the sixteenth century museum is constantly used in both senses.

of Leipsic. Travels,. 172. In the German version it is " Raritaten-Kammer," p. 293, Niirnberg, 1686. Neickelius gives "Eine Schatz-Raritaten-Naturalien-Kunst-Vernunfft-Kammer, Zimmer oder Gemach." Museographia, p. 409. In the Thesaurus Ey-tiditionis Scltolasticae of Basil Faber, Francof., 1749, fol., Kunst-Kammer and Gallerie are with Bilder-gemach given as the equivalents of Pinacotheca.

"Material-Kammer" is a collection of simples, or more generally of the substances used by the druggist.

Goltz uses museutn and nuinismatarchia for a coin cabinet, in the Dedication to the Patrons of Antiquities in his C. Ivlivs Caesar, Drug., 1563, fol. In 1569 Enea Vico of Parma edited certain bronze tables containing Egyptian hieroglyphics " ex Torquati Bembi Museo " which was reprinted at Venice, 1600, fol. Fuiren's collection was a " Museum," Rariora Musaei Henrici Fuiren, AI. D., quae Academiae regiae Hafjiiae legavit, publici juris facta a Thoma Fuiren, Hafniae, 1663, 4to. From Paris we have Selecta Numismata antiqua ex Musaeo Petri Seguini, Paris, 1666, 4to, and Selectiora Numismata e Museo Francisci de Camps, Lutet., 1695, 4to- In 1692 the collection of coins and gems of Jacob de Wilde of Amsterdam, and in 1740 that of Baron de Grassier are styled ' musaeump See Selecta numismata aittiqua ex musaeo Jacobi de Wilde. Amst., 1692, 4to. Signa antiqua e museo J. de W., veterum poetarum carminibus illus-trata. Amst., 1700, 4to. Ge7nmae selectae antiquae e museo y. de W. Amst. 1703, 4to. Descriptio Gemmaruni quae in museo G. Baronis de Grassier. asservatitur. Leodii, 1740, 4to. Baron de Grassier also collected coins, statues, and other antiquities of which he printed a Catalogue. Liege, 1721, 8vo. The great collections at Florence are termed a Museum in 1731, Museu7n Flore)itinum, exhibens insigniora Vetustatis monumenta, quae Floreiitiae sunt in Thesauro Mediceo. Florent., 1731-66. 12 vols., fol.

The collection of gems and coins made by Queen Christina of Sweden, and acquired by the Duke Odescalchi, was also styled "museum." See Museum Odescalchutn. Romae, 1751, 2 vols., fol. Her collection is styled "nummophylacium" or "cabinet" in Nummophylacium Reginae Christinae, by Havercamp. Latin and French. Hag. Com., 1742, fol.

The elder Scaliger improves upon museum by the phrase " Musarum thesaurus." Supra, p. 25.

Some of the exhibits of the old museums unicorn's horn, giants' bones, petrified toad-stools, and the like strike us as somewhat extraordinary, but they were placed there in accordance with the opinions and teaching of the time. Our point of view is so different that we are inclined to look upon much of the material of the old collections as rubbish, and it is apt to be so treated by keepers only interested in the current views of museum management, but this is a mistake. Many of these objects are of much interest in the history of science, and to the discussion and controversies, which some of them evoked, we are indebted for the science of to-day. The illustration of the growth and development of culture and civilisation is one of the aims of the modern museum; and we have rooms filled with objects, chronologically arranged, to show the progress not only of such things as costume, weapons, and furniture, but of trade and navigation and the industrial arts, of geography, of education, of surgery, and of physical research, but it does not seem to have occurred to anyone to illustrate in a museum the iory of the idea of the museum, its arrangement and contents. The nearest approach to this, so far as I can remember, is the old apothecary booth and chemical laboratory in the German National Museum at Nuremberg, and another in the Bohemian National Museum at Prague.

Some explanation of the current opinions regarding a few of these exhibits may enable us to understand why they found a place in the older museums and something of the nature of these collections.

UNICORN HORN.

No museum of any repute was considered complete without one or more specimens of unicorn's horn, an article which was believed to possess wonderful virtues, and was much employed in medicine. It was a recognised preservative against poisoning, and a piece was placed in the drinking cup of the King of France till almost the close of the monarchy. At the reception of Louis Seigneur de la Gruthuyse, by Edward IV. in England, in 1472, the king gave him a golden cup with a piece of unicorn horn in it, seven inches in circumference. The Grand Inquisitor Tor-quemada always carried about with him the horn of a unicorn to protect him against poison and assassins.

Fiihrer durch die Sammlungen des Museums des Kbnigreiches Bohmen in Prag, p. 70, Prag, 1897, i2mo; Die Ku7ist- und Kultur-geschichtlichen Satmnlungen des Germanischen Museums p. 159, Niirnberg, 1899, i2mo.

This, however, is only a reproduction of an old idea. There was a laboratory and apothecary's booth in the Dresden Museum in the seventeenth century.

See Leibnitz, Protogaea, 35, Goetting., 1749, 4to.

Archaeologia, xxvi., p. 277.

Collin de Plancy, Dictionnaire des Reliques, ii., p. 121, Pari. f

Above the drug cases in one of the old apothecary-booths exhibited in the Prague Museum the Apotheke, "Zur goldenen Krone" are two conventional unicorns' horns. Above one of those in the Nuremberg Museum, the horn of a narwhal the sea unicorn is suspended, reminding one of Shakespeare's apothecary: in his needy shop a tortoise hung, An alhgator stuffd, and other skins Of ill-shapd fishes.

The " true" horn commanded a very high price. At Rome as much as 90,000 crowns were given for a single horn. The Republic of Venice, in 1595, gave 30,000 ducats for another; and Brantome mentions a nobleman who sold an estate for 50,000 crowns, of which he took payment as regards 45,000 in gold and silver, and for the balance of 5000 crowns a piece of unicorn horn. In the Jewel House in the Tower there were in 1649, "The unicornes homes weighing 40 lb. 8 oz., valued at 600." Bankers and moneylenders often advanced large sums of money upon no other security than the pledge of a bit of this horn. The existence of the horn was proof positive that the

Hill, writing in the middle of the eighteenth century, mentions that the narwhal's horn was "kept as an ornament to druggists' shops." History of the Materia Medica, p. 842, London, 1751, 4to. In Germany, "Einhorn Apotheke" is still to be seen amongst the street signs.

"Romeo and Juliet, Act v. Sc. i. See also Hudibras, Part iii., Canto ii., 1074.

Bartholinus, Historiarton attatomicaruin Rariora, Cent, iv., Hist. 4,

"6, Hafniae, 1657.

. arousse. Grand Didionnaire miiverseldu xix Siecle, x., s. v. Licorne.

y; op. laud., p. 841, mentions that one of the French kings had a hisii valued at 20,000. Archaeologia, xv., p. 274.

4-etius, Gemmartcm et lapidum Historia, p. 435, Lugd. Bat., 1647.

unicorn itself existed. " Some have made doubt," says Guillim, " whether there be any such beast as this or no. But the great esteeme of his home (in many places to be seen) may take away that needless scruple." Another old writer is more precise, "Albeit there be many horned beasts which may improperly be called unicorns, yet that which is the right unicorn indeed is like unto a colt of two years and a half old, which hath naturally but one horn, and that a very rich one, which groweth out of the middle of his forehead, being a horn of such virtue as is no beasts horn besides; which, whilst some have gone about to deny, they have secretly blinded the eyes of the world from their full view of the greatness of God's great works. " Many reputable travellers reported that they had seen it. Sometimes it was said to be in India, at other times in South Africa, and latterly in West Africa, but although constantly sought after, the animal itself was never brought to Europe. Still the horn was forthcoming.

A Display of Heraldry, p. 259, London, 1660, fol. 2 Swan," Speculum Mundi or a Glass of the World, p. 389, London, 1670, 4to.

The unicorn has appeared as one of the supporters of the Royal Arms of Scotland since the reign of James IIL, and since the union of the crowns it has occupied the same position on the arms of the United Kingdom. Woodward and Burnett, Heraldry, British atid Foreign, pp. 296, 632, Edinburgh, 1892, 8vo; Nisbet, Sysievt of Heraldry, i., p. 311, Edinburgh, 1722, fol.

Ludovico di Varthema saw two live unicorns in the temple at Mecca. Travels, p. 46, London, 1863, 8vo (Hakluyt Society, vol-Kyj") Scaliger founds upon this passage in order to con– P- l. ven-Cardan who had doubts as to the existence of the un I

De Subtilitate, Exercit. 205, p. 659, Francof., 1582. W,

Bartholinus, Historiarum anato nicarum Rariora, L"

p. 251, Amstel, 1654. Varthema, Op. laud., p. 47 n. i

Other one-horned animals, notably the rhinoceros and narwhal, or Unicornu Gronlandicum, as it was termed, were to be found in plenty, and it was ascertained by experiment that their horns possessed the same qualities as those of the " true" unicorn, although in a less degree. Certain small differences existed which could only be detected by an expert, and his services were in as much demand as those of an assayer at the present time.

Besides the horns of existing animals, fossil horn was in request. This was horn embedded in the earth, generally some species of ivory,- and was found principally in caves. Cave-hunting was in consequence carried on in the seventeenth century almost as assiduously as in the nineteenth; the Baumanshole at Riibeland in the Harz and a cave at Scharzfeld in the duchy of Grubenhagen were explored, and others were opened up in the neighbourhood of Hildesheim, and many in Hungary, Moravia, Silesia, Saxony, and elsewhere. The nature of these bones was much discussed, and many curious theories were propounded. The supposed skeleton was set up with one prominent horn on its head and is fio-ured in books.

Museum Wormianum, p. 286; Boetius, Op. laud., p. 429; Schroder, Pharmacopoeia Medico-Chymica, lib. iii., p. 42; lib. v., p. 292.

Woodward, An addiion to the Catalogue of the Foreign and Extraneous Fossils, p. 13, London 1728, 8vo.

Boetius, Op. laud., p. 425; Philosophical Tratisactions, vi. (bli), p. 3016; Briickmann, Epistolae Itinerariae, 34, "JT, Cent. i.; Valentini, Museum Museorutn, vol. ii., p. 49; Leibnitz, Protogaea, 34, 36, 37, Goetting., 1749, 4to; Parkinson, Organic Remains of a former World, iii., p. 415 sqq.; Boehmer, Bibliotheca Scriptorum historiae naturalis, iv., 2, p. 355, Lipsiae, 1789, 8vo; Dryander, Catalogus Bibliothecae histonco-naturalis fosephi Banks, iv., p. 56, Lond., 1799, 8vo.

Valentini, Museum Museorwn, i., p. 479.

As time advanced the existence of the unicgrn itself became matter of discussion, and much labour wa expended in ascertaining the characteristics of the various one-horned animals that could be ad ced. Ambroise Pare (1509-1590), the great French surgeon, doubted whether there was such an animal, and disputes the virtues attributed to the horn." As information accumulated, and was sifted, the truth was gradually arrived at, but by a long and tedious process; and even yet there are some who live in hopes of seeing a "true" unicorn, Lord Bacon, writing in 1623, mentions that unicorn horn had lost its reputation as a cordial, but sixty years later Nehemiah Grew, and the rest of the Faculty, still believed in it for producing perspiration in fevers and curing other ailments.

Boetius, Op. laiid. p. 429; Bartholinus, iit supra; Museum Wormi-anum, p. 287.

Discours asqavoir de la Mumie, des Venifis, de la Licorne et de la Peste, Paris, 1582,410. The work is illustrated with curious woodcuts. Reprinted in his Oeuvres completes., by Malgaigne, iii., p. 492 sqq., Paris, 1841, 8vo. He takes the same view in his Chirurgie, xxi., c. 39, English translation, p. 533, London, 1649, fol.

His opinions were challenged, and he replied to the criticisms in Replique dambroise Pare. a la Response faicte contre son Discours de la Licorne., Paris, 1584, 4to.

Mr. G. Percy Badger, writing in 1863, is inclined to believe the stories of the old travellers, and that the unicorn, as they described it, really existed. He thinks "that further research in the unexplored parts of Central Africa, or among the mountains of Tibet, may yet bring it to light." Varthema, Travels., p. 48 n., London, 1863, 8vo.

Historia Vitae et Mortis., p. 188, London, 1623, 8vo; Works, ii., p. 156, ed. Spedding; see Hill, Op. laud.; Hoffmann, Clavis pharma-ceutica Schroderiana, p. 691, Hal. Sax., 1675, 4to 5 Alston, Lectures on the Materia Medica, ii., pp. 527, 528, London, 1770, 4to.

Grew, Musaeum Regalis Societatis, p. 84; Schroder, Pharmacopoeia

Ralph Thoresby had in his museum "a thin slice of the sea-unicorn's horn, white and solid; the present of Mrs. Dorcas Dyneley, to whose great-grandmother, Frances, then daughter-in-law to Archbishop Parker, and after the wife of Archbishop Matthews, Queen Elizabeth gave this very piece." Unicorn horn, veritable and substitute, living and fossil has a considerable literature full of curious learning.

GIANTS BONES.

The belief in giants was universal. They were mentioned in Holy Writ and by classical authors. Their bones, as already mentioned, figured in the museum of Augustus, and formed conspicuous objects in many museums of the sixteenth and seventeenth centuries. In some instances they were even passed off as the bones of saints These were not parts

Medtco-Chytnica, lib. iii., p. 42, Ulmae, 1644, 4to; Salmon, Neiv London Dispensatory, p. 422, London, 1696, 8vo.

"A Catalogue and Description of the Rarities in this Museum," p. 7, in Ducatus Leodiensis, vol. ii., 1816, fol.

Rev. John Ward has a curious anecdote regarding a piece of unicorn horn. Diary (1648-79), p. 171, London, 1839, 8vo.

- Hoffmanni, Lexicon, s. v. " rhinoceros," " unicornu," has some interest- ing notes on the unicorn. The whole subject has, in recent times, been I fully dealt with by J. W. von Miiller, Das Einhorn vom geschichtlichen und naturalwissenschaftlichen Siandptinkt, Stuttgart, 1853. Reference may also be made to E. P. Evans, Animal Symbolistn in Ecclesiastical

Architecture, p. 105 sqq., London, 1896; Charles Gould, Mythical

Monsters, p. 338 sqq., London, 1886; Thomas Hawkins, Book of the j Great Sea Dragons, London, 1840, fol.

I "Nullum fere Musaeum giganteis dentibus caret," Bartholinus, Historiariini anat07nicarum Rariora, Cent, i. Hist. 96, p. 144, Amstel., i 1654, i2mo; 77 1? Philosophical Transactions, xxii. (1700), p. 489. Major,

Bevolckertes Cimbrien, p. 53 sqq., Plon, 1692, fol.

In the Jesuits' Church at Munich they had in the seventeenth century "a vertebra or joint of the back-bone as big as that of an of the skeletons of ordinary men, but were bones dug up from the earth Hke the fossil unicorn horn. The body of Pallas, son of Evander, was reported to have been found in Rome in the time of the Emperor Henry III. in 1041 or 1054, and was of such size that it exceeded the walls of the city in height. Boccaccio, as we have seen, mentions the finding of a giant in Sicily. In 1577 another was disinterred near Lucerne. Felix Plater (1536-1614), the learned physician of Basle, made a drawing of the skeleton, which he computed to be nineteen feet high, and the Lucernese adopted the giant for a supporter of the city arms. In 1613 some bones of extraordinary size were found in Dauphin, which were brought to Paris by a physician named Mazurier and exhibited as a show. To attract visitors he issued a pamphlet descriptive of the bones in which he attributed them to Teutobochus, King of the Teutons. This opinion was adopted by Nicholas Habicot (1550-1604), a well-known surgeon and anatomist. His opinion was immediately challenged by Jean Riolan (1577-1657), professor of anatomy, in several publica- elephant or some huge animal; and this great bone, as we were informd, is in great veneration with them, as being one of the vertebrae of the huge St. Christopher." Misson, A New Voyage to Italy i., p. 88, London, 1699, 8vo; Keysler, Reisen, p. 56, Hannover, 1751, 4to.

As to Giants' bones in churches, see supra, p. 11. Briickmann enumerates several other instances, Epistolae Itinerariae, 12, 35, Cent. i.

Aldrovandi, Musacum Meiallicufn, p. 236, Bononiae, 1648, fol.; Dom Calmet, Dictiofinaire de la Bible, s. v. Geant, i. 318, Paris, 1722, fol.; Martene, Thesaurus Anecdotarum, iii., p. 576, Paris, 1717, fol.

Platerus, Observationum. Libri tres, p. 566, Basil, 1680, 8vo; Bartholinus, Historiarum anatotnicarum Rariora, Cent, i. Hist. 98, p. 147, Amstelod., 1654, i2mo. Infra, p. 98.

Histoire veritable du g ant Teutobochus. Paris, 1613, l2mo.

tions, most of which he issued anonymously, and in which he personally attacks Habicot. After all, the bones, it is said, were those of a fossil salamander. Thomas Bartholin, the elder (i619-1680), of Copenhagen, an excellent anatomist and author of a standard work upon his subject, which was translated into English, had no doubt at all as to the former existence of giants, but on the contrary satisfied himself of the fact by careful measurements of a tooth in Olaf Worm's museum, which proved that it was in exact proportion to the human tooth, and must have belonged to another Og. He visited Malta in 1644, and in his description of the island mentions that it was formerly inhabited by giants, and that in the museum of John Francis Abela (1582-1655), Vice-Chancellor and Commander of the Knights of Malta, there were preserved the hip bones, a tooth, and a rib of one of them. When the remains of the mastodon were first discovered, near Albany, i 712, they were believed to be bones of giants and a confirmation of the Mosaic account of gigantic races of men. One would suppose that an anatomist

An account of the controversy is given by Habicot in his Anti-gigantologie, ou contre discours de la grandeur des Geatts. Paris, 1618, 8vo.

- Bartholimis Anatomy. in four books and four tnanuals. published by Nich. Culpeper, Cent., and Abdiah Cole, Doctor of Physick. London, 1668, fol.

Historiaru7n anatomicarum Rariora, ut supra, p. 144. Museujn IVormianum, p. 343.

His account is contained in a letter to Joseph Donzelli, Epistolae Medicinales, Cent, i., Epist. 53, p. 223, Hafniae, 1663, and again, Hag. Com., 1740, i2mo.

The remains of a species of small elephant have been found in caves in Malta. Boyd Davvkins, Cave Huttiing, p. 377. London, 1874, 8vo.

Letter, Dr. Mather to Dr. Woodward, The Philosophical Transactions vol. xxix. (1712), p. 62.

should have no difficulty in distinguishing between the bones of a man and of other animals, but Cuvier says that this is not so, and that there is considerable resemblance between some of the human bones and those of the elephant.

The existence of giants was, however, disputed by some. Jan van Gorop, surnamed Becanus (1518-1572), physician to the Lady Mary, sister to the Emperor Charles the Fifth, Queen of Hungary and Regent of the Netherlands, writing in 1569, says that the so-called giant's bones are bones of large animals, not of man " but this heterodox opinion was at once disputed by Jean Chassanion. Michael Mercati, while doubting the existence of giants, maintained that men and other animals were not larger in former times than they are now. Some, he says, explained the great size of the fossil bones by the suggestion that they increased in size while lying in the soil.

Recherchcs siir les ossefnens fossiles, i., p. 75, 3" ed., Paris, 1825, 4to. Cuvier has here collected a vast amount of information on the subject of giants' bones, which is reproduced and abridged by Pidgeon, Fossil Remains of the Animal Kingdom p. 41 sqq. London, 1836, 8vo; and by Edward J. Wood in Giatils and Dwarfs London, 1868, 8vo.

2 Origines Antverpianae. Book ii., entitled Gigantomachia, p. 242. Antverp., 1569, fol. There is a long notice of this work in Clement, Bibliotheque Curieuse, ix., p. 243.

Becanus maintained that German was the first and most ancient language m the world, and assumed that it was spoken in Paradise. In allusion to this Butler says that Sir Hudibras knew all about Adam and Eve and the Fall,

Whether the devil tempted her By a High-Dutch interpreter.

Hudibras, Part i. Canto, i., 180. See Lord Fountainhall's Journals, p. 81, Edinburgh, 1900.

Cassanion, De Gigantibus eorumque reliquiis. Basil., 1580, i2mo; Spirae, 1587, i2mo.

This he denies, and holds that the bones are produced by the earth itself. On the other hand, Nicolas Steno, whose views on the formation of fossils were sound, was of opinion that giants had existed and that the bones which were found were their very bones in a fossilised condition." In 1696 a skeleton was found at Tonna in Gotha, which the physicians, consulted by the Duke, declared to be a lus7is naturae. Tentzel, the Duke's librarian, compared each bone separately with those of the elephant, and found that they were identical. Many other finds were made in Germany and in Italy, and it gradually came to be accepted that the bones were those of elephants and not of men Then came a difficulty, how to account for their presence, as the elephant is not a European animal. As regarded Italy, an easy explanation was found in the suggestion

Metallotheca, pp. 325, 326.

"Prodromus to a Dissertation concerning Solids naturally contained within Solids. Englishd by H. O. Henry Oldenburg, p. 89, London, 1671, 8vo. Originally published in Latin at Florence, 1669, 4to.

The Prodromus is an excellent discussion of present geological doctrines. the deposition of horizontal strata by water, their dislocation by fire, gas or other upheaving force, the scooping out of valleys, and the formation of mountains. The whole surface of the earth has been repeatedly submerged and again elevated. Fossils, he maintains, were originally living organisms converted into stone by certain elements in the earth. He entirely repudiates the doctrine that they grew in the earth.

His account is printed in the Philosophical Transactions, xix. (1695-97), p. 757. Separately, Epistola de sceleto Elephantino Tonnae nuper effoso, 1 " ed., Jenae 1696, 8vo; Briickmann, Epistola Itineraria, 12, Cent. i.

G. A. Helwing Lithographia Angerbnrgica, p. 92, Regiom., 1717) mentions the frequent finding of large teeth attributed to giants, but he did not think that they were such.

Briickmann devotes a letter to the subject, Epistola Itineraria, 12, Cent. i. See also Epistolae 5, 11, 34, 35, 36, 55, 56, 61, Cent. i.; Keysler, Rdsen, pp. 96 sqq., Hannover, 1751, 4to, ist ed., 1740, 4to.

that the bones were those of elephants brought by the Carthaginians or the Romans. As this could not apply to Germany, it was necessary to fall back upon an elephant sent to Charlemagne by the Caliph Haroun-al-Raschid, which had to do duty for scientists in all parts of the country. The difficulty as regarded England w as still greater. Some thought that the Emperor Claudius might have brought an elephant with him, and that it died here. But this supposition, being unsupported by evidence, was rejected. A live elephant was shown at Oxford in 1676, when Dr. Robert Plot, afterwards the keeper of the Ashmolean Museum, took the opportunity of comparing its teeth with one of the fossil grinders, and finding that they differed, triumphantly decided in favour of giants. The first complete account of the anatomy of the elephant was by Mr. Patrick Blair, the botanist, then a surgeon in Dundee, who dissected and set up one which died near that place in 1706. His account occupies no less than 116 pages of the

Philosophical Transactions. The drawings were made by Mr. Blair and engraved in Dundee by Gilbert Oram.

MUMMY.3 In old times Egyptian mummies were to be come by only with difficulty, and were rarely to be found in Europe. When one was obtained for a museum, it formed a prominent object in the collection, and

The Natural History of Oxfordshire p. 136, London, 1705, fol.

"The Philosophical Transactions, xxvii. (1710-12), p. 53 sqq. xxx. (1717-T9), p. 385; and separately, Osteographia Elepjtantitia, 1713, 4to.

An account of Dr. Patrick Blair will be found in Pulteney, Sketches of the Progress of Botany, ii., p. 134.

3 Kundmann, Promtuarium, p. 120, Vratislav., 1726, 4to.

became the subject of elaborate description Father Montfaucon figrures several; one of them had been brought to Paris in 1692; two of the others were in Father Kircher's museum at Rome. The town of Leipsic purchased one in 1693, which was placed in the town library, and an account of it occupies nearly four columns of Zedler's Lexicon. The Jesuits of Presburg had one in their Pharmacy (Apotheke), which was believed to be that of Cleopatra. There was one in the Copenhagen Museum, one in the Gottorp Museum, and others in those of Tobias Reymers of Luneburg and Robert Hubert of London. In the Leyden Museum they had " The Mumie of an Egyptian Prince about 1800 years old," and "The Mumie of an Egyptian Princes above 13CXD yeares old." The Royal Society of London had a mummy taken from the Royal Pyramids, and presented by the Duke of Norfolk. It was unrolled, and various experiments were made with the body, which enabled Dr. Grew to advance certain opinions regarding the method of embalming practised by the Egyptians, but everything concerning the personality of the mummy remained a mystery. Information regarding ancient Egypt and her people was principally derived from Herodotus

Zedler, Universal Lexuo? t, s. v. " Mumie." The Leipsic mummy is described and figured by Bruckmann, Epistola Itineraria, 13, Cent, iii., p. 135.

-Antiquity Explained translated by Humphreys, v., p. 121, London, 1722, fol.

Valentini, Museum Museorum, vol. ii. Appendix x., p. 26.

A Catalogue of many Natural Rarities, with great industry, cost, and thirty years' travel in Foraign Countries, Collected by Robert Hubert, alias Forges, Gent., and sworn servant to His Majesty, p. i, London, 1665, i2mo.

This was a famous specimen, and is referred to by Valentini, Museu)n Museorum, i., p. 418.

and Diodorus Siculus, and abounded in the marvellous; while the writing, with which mummy cases and wrappers were covered, had long baffled all the attempts of scholars to interpret it, so that a mummy was in truth a curiosity.

Embalmed bodies were found to be endowed with extraordinary virtues. Francis I. always carried about with him a little packet containing some mummy mixed with pulverized rhubarb, ready to take upon receiving any injury from a fall or other accident that might happen to him. According to Cardan, mummy was a most valuable medicine for staunching blood, and for healing fractures and bruises, an opinion which has the support of Robert Boyle and Lord Bacon. " Mummy," says Ole Worm, "is of great use for contusions, dissolves clotted blood, assists labour, relieves spasms and convulsions, and cures all wounds, external and internal, ulcerations, and other ailments of that kind." This was disputed by Ambroise Pare and others, but it was the current opinion of the time. Mummy accordingly formed an important item of the Materia Medica, and was to be found in every apothecary's shop, and appears in

Belon, Obsenuitiotis de phtsieiirs Singularitez et Choses memorables, p. 261; quoted by Pettigrew, A History of Egyptian Mummies, p. 9, London, 1834, 4to.

De Subtilitate, lib. xviii., p. 645, Lugduni, 1580, 8vo.

Sylva Sylvarum, Cent, x., 980; Works, ii., p. 665, ed. Spedding.

"Museum Wormianutn, p. 344, Lugd. Bat., 1655, fol.; see further, Aldrovandi, Musaeum Metallicujn, p. 403; Zedler, Universal Lexicon, s. v. Mumie."

Discours, supra, p. 44; Oeuvres, iii., p. 468; Chirurgie, ii., c. 7, Oeuvres, ii., p. 202; English translation, p. 332, London, 1649, fol.

the Scottish Customs Tariff of 1612, The mummy of commerce was of various colours. Pierre Pomet of Rouen (1658-1699), chief druggist to the Grand Roi, recommends one to choose what is of black colour. "This is reckond proper for contusions and to hinder the blood from coagulating in the body; but its greatest use is catching fish."-

Although all museums could not attain to an entire mummy, nearly every one had one or more fragments. Thus, besides the whole mummies in the Leyden collection, they had "The head and foot of a Mumie," "The cheek-bone of a Mumie," "The arme of an Egyptian Mumie." In the old pharmacy in the German National Museum at Nuremberg there is a piece of black mummy amongst the assortment of drugs. Franz Ernst Briickmann of Wolfenblittel had the whole left I foot of an Egyptian mummy, with all the toes; and Jakob von Melle of Liibeck had a bit in his cabinet, I which is still preserved in the town museum. There i was another fragment in the Balfour Museum, pre-i sented by Sir Robert Sibbald to the University of Edinburgh.

I But while mummified portions of human bodies were always obtainable for pharmacies or museums, it is to

Ledger of Andretu Halyburto7i p. 301, Edinburgh, 1867 (Lord Clerk Register Series).

- Histoire getterale des Drogues, Paris, 1694, fol., English translation, ii., p. 229, London, 1712, 4to. The copy of this translation in the British Museum bears on the title-page the autograph " James Petiver, S. R. S." Stt post, p. 135.

Epistola Itineraria, 58, Cent, i., Wolffenb., 1737, 4to.

Festschrift zur XXVIII. Versammlung dcr deutschen anthropologi-schen Gesellschaft, p. 16, Liibeck, August, 1897.

Auctarium Musaei Balfourtani, p. 32.

be feared that very few of them were parts of embalmed bodies. "All the kinds of Mummy are brought from yegypt, but we are not to imagine that any body breaks up the real Egyptian Mummies to sell to the druggists, as they make so much better a market for them in Europe whole, when they can contrive to get them. What our druggists are supplyd with is the flesh of executed criminals, or of any other bodies the Jews can get, who fill them with common bitumen, so plentiful in that part of the world; and adding a little aloes, and two or three other cheap ingredients, send them to be baked in an oven till the juices are exhaled, and the embalming matter has penetrated so thoroughly, that the flesh will keep, and bear transporting into Europe." Fortunately, just as the horn of the narwhal was found to possess all the qualities of the " true" unicorn, so artificial mummy was found to be quite as efficacious as the genuine article.

Dr. John Schroder (1600-1664), whose Pha7ma-copoeia was for more than a century a standard authority on the simples, advocates the use of artificial mummy as being fully as good in all respects as the best Egyptian, provided it be properly prepared. The coarse work of the Jew dealers was not in much esteem; but a receipt for the preparation of the artificial article by Oswald Croll was highly recommended. From this were prepared tincture of mummy, elixir of mummy, and balsam of mummy. The latter "has

Hill, History of tjie Materia Medica, p. 875, London, 1751, 410; Alston, Lectures on the Materia Medica, ii., p. 543, London, 1770, 4to; Zedler, Op. laud.; Valentini, Museum Museortim, vol. ii. Appendix xxi., p. 83; Pettigrew, A History 0Egyptian Mummies, p. 8, London, 1834,4to.

2 Alston, Op. laud., i., p. 24.

such piercing qualities, that it pierceth all parts, restores wasted limbs, consumptions, heckticks, and cures all ulcers and corruptions."

HU- LA. SKULL.

A collection of human skulls is one of the features of a modern anthropological museum; but although skulls were to be found in the old museums, they were not exhibited for anthropological purposes, but as common simples of the Pharmacopoeia. A man's skull was a specific in the cure of most diseases of the head, and was administered as a magistery and in various other forms. Human brains again, either in the form of a spirit or an oil, was a noble anti-epileptic. Nehemiah Grew catalogues two skulls in the Royal Society's museum amongst " Human Rarities," The one was, "A human skull that was never buried. Whereof there are several medicines prepard, as Cranium htimamiin praeparatum, Cra imm humatium calcinatutn, Cra iii huniani magistermm, Spiritus essentificatus, Oleum, Sal volatile, Ti? ictura, Galreda, i. e. Extractum cranii Theophrasti. But the Cranium praeparatitm and the spirit are the most, and most deservedly, in use." Directions for the preparation

Salmon, New London Dispensatory, pp. 194, 195, London, 1696, 8vo; Schroder, Pharmacopoeia Medico-Chymica, lib. v., p. 277, Ulmae, 1644, 4to; Hoffmann, Clavis Pharmaceutica Schrbderiana, p. 673, Hal. Sax., 1675, 4to.

Salmon, Op. laud., p. 195; Daniel Beckher (1594-1655;, Professor at Konigsberg, wrote Medicus Microcosmus, sive, Spagyria Microcosmi, tradens Medicinatn e corpore Hominis, turn vivo, turn extincto, docte eruendam, scite praeparandam et dextre propinandam, Rostochii, 1622, 8vo; Lugd. Bat, 1633, 4to; Lond., 1660, i2mo, in which this and similar subjects are discussed.

Grew, Musaeum Societatis Regalis, p. 6, London, 1681, fol.

and use of all these and many others are given in the Neiv London Dispensatory In the Balfour Museum, presented by Sir Robert Sibbald to the University of Edinburgh, there was a similar skull. Another was "A humane skull coverd all over with moss, by the Paracelsians called usnea. This moss is by them commended by its peculiar virtue in stopping of bleeding at the nose." In consequence of a schism in the sympathetical school of curers, a serious discussion was long maintained "Whether it was necessary that the moss should grow absolutely on the skull of a thief who had hung on the gallows?" The general opinion was that the virtues attributed to skulls belonged only to those which had never been buried, and particularly of persons who had died violent deaths, and had lain some time on the ground, or hung on the gibbet or the like. The skulls of commerce were generally those of criminals, and in the old days of hanging there was always a plentiful supply. French writers love to give colour to tl subject, and Pierre Pomet, when treating of skulls, says, "The English druggists generally bring these heads from Ireland, that country having been remarkable for them ever since the Irish massacre." About

Salmon, Neiv London Dispensatory, p. 195; Schroder, Pharmacopoeia Medtco-Chytnica, lib. v., p. 280; Hoffmann, Op. laud., p. 676.

2 Sibbald, Auctarium Musaei Balfouriatii, p. 197, Edinburgh, 1697, 1 i2mo. There was one in the Anatomy School at Oxford. Fountainhall, Journals, p. 170, Edinburgh, 1900; see also Museum Wormianitm, p. 344; Salmon, Op. laud., p. 79; Robert Boyle, Works, ii., p. 177; iv., 767, London, 1772, 4to.

Pettigrew, Superstitions comiected with the History atid Practice of Medicine and Surgery, p. 162, London, 1844, 8vo.

Pomet, Op. laud., English translation, p. 229; Boyle, ut supra.

the same time it was said that the Germans got their supply from the last Turkish war.

HUMAN SKIN.

The seat on which the Persian judges sat was covered with the skin of their unjust predecessor, with the inscription, "Remember whereon thou sittest." Amongst European nations the skin of an enemy or of a notorious criminal was often tanned and preserved out of revenge or as a terror to others. In many old collections pieces of tanned human skin were to be seen," but these were placed there not as ethnographical objects, but as specimens of officinal preparations, as this material was said to be possessed of many virtues. " Celebres sunt corii humani praeparati in medicina usus." A belt of human skin was used as a remedy for hysteria, and was found to be useful in spasms of the hands and feet. A bandao e round the wrist checked convulsions, and a thong round the neck cured a paroxysm of epilepsy.

The origin of this strange belief is illustrated by the practice of uncivilised people of the present day. Some of the aborigines of Queensland carefully flay their slain foes, and preserve the skin with the

Valentini, Museum Museorujii, i., p. 419. 2 E. g. in the Anatomy Hall of Leyden.

Bartholinus, Historiariim anatomicarinn Rariora, Cent, iii., Hist. 87, p. 177, Amstelod., 1654.

Rattray, Aditus itoviis., p. 25, Glasguae, 1658, i2mo; Schroder, Op. laud., lib. v., p. 279; Hoffmann, Op. laud., p. 679. Briickmann disputes this, Epistola Itineraria, 17, Cent. i.

Bartholinus, Op. laud. As the tanning of human skin was a disagreeable and somewhat difficult art, Bartholin gives directions how it is to be done.

hairy scalp and even the finger nails attached. They look upon it as a powerful medicine, and cover their patients with it as with a blanket. In some parts of Africa the natives cover their idols with human skin.

THE STAG AND THE ELK.

Hartshorn (the antlers of the cervus elephas) is a familiar term in pharmacy, and oil of hartshorn, spirits of hartshorn, and the like are still ordinary domestic remedies; but in old days so many medicines were compounded from various parts of the stag that they formed the subject of entire volumes, and inspired a poem. The animal itself was described as "a world of remedies, of commodities and advantages, for men." The horn that was most in repute was that of the red deer, the exetpa? of the Greeks, but, as it was scarce in England, the horn of the fallow deer was used instead. The old Schloss Merlan at Grumberg in Hesse-Darmstadt was so set out with rare, cu,, and valuable stag-horns of all descriptions as to be in itself a museum. In the Dresden Museum there were various stag-horns and preparations from stags, and in the Court Pharmacy there were fifty-one of such preparations, a selection from which was presented

Frazer's Paiisanias, ii., p. 477, who refers to Fison and Howitt, Kamilarot and Kurnai, p. 223, Melbourne, 1880, 8vo.

2 Boehmer, Bibliotheca Scriptorutn historiae naturalis ii., 2, pp. 360-7.

Balduin Ronsseus, Venatio Aledica, Lugd. Bat, 1584 and 1589, 8vo; and in his Opuscula Medica, Lugd. Bat., 1618 and 1654, 8vo.

Valentini, Aluseum Museoritm i., p. 430. There is a large collection at the present day in the Schloss Erbach in the Odenwald.

Beutel, Cedern-Wald, Dresden, 1671, 4to; Happel, Relationes Curiosae, iii., p. 121, Hamburg, 1687, 4to.

"Happel, Op. laud., iii., pp. 121, 122.

by the Elector John George II. (1656-1680) to the Grand Duke of Tuscany.

Stag's horn was esteemed of great use in cases of poisoning and of malignant diseases. Snakes, it was said, would not touch a person clad in deer-skin. The smell of burnt horn drove away serpents and gnats. Venison was a specific for fevers. A stag could not only swallow a snake with impunity, but turned it into stone in its stomach." Stag tears, "a thickend excretion from the inward angle of his eye," had a great reputation; and were " affirmed to be sudorifick and of an alexipharmic nature "; and Dr. Grew wickedly adds, "If they were as easie to be had as some women's it were worth the trying." But they were scarce, and so valuable as by some to be preferred to all the treasures of a king. The elder Scaliger had one which he considered the gem of his collection.

Another esteemed remedy was Ossa de Corde Cervi, a kind of ossification occasionally found in the hearts of stags and of oxen. These were imported from Italy and sold by the thousand," and we find them in use in

Major, Dissertatio Epistolica de Cancris et Serpentidus petrefaclts, p. 9, Jenae, 1664, 8vo.

2 Major, Op. laud., pp. 7 sqq., 36; Sachse von Lowenheim, Op. laud., p. 58.

Grew, Afusaeum Regalis Socle talis, p. 21. Hoffmann, Clavis phar? naceutica, p. 659.

De Subtilitate, Exercitatio 112, p. 422, Francof., 1612, Bvo. Schroder mentions that he had the gift of a small piece from Sophia Eleonora, Princess of Saxony, wife of George, Landgrave of Hesse. Pharinacopoeia Medico-Chyrnica, lib. v., p. 266, Ulmae, 1644, 410.

"Valentini, Museum. Museorum, i., p. 431.

Scotland in 1612. So numerous were their merits that these afforded material for a graduation thesis.

The elk and its parts were to be found in museums and in apothecaries' shops. Elk's hoof was a specific remedy for epilepsy, and was always kept in druggists' booths and often placed in museums. That which possessed the greatest power was the hoof of the left hind foot. The elk, it was said, was itself subject to epilepsy, and cured itself by putting that foot into its ear. Judging from the form of the animal, such cures must have been few and far between.

The medicinal virtues of these various substances were not arrived at haphazard, but were ascertained by observation and by what were believed to be careful experiments. Very few of them were of any real toxicological value; but that cures followed many of the prescriptions there is no doubt. In some raco-the remedy did effect a cure. In other cases the natural event of the disease was mistaken for the effect of the medicine last administered, or at least of the use of some medicine. Imagination, too, plays an important part in the human economy, and in our own day many

Andrew Halyburtofis Ledger, ut supra, p. 301.

"Os de corde cervi gestantem reddit immunem a venanatorummorsibus." Rattray, Aditus novus, p. 26, Glasguae, 1658, i2mo.

"Adami, Dissertatio i? iauguralis de Osse Cordis Cervi, Giessae, 1684, 4to.

Ray notes the horns and feet of the elk in the museum of Jan van Der Mere of Delft, and the horns (25 lbs. in weight) in the shop of Mr. Holney, apothecary in Lewes. Travels through the Low Countries, ii., p. 24, London, 1738, 8vo.

Valentini, Museum Museorum, i., p. 428; Schroder, Pharmacopoeia Medico-Chytnica, lib. v., p. 252; Salmon, Neiu London Dispensatory, p. 197.

Alston, Lectures on the Materia Medica, i., p. 24, London, 1770, 4to.

wonderful cures have been apparently effected by remedies which were in fact powerless; a subject which has been discussed by Dr. T. J. Pettigrew who records many interesting cases. " Imagination," says Lord Bacon, " is next akin to miracle a working faith." In old days it was dangerous, however, to apply a harmless remedy and leave it to the imagination to do the rest. Sir Georcre Mackenzie mentions the case of a poor woman who was charged with witchcraft because she cured another by applying a plantain leaf to the left side of her head, and binding a paper to her wrist, upon which was written the name

Jesus.

FIGURED STONES.

Everyone knows what is meant by a "fossil"; but the present meaning of the word is somewhat late. The old writers understood by fossils whatever was extracted from the earth, and divided them into three classes: media mineralia, stones, and metals. Media mineralia were of a nature intermediate between stones and metals, and comprised earths, salts, sulphur, and bitumen. This classification, or some modification of it, was the groundwork of the arrangement of all old

On Superstitions connected with the History and Practice of Medicine, p. 89 sqq., London, 1844, 8vo. See also Thomas Fien, De Viribus Imaginationis tractatus, Lovan., 1608, 8vo; Lugd. Bat., 1635, i2mo; Robert Boyle, Works, ii., p. 174, London, 1772, 4to; Haygarth, Of the Imagination as a Cause and Cure of Disorders of the Body exemplified by Fictitious Tractors and Epidemical Convulsions, Bath, 1800, 8vo; D. H. Tuke, Illustrations of the Infiuence of the Mind upon the Body in Health and Disease, designed to elucidate the Action of the Imagination, London, 1872, 8vo. Pleadings in some remarkable Cases, p. 192, Edinburgh, 1673, 4to- Albertus Magnus, De mineralibus et rebus metallicis, lib. v., c. i.

museums, and must be kept clearly in view in studying their catalogues and in reading the descriptions of their contents. Fossils, it was held, were endowed with the power of growth and reproduction; there was thought to be a seminal quality or plastic power vis plastica, fiisus formativtis) in the earth by which fossils were produced, by which they grew and took shape.

Stone was defined to be a fossil body, hard, inductile, not soluble in water, generated from a strong juice succus in which is the stone-forming spirit lapidificus spiritus), petrescent liquor or petrifick spirit, as Robert Boyle called it. One of the principal divisions of stones was lapides Jigurati or lapides isio-jlopcpoi, s. ejujuopcpoi, " formed stones," otherwise lapides regiilares or "regular stones," that is, stones which had a specific form or shape, or resembled in shape some known object, animal or vegetable, '–tinguished from lapides auopcpoi. For example, the Jew stone lapis yudaiacs was of various shapes, resembling a pear, an almond, an acorn, or an olive; and had many virtues. These stones were of two 1" Quis non obstupescit animo, cui hominum, piscium, serpentum, ostrearum, concharum, et infinitarum aliarumque rerum, ab archaeo subterraneo fabricatae et lapidibus metallicis impressae, occurrunt imagines."' Zacharia-Pillingen, Bitumen et lignum fosstle biiumt? tosum, p. 8, Altenb., 1674, 8vo. To the same effect, see Museum Wormianum, p. 81.

"Museum Wormianum, p. 36; Aldrovandi, Museum Metallicum, p. 818, Bononiae, 1648, fol.; Agricola, De ortu et causis Subterraneorum, lib. iv., with his De re metallica, p. 512 sqq., Basil, 1657, fol.; Boetius, Gemmarian et lapidum Historia, pp. 13, 24, 29; Valentini, Museum Museorum, ii., Appendix xxi., p. 92.

Steno, Prodromus Efiglishd by H. O. Henry Oldenburg. Preface, London, 1671, 8vo. Boyle thought that there were also both Metal-lescent and Mineralescent juices.

kinds, male and female, the former covered with points, the latter smooth, and found in Palestine; and were supposed to grow like other stones. They were, in fact, the spines of an echinus. Belemnites, the English "bolt-head" so called from its resemblance to an arrow; in Scotland known as an elf-arrow, and in Germany as Alpfschos, because they are vulgarly believed to be shot by fairies are the petrified internal bone or shell of a kind of cuttle-fish; the ammonite or cornu Ammonis, so called from its resemblance to the horn on the statue of Jupiter Ammon, is a fossil shell. Then we have bucardia or ox-heart stone, echmites or button-stone, pear stones, apple stones, gourd stones, stone teeth, and so on. Some of these were only accidentally shaped, but the greater part of them are animal remains which have been petrified. In the old museums they were, however, treated as natural growths. Thus, in the beautiful collection in the Schloss Amras near Innsbruck, were "stones which represent trees, fruits, shells, and animals, all which are the pure product of nature." The stone oranges, figs, melons, nutmegs, mushrooms, and the like, regarding which the most miraculous stories were current, were fossil zoophytes. The bufoniies,

These were not petrified teeth, but figured stones, or perhaps some kind of coral. Briickmann, Episiola Itmeraria, 64, Cent. i.

Misson, A New Voyage to Italy, i., p. 113, London, 1699, 8vo. Misson was anything but credulous. When they showed him at Ley den 1 a serpent's skin with Arabic letters on it naturally formed, he at once rejected it and very justly adds, "There is so universal, and so odd a 1 diversity in all things in the world, that woud be easie to find the i like figures on the first thing we meet with, if we would give ourselves the trouble to look for em." Op. laud., i., p. 15.

Parkinson, Organic Remains of a Former World, i., p. 460.

the English toad-stone, a semi-oval or semi-globular stone, was supposed to be engendered in the heads of toads and frogs, but is in reality a petrified portion of the teeth or dentary plates of fishes; although, when this was demonstrated, the defenders of the old opinions produced another stone, convex above and concave below, which they said was the real toad-stone. The fact that animal or vegetable remains could be petrified was only recognised comparatively recently. It was opposed to the science of older times, and even when sounder views began to prevail they had to encounter theological objections, which stood in the way of their acceptance. What we now know as fossils were popularly explained by some to be sports, lusus naturae, by others, to be the product of the plastic quality of " th, which by its inherent power in certain places produced stones having these particular shapes. Stones, it was said, grow; vegetables grow and live; animals grow, live, and feel.

Another group of stones falling within the class of lapides Jigurati, or regular stones, were cerauniae, the stone axes and stone hammers of modern archaeologists. These were popularly believed to fall from the clouds, and had for centuries been regarded with superstitious awe. Our English encyclopaedist, Bartholomew de

Plot, The Natural History of Oxfordshire p. 129, London, 1705, fol.

2 Linnaeus, Fundainenta Botanica, 3; Alston, Lectures on the Materia Medica, i., p. 22.

Stone celts are still viewed as thunderbolts by the modern Burmese. P. R. I. A. 2'S., i. (1870-1879), p. 396. See other references in Reinach, Antiquith nationales, i., p. 79. Paris, 1889.

As to charms in the form of stone axes, see Materiaux, x. C1875), p. 290,

Glanville r, 1250, gave currency to the current doctrine, and quotes the curious poem of Marbode, Bishop of Rennes (f 1123):

Cum tonat horrendum, cum fulgurat igneus Aether Nubibus illisis caelo cadit ille lapillus.

Illis quippe locis, quos constat fulmine tactos, Iste lapis tantum reperiri posse putatur.

Qui caste gerit hunc a fulmine non ferietur Nee domus, aut villae, quibus asseruit lapis ille.-

The stone axes in the Cathedral of Halberstadt and in Martha's Hof, Bonn, before alluded to, exemplify this belief.

When the stone fell it buried itself in the earth as deep as the highest church tower is high. Every time it thundered it began to rise nearer to the surface, and after seven years you may find it above ground. According to others the thunderbolt penetrated the earth to a distance of nine fathoms, and rose up a fathom each year until it reached the surface. Agricola

De Proprietatibus rertim, lib. xvi., c. 32. He relies on Isidore as his authority.

Marbode, Liber de Gemnn's, 28, in Migne, Pairologiae Ciirsus coni-pleius, torn. 171, p. 1756. Ropartz, Poenies de Marbode (Latin and French), p. 176, Rennes 1872, 8vo. This is a locus classiais quoted since its date by everyone who has touched upon cerauniae. It was copied on a slip and attached to a Fubninis sagitta in the museum at Leyden in 1634. Brereton, Travels, P- 41. (Chetham Society.)

Grimm, Teutonic Mythology, translated by Stallybrass, i., p. 179. London, 1882, 8vo.

Gesner, De rerutn fossiliuin, lapidu7n et gcmniarum Liber, p. 66; Aldrovandi, Mtiseum jnetallicum, p. 609; Von Scheelenberg in Zeitschrift filr Etjmologie, xii. (1880), p. 255.

mentions the common belief, but without saying that he accepts it and in this he is followed by Gesner." De Boodt says that so strong was the vulgar notion that anyone who disputed that such things fell from the clouds would be thought a fool. Many, however, he adds, are doubtful, while others explain the phenomenon by the theory that cerauniae were the product of an exhalation from lightning acted on by moisture and heat which caused them to assume their specific shapes and produced their various colours. But if this explanation be well founded, it is strange, he adds, that the stone is not entirely round, and that it is perforated. Others, again, could not understand how stones came to be formed in the clouds, anu suggested that the cerauniae or the material which composes them, were swept up from the earth by whirlwinds and hurled down again by thunder clouds. This de Boodt considered unsatisfactory. Ulisse Aldrovandi, the great naturalist of Bologna, thought that they were produced like other stones, by the plastic power of nature, and this was evidently the opinion of Agricola, of Gesner, and of de Boodt.

While so many imaginary virtues were attributed to celts it is interesting to know that they are possessed of some very curious dynamical properties. A few years ago an Aberdeenshire farmer ascertained that a perforated celt spins perfectly when turned in one

De naiura fossiliutn, lib.-., p. 6io, with the De re metallica. Basil., 1657.

Ut supra, p. 65.

This is explained at some length by Lodovico Moscardo, Note ovvero Memorie del suo fnuseo, p. 144. Padua, 1656, fol.

See Von Scheelenberg, ut supra, p. 255.

direction, but will not do so when spun in the opposite direction; a phenomenon which was subsequently investigated and explained by Mr. G. T. Walker of Trinity College, Cambridge.

Another thunder-stone was known by the name of brontea (German Trottenstein) and a third as ombria. The latter falls, says Pliny,- " with showers and lightning, much in the same manner as the ceraunia and brontea, the properties of which it is said to possess." The bronteae were in reality petrified bodies, the ceratluiae were the product of human handicraft, yet both were treated as stones which had assumed their particular shapes by virtue of an occult power in the earth. Bronteae, says Mercati, " are not thunderbolts but naturally-formed stones," by w hich he meant lapides i iofx6p(poi. Besides thunder-bolts there were also thunder-balls globuliftuminares, Donner-Kugeln), which were likewise thouq-ht to be o'enerated in the air and thrown down by thunder clouds. These were egg-shaped in form, and were apparently merely rolled stones."

Stones have often an accidental resemblance to some known object, such form being produced by weathering, by ice, water, or other external cause, and it is sometimes difficult to distinguish between such

Proceedings of the Cambridge Philosophical Society, viii. (1895), P- 2 S-

Valentini notes that the perforation is through the point of equilibrium. Museum Museorum, i., p. 54.

Historia Naturalis, xxxvi. 65.

Metallotheca, p. 246.

Briickmann, Epistola Itineraria, 32, Cent, i., and Supplement, p. 26. He mentions, Epistola 15, a curious story of meal which some credulous peasants believed to have fallen from the clouds.

a Sport and an object artificially formed. A large number of the stones which were grouped according to a fancied likeness to some natural object were of this character. The result was that petrifactions, artifically shaped stones and mere sports were placed in the same group, which was based on figure, and such figure, it was assumed in each case, was produced by the plastic power of the earth.

Glossopetrae were a class of stones which caused much discussion, Pliny says that the glossopetra resembles the human tongue, is not engendp- d in the earth, but falls from the heavens dunng the moon's eclipse, and is considered highly necessary for the purposes of selenomancy. He does not, in terms, refer to flint arrowheads, but that he did was assumed by many of the older antiquaries, who classed these objects under the head glossopetrae, and attributed to them all the virtues mentioned by Pliny and many others besides. Glossopetrae were found in great numbers in Malta, and were known as " Serpents' tongues " from the belief that they were the tongues of serpents which had been turned into stone by the preaching of St. Paul.- This, says de Boodt, is all wrong; "they are stones of their own kind," that is, stones which so grew. Michael Mercati, after mentioning that there are three kinds of glossopetrae, large, middling, and small, says that some people

Historia Aaturalis, xxxvii. 59.

-Bartholinus, Epistolae Medicinales, Cent, i., Epist. 53, p. 223. See also lb., pp. 216, 240, 241, 242; Major, Bedencken von Kiinst- und Naturalicn-Kammern, c. x., p. 59, in Valentini, Museum Museorum, vol. i. See also Valentini, Op. laud., i., p. 65.

Getmnarznn et lapiduni Historia, p. 340.

confound the large kind with the teeth of the lamia or shark, and that their mistake is excusable as there is a great similarity. He figures the open mouth of a shark and separately one of its teeth and also a glossopetra. He then goes on to point out wherein they differ. Giossopetrae, as a rule, are thinner and less bright; sharks' teeth are always bright, while giossopetrae vary in colour. It was the middle size which were taken for serpents' teeth, which, says Mercati, is an error; they are nature's own handiwork, "privatum naturae opus." Yet they are undoubtedly the fossilised teeth of certain kinds of shark. The identification, which was only accepted after a long controversy, was one of the first steps towards determining the true nature of fossils. Fossil shells, according to the opinion of the ancients, were the remains of fish that had once lived, but curiously enough this view was not accepted by scientific men of the sixteenth and seventeenth centuries. According to their doctrine, fossil shells were not regarded; is having any connection with actual shells, but were attributed to a vegetative virtue in the particular soil in the places where they were found, which determined them to that particular and regular shape. An argument against their ever having been the coverings of molluscs was that they were found far from the sea.

Metallotheca, p. 333. His account of the lamia he takes from Ron-dolet, De piscibtcs marinis, p. 390. Lugd., 1554, fol.

Pidgeon, The Fossil Remains of the Animal Kingdo7H, p. 428, London, 1836, 8vo; Hill, History of the Materia Medica, p. 307.

An interesting abstract of the opinions of the older writers tending to prove that fossil shells were once real shells is given by John de Laet, De ge7? iinis et lapidibiis, p. 177 sqq. Lugd. Bat., 1647, 8vo.

Glossopetrae for instance were found in the sands of Deventer and in the alum pits at Ltineburg as well as in Malta, and sharks, it was argued, could not by any possibility have been in such inland places. John Baptista Olivus or Oliva of Cremona, writing in 1584, states that they were believed to be sharks' teeth. " dentes lamiarum credunt." Fabio Colonna (1567-1660), a physician in Rome, an exact and erudite observer, published a treatise in 1616, Glossopetris, in which he maintained that they were the teeth of sharks. In 1669 Niels or Nicolaus Steno (1631-1687), a Danish naturalist resident in Italy, argued that they were the teeth of sea doq-s Aorostino Scilla, a Sicilian painter, writing in 1670, pointed out the close resemblance in several particulars between the fossil teeth found in Malta, Calabria, and other places, and the teeth of living sharks, and added that they are just such teeth converted into stone. John Reiske (1640-

Boetius, Geinmarum et lapidum Historia p. 341.

- De recondifis et praecipuis collcctaneis in Musaeo Calccolarii, p. 42. Venet., 1584, 4to.

With his treatise, De Purpura, Romae, 1616, 4to; reprinted separately in an enlarged form, Romae, 1627, and with Agostino Scilla De Corportbus marinis lapidescentibiis. Romae, 1752, and again 1759, 4to. He had advocated the same views in his De aquatilibus aliisque anitnalibus qtdbusdaih panels Libelbis. Romae, 1616, 8vo.

An account of Colonna's museum will be found in Major, Bedencken von Kunst- und Ahituralieti-Katnniern, p. 68, in "alentini, Museum Museoriun, vol. i.

De Solido intra Solidum naturaliter contento dissertationis Prodro-? nus. Florent., 1669, 4to; Lugd. Bat., 1679, i2mo; translated into English by H. O. Henry Oldenburg, London, 1671, 8vo. In Italian, Pistorii, 1763, 4to, supra, p. 49.

La vana speculaziotie disingafmata del Senso. Naples, 1670, 4to; in Latin, Rome, 1752, 1759, 4to. Abridged in The Philosophical Trans-actiofts, xix. (1695-97), p. 181 sqq., by Dr. Wotton. The subject was 1701), Rector of the Gymnasium at Liineburg, took a different view, combatted the doctrines of Colonna, Steno, and Scilla, and advanced as his own opinion that glossopetrae were neither tongues nor parts of animals but simply stones, that is, figured stones which had so grown Still later, Ole Worm (1667-1708), grandson of the great collector of the same name, gives it as his opinion that the glossopetra was a stone condensed by some saline, nitrous, and bituminous juices in the bowels of the earth, as well on the sea shore as on the tops of mountains." In 1717 Georg Andreas Helwing (1666-1748), pastor of Angerburg, refutes the old story of glossopetrae being serpents' tongues and describes several species of sharks' teeth under the titles Glossopeh a and Odo7itopeira He was, taken up and discussed by Dr. John Arbuthnot. An Exaj)iitiatio)i of Dr. Woodward's Account of the Deluge., etc., London, 1697, 8vo, in which he deals not only with Dr. Woodward, but also with Steno, Scilla, and Wotton.

An interesting account of the whole question and of the views of Robert Hooke is given by Ray, Travels througji the Loiu Countries., i., pp. 96-iio, 252, 267, London, 1738, Svo.

Scilla's collections are in the Woodwardian Museum, Cambridge.

De Glossopetris Lihiebiirgensibus. Lips., 1684, 4to; Norimb., 1687, 8vo.

"De Glossopetris dissertatio. Hafniae, 1686, 4to.

Lithographia Angerburgica, pars i. Koenigsb., 1717; pars ii. Lips., 1720, 4to. Prefixed to Part i. is a very quaint engraving of Angerburg. De lapidibus et fossilibus. Koenigsb., 1717. His chapter (Part i., c. vii., p. 79 sqq) on Thunder-bolts lapidesfulininares) is reprinted in Materiaux., X. (1875), P- 297 sqq. See also lb., p. 98.

In his plate x. he gives representations both of stone and bronze axes and fibulae.

'This was pretty much Scilla's view, that minerals and metals were generated by a penetrating juice or vapour, arising out of the bowels of the earth, which alters and turns all manner of earth into itself.

Briickmann deals fully with the subject in Epistola Itineraria., 29, Cent. i.

however, a believer in fossil man, and describes many petrified parts of the human body and stones bearing the figure of man. A few years later, Dr. John Woodward 1665-1728) catalogues a large number of objects, which had been sent to him by Scilla, as fossil sharks' teeth. Chemistry was dragged into the dispute. Elias Camerarius (1672-1734), Professor of Medicine in the University of Tubingen, was unable to persuade himself that the glossopetrae could ever have been the teeth of any fish because of the small quantity of volatile salt and oil which they afforded on distillation. To which Woodward replied that they no doubt lost the best part of their volatile principles from being so long buried in the earth. Camerarius next objected that when exposed to the naked fire they turn to a coal and not to a calx as asserted by Colonna.

To this Woodward answered that it was quite probable that in burning they might assume the form of a coal before it arrived at that of a calx.

Fossil bones which were not petrified were treated just the same as teeth that were petrified. It was assumed that they were not bones at all. By some it was thought that they were produced naturally in the earth. Others were of opinion that stone marrow op. laud., part i., p. 55 sqq.; ii., p. 127.

"Catalogue of foreign fossils. Part ii., pp. 23-29. London, 1728, 8vo.

3 Woodward, Naturalis historia Telluris illustrata et aucta una cum ejusdem defensione praeserfim contra jiuperas objectiones El. Camerarii, London, 1714, Svo. In English, London, 1726, Svo; in French, by Noguez, Amst., 1735, o me7-ga), being dissolved and percolating through the earth, ultimately assumed the form of bones.

Glossopetrae, like arrow-heads, were used as charms. At one time, too, they occupied a prominent place in the pharmacopoeia and were administered in various forms as a remedy for snake bites and for the cure of many diseases; but latterly they were less esteemed and, like the teeth of present-day sharks, were used only for tooth powder.""

Nearly every stone, figured and otherwise, was used in medicine in old days. Cerauniae stone axes when reduced to powder, was a famous remedy for jaundice, and belemnites the bolt-head was an accepted cure for nightmare!

THE BARNACLE GOOSE.

An exhibit which was eagerly sought after was the Claik or Barnacle Goose, the French IMarguerooue or Macreuse the origin of which long vexed the

As to merga, see Agricola, De natura fossiliiim, lib. ii., with the De re metallica, p. 578. Basil., 1657. Aldrovandi, Mtisaeum metalliaivi, p. 630; Valentini, Museum Aluseorum, ii., pp. 3,4; Leibnitz, Protogaea, 36; Schroder, Pharmacopoeia, lib. iii., p. 42.

Boetius, Op. laud., p. 426; Valentini, Op. laud., ii., Appendix i., p. 92; Hill, History of the Materia Medica, p. 260.

3 One is figured in Materiaux, xi. (1876), p. 540.

Hoffmann, Clavis pharmaceutica Schroderiatta, p. 131, Halae, 1675, 4to; Alston, Lectures on the Materia Medica,., p. 271; Valentini, Museum Museoruni, i., p. 66. Keysler, explains their virtues by the presence of coralline salts. Reisen, p. 102, Hannover, 1751, 4to.

Leibnitz, Protogaea, 32; Rondelet mentions De piscibus marinis, P- 393) Lugd., 1554, fol.) that from sharks' teeth the best dentifrice is made. It whitens the teeth by reason of its hardness. Goldsmiths, he says, covered the teeth with silver and called them " Serpents' teeth," and mothers hung them round their babies' necks in the belief that they assisted dentition and kept off frights.

scientific world. Hector Boyis, "a man nocht les notable in lugement, than famous in eruditione, and a maist curiouse sercher out of this secrete and nature of this foule," had given currency to the fable that they were produced either in rotten timber floating in the sea, or from the fruit of certain trees when it fell into the sea; which are actually figured by Gerarde and Aldrovandi. Michael Maier (1568-1622), physician and alchemist, Count of the Imperial Consistory, wrote a special treatise upon these birds The elder Scaliger disputed that they grew upon trees, but was satisfied that they sprang from floating wreckage. Sir Robert Moray, the President of the Royal Society, declared, in 1678, that when he was last in the Western Islands of Scotland he saw multitudes of shells adhering to trees, "having within them little Birds perfectly shapd." He opened several of them and found, he says, nothing wanting for " making up a perfect Sea Fowl," a statement which is alluded to in Hitdibras (Part iii., Canto ii., 652):

And from the most refind of saints,
As natrally grow miscreants,
As barnacles turn soland geese In th islands of the Orcades.

The Historie of Scotland, by Leslie, translated in Scottish by Dal-rymple, i., p. 60, Edinburgh, 1888, 8vo.

- Boece's History was published in 1527. The stor) is to be found three hundred years earlier in the Speculum of Vincent de Beauvais (t 1264).

Boethii, Scotorum Historia, p. 8, verso. Paris, 1574, fol.

Herball, p. 1391. London, 1597, fol.

Tractatus de Volucre Arborea, absque patre et matre in Insulis Orcadum forma Anserculorum proveniente. Francof., 1619; i2mo.

De Siibtilitate, Exercitatio 59, p. 215. Francof, 1612, 8vo. See Gassendi, Vita Peirescii, p. 42, Hag. Com., 1656, 4to.

Philosophical Transactions, xii., No. 137, p. 925. John Ray, who was

Ole Worm adopted the popular belief, with some additional marvels taken from John Monipennie's A bridge7ne7it or Sumniarie of the Scots Chronicles. "At Dumbarton, directly under the castle, at the mouth of the river of Clyde, as it enters in the sea, there are a number of clayk geese, blacke of colour, which in the night time doe gather great quantity of the crops of the grasse, growing upon the land, and carry the same to the sea; then assembling in a round, and with a wondrous curiositie, do offer everie one his own portion to the sea fioud, and there attend upon the flowing of the tide, till the grasse be purified from the fresh taste, and turned to the salt; and lest any part thereof should escape, they labour to hold it in with their nebs; there after orderly every fowie eats his portion; and this custome they observe perpetually. They are very fat and delicious to be eaten."- In some places they were eaten instead of fish, and not being flesh or being produced from flesh, the Theologians of the Sorbonne, it is said, decided that they were to be a fellow of the Royal Society, writing in 1663, says that the story is " without all doubt false and frivolous." Travels through the Low Countries i., p. 250. London, 1738, 8vo.

Museum IVormianum, p. 257.

Edinburgh, 1671, p. 289; Glasgow, 1820, p. 202. The first edition was published, London, 1612, 4to. Again, Edinburgh, 1633, i2mo; Glasgow, 1750, i2mo.

The Claik is still found on the Clyde and Loch Lomond, but the picturesque details of the old chronicler have vanished. See Lumsden and Brown, Guide to the Natural History of Loch Lo7no? id and Neighbourhood, p. 47, Glasgow, 1895, 8vo.

3 Worm, Op. laud.; Dr. Tancred Robinson, "On the French Macreuse and Scotch Bernacle," in The Philosophical Transactions, xv. (1685), pp. 1036, 1041.

classed with fish, and not with birds; they were therefore deemed suitable for use during Lent, and used to be sent from Normandy to Paris in great numbers at that season. Andre Graindorge of Caen (i616-1676) rejected all such stories and decided, in accordance with the opinion of many writers, whom he quotes, that they were hatched from eggs like other birds." Sir Robert Sibbald, about the same time, examined the whole subject personally, and showed that the Barnacle goose Bernicla leucopsis) was a bird produced from an g'g, and that the Barnacle shell Concha miatiferd) instead of being that g was a pholas the Scots piddocks.

It still, however, held its place in the Phar7nacopoeia, and Salmon repeats the old story that "they breed unnaturally of the leaves or apples of a certain tree in Scotland." It agreed in nature and virtues with the common goose. The grease is exceeding good against

This was still the case in 1698. Lister, A Journey to Paris, in 1698, p. 156, London, 1699, 8vo.

2 Traite de Vorigine des Macrckscs par feu M. de Graifidorge, doctcur de la Faculte de Medecine de Motitpellier, et fiiis en lumiere par M. Thomas Malouin, Docteur de la Faculte de Medecine en PUniversite de Caen. Caen, 1680, 8vo. Reprinted by P. J. Buchoz in Traites fres-rares, con-cernant Vhistoire naturelle et les arts. Paris, 1780, i2mo.

Pfody-omus Naturaus Hisioriae Scotiae, Pt. ii., lib. 3, pp. 21, 27, and Appendix, p. 36, Edinburgh, 1684, fol.; Auctarium Musaei Balfouriani, p. 170, Edinburgh, 1697, i2mo. See Wallace, Description of the Isles of Orkney, pp. 21, 189, and Plate ii., ed. Small, Edinburgh, 1883, 8vo. Deusing, Dissertatio de anseribus Scoticis, in his Dissertationum Fasciculus, Groning., 1660, i2mo; Valentini, Museum Museorum, i., p. 465; Laskey, Account of the Hunterian Museum, pp. 30, 99, Glasgow, 1813, 8vo. Migne, Dictionnaire des Superstitions, s. v. Paris, 1856.

An interesting account of the Barnacle goose myth is given by Max Miiller in Lectures on the Science of Language, 2nd Series, pp. 536-551. London, 1864, 8vo.

palsies, lameness, and the like; the blood is an antidote against poison; the gall with honey helps contused eyes; the dung is excellent against scurvy and dropsy, gout and jaundice; the skin of the feet dried and given in powder was a specific for certain ailments.

Salmon, Ncio London Dispensatory, pp. 223, 224, 5th ed., London, 1696, 8vo; Schroder, Pharmacopoeia medico-chymica, lib. v., p. 295, Ulm., 1684, 4to.

Passing by national collections such as those of Rome, Florence, Vienna, Dresden, Munich, Berlin, Paris, Brussels, and London, and Galleries of Art and special collections, as of coins, medals and gems; and anatomical and pathological preparations, it may be instructive to run over some of the more important museums of the seventeenth and eio-hteenth centuries. One of the earliest and most notable was that of the great naturalist Ulisse Aldrovandi (1527-1605), " omnis fere eruditionis oceanus " which is still preserved at Bologna, a monument of his industry and learning. His ambition was to describe and illustrate all external nature. For thirty years he employed and paid a painter two hundred crowns a year, and spared no expense in obtaining the assistance of the first artists of the day; but his labours exceeded his strength and wealth, and he died poor and blind in the hospital of his native city.

See supra, p. 24; itifra, p. 145.

C. S. Schefifel, Vita Schelhammeri, p. 25, in Ad G. C. Schelhavimerum Epistolae selectiores, Wismar, 1727, 8vo. " Rondeletius, Gesnerus at Aldrovandus, qui tres constituunt trigam historicorum physicorum absolutissimam," Alsted, Scientiarum omnium Eficylopadia, xxxii. 10, 4.

His works published in 1599 and subsequent years fill no less than thirteen folio volumes, and were in part edited by Thomas Dempster of Muresk, then professor of humanity in the University of Bologna. " But above all, I must entreat you," writes a learned Scot, " buy me Aidrovandiiss workes, which are 13 or 14 Tomes in Folio; you may buy them in sheets and have them packt up in your own things for Venice, where you will not fail to meet with frequent occasions of sending them to London."" One of the rarest of these volumes is the Musaezmt metallicwn a description of rocks and earths, minerals and metals, including amongst rocks, fossil plants, shells and fish, and such artificial productions as stone axes and flint arrowheads. It is copiously illustrated and brings together all

After Aldrovandi's death the Senate of Bologna employed Dempster along with John Cornelius Uterverius of Delft, who was also a professor at Bologna, to assist in preparing his MS. material for the press. Only a portion was published. There still remain in manuscript between two and three hundred memoirs. Maximilian Misson, who visited the combined museums of Aldrovandi and Cospi in 1688, says, "But there is nothing in both those cabinets so rare and surprising as what I am going to relate to you. In a chamber near to the first we saw a hundred and eighty-seven volumes in folio, all written by Aldrovandus his own hand, with more than two hundred bags full of loose papers. Tis true the margins are large, and the lines at a considerable distance." A Neiu Ioyage to Italy, ii., p. 197, London, 1699, 8vo.

-Letters written to a friend by tjie learned a)id judiciotts Sir Atidrcw Balfour, M. D., pp. 213, 268, Edinburgh 1700, i2mo. See the remarks of Schelhammer in notes on Conringii, In 7tniversam artein niedicam Intro-ductio, p. 293. Spirae, 1688, 4to.

Musaetim 7netallicum in libros iiii. distributum, Barth. Ambrosinus composuit. Bononiae, 1648, fol. Bartholomeo Ambrosini, the editor, was Director of the Botanic Garden of Bologna. The Musaeum was abridged by David Kellner, Synopsis Musaei Metallici U. A. Lipsiae, 1701, i2mo.

the information of the time, which instead of being a blemish, as Buffon suggests, adds considerably to the utility of a work whose value is nowadays, to a great extent, historical. In treating of the metals Aldrovandi deals with them not only in their native but also in their manufactured condition, and enumerates and describes the uses to which they are put for weapons, utensils, and otherwise. Although he mentions that in India the natives used stone knives and stone axes, and figures beautifully hafted examples of both, it apparently did not occur to him that they corresponded with the cerauniae which he describes at length. He represents a stone arrowhead as lapis sagittariils or artificial belemnite, and mentions that these objects were used by the old Romans in warfare.

There was another contemporary museum at Bologna, that of Giacomo Zanoni (1615-1682), the botanist, which was remarkable for its collection of stones, learnedly termed a XSotafxelov " Dr. Mont-albanus," says John Ray, writing in 1663, 'very civilly brought us to the house of Jacobus Zenoni, an In treating of bronze he refers to frequent finds of bronze objects in the earth, and concludes that the ancient Saxons used weapons of bronze. Musaeum Metalltcum, p. 122.

Musaeiim Aletallicum, pp. 156-158.

Op. laud., p. 606, et sqq. He repeats the illustrations of Gesner and adds some of his own.

Op. laud., pp. 618, 634, 635. alentini comments on the passage, Museum Museoru? n, ii., p. 16.

C. S. Scheffel, Vita Schelhajnmen, p. 25, in Ad G. C. Schel-hammerum Epistolae Selectiores. Wismar, 1727, 8vo. See also Jocher Gelehrteti-Lexicon, s. v.; Fantuzzi, Scrittoh Bolognesi, viii., p. 412.

Zanoni was the author of Istoria Botanica (Bologna, 1675, fol.); translated into Latin by Cajetano Monti, Bologna, 1742, fol.

apothecary, a skilful herbarist, and a collector of rarities; who among other things shewed us three pieces of rock-chrystal, with drops of water inclosed in the middle of them, which we could plainly perceive when the chrystal was moved to and fro." The museum was maintained by Zanoni's son, Pelleorino."

When at Bologna, Ray mentions that he visited " Signor Gioseppi Bucemi, a chymist, who prepares the Bononian stone or Lapis phosphortts, which, if exposed a while to the illuminated air, will imbibe the light, so that withdrawn into a dark room, and there lookd upon, it will appear like a burning coal; but in a short time gradually loses its shining, till again exposed to the light."

At Modena, Ray saw the Duke's palace, but " what we most minded was the cabinet or musaeum, furnished with choice of natural rarities, jewels, ancient and modern coins and medals, ancient and modern en-taglias, curious turnd works, dried plants pasted upon smooth boards whitend with ceruss, which may be put in frames and hung about a room like pictures; and a great collection of designs of the best painters. Among other things we took notice of a human head

Ray, Op. laud., i., p. 200.

Paolo Boccone in A conipleat Volume of the Memoirs for the Curious, ii., p. oz sqq. London, 1710, 4to. He mentions several other museums in Bologna and the neighbourhood.

As to the Bononian stone, see Robert Boyle, Works, iv., p. 380; The Philosophical Transactions Abridged, by Hutton, i., p. 139; ii., pp. 382, 515; Grew, Musaeum Regalis Societatis, p. 311; Valentini, Museilm Museorum, ii., p. 56; Beckmann, History of Inventiofts, ii., p. 429; and list of treatises in Dryander, Catalogus Bibliothecae historico-naturalis Josephi Banks, iv., p. 254.

petrified; a hen's egg having on one side the signature of the sun, which I the rather noted, because some years before Sir Thomas Brown of Norwich sent me the picture of one, having the perfect signature of a duck swimming upon it, which he assured me was natural. Moss included in a piece of chrystal, silver in another. A fly plainly discernible in a piece of amber. A Chinese calendar written on wooden leaves."

This description gives, in short compass, an excellent idea of the contents of a seventeenth century museum, and tells us, not merely what attracted the ordinary visitor, but what the scientific traveller looked at and deemed to be of importance.

Mercati's museum, already referred to, was an excellent one, and he was himself a good observer and a man of considerable independence of judgment. He was among the first to establish that flint arrowheads, known in Italy as " saette," were really manufactured weapons. He appeals to history, and refers to the use of flint knives amongst the Jews, and to the employment of stone for tools and weapons by the American Indians. The early inhabitants of Italy likewise, he thought, used stone, which gave way to iron only on the introduction of the latter by commerce. He describes true meteorites, and distinguishes them from cerauniae 1 As to signatures, cf. p. 85 and see Prof. P. J. Veth of Arnheim in hiternationales Archiv fiir Ethnographie, vii. (1894), pp. 75, 105.

2 Ray, op. laud., i., p. 201. His remarks on the Florentine museum are in the same strain. lb., p. 285.

Metallotheca, pp. 243-245. He figures nine examples. The passage has been reproduced in Matdriaux pour Phistoire primitive et naturelle d P horn me, x. (1875), pp. 49-57.

and other stones supposed to have fallen from the clouds. Ceratmtae, that is, stone celts cerauniae CHiieaiae), he mentions, were used in his day for burnishing gold and silver, and by the shoemakers of old for polishing women's shoes,- Mummy, he points out, is not a bitumen, as fancied by the Arabians, but human remains preserved by spices. It is an excellent remedy, he explains, for ruptures and contusions, and for stopping bleeding, either taken internally or applied externally. Pit-coal he treats as a mere museum curiosity. It is not used for cooking, he says, on account of its heavy smell. " Francesco Calzolari or Calceolari of Verona added greatly to the museum which had been commenced by his father of the same name from whom the well-known yellow flowers, with long baggy lips which ornament our o reen-houses and wardens, are said to take their name who was an intimate friend of Mattioli and Aldrovandi. He grudged neither trouble nor expense in obtaining specimens from all parts

Op. laud., p. 248.

Op. laud., p. 241. This seems to have been a fairly general practice. See Evans, A? tdent Stone Implements, p. 440, 2nd ed. London, 1897.

Op. laud., pp. 84, 85.

Op. laud., p. 87.

So say the scientists. Father Feuillet, the distinguished French traveller and observer, is said to have given the name in honour of Calceolari. The Dictionary-makers English, French, and German on the other hand derive the name from calceohis, a slipper. With strange inconsistency Pierre Larousse, in that most useful work Grand Dictionnaire Universel du xix Steele, on the same page (Tom. iii., p. in) gives the slipper etymology, and mentions that Father Feuillet bestowed the name in honour of the Italian botanist. The plant does not appear in Boehmer, Commentatio botanico-literaria de Plafitis in memoriam Cultorum noininatis, Lipsiae, 1799, 8vo.

of the world, and made the collection one of the most complete and valuable in Italy. An account of the museum, as it existed in the father's time, was drawn up by John Baptista Oliva of Cremona; and a detailed account of the enlarged collection, prepared by Benedetto Ceruti and Andrea Chiocco, was published in 1662." Prefixed is a view of the interior of the museum. The collection passed into the hands of Ludovico Moscardo, a nobleman of Verona, who added it to his own which was particularly rich in antiquarian objects inscriptions, statues, fibulae, lacrymatories, lamps, weapons, implements. Of these he wrote an account and gave drawings of all the more important.

De 7econditis et praecipuis collectaneis ab honestissimo et solertissimo Francisco Calceolario Verojicnsi in Miisaco adserieafis, Venet., 1584, 4to. Prefixed is a tabular index.

Musaeuin Francisci Calceolari Jnnioris a Benedicio Cervto, nudico, incoeptitm et ab Andrea Chiocco luculenier descriptiirn et perfectum. Veronae, 1622, fol., with plates. Tiraboschi, Storia delta Letteratura Italiana, viii., p. 124. It was a scarce and dear book in 1719. Nichols, Literary Illustrations of the Eighteenth Century, i., p. 358.

Note, ovvero Memorie del suo Aluseo. in tre libri distinte, Padoa, 1656, fol., with plates; and enlarged, Verona, 1672, fol. The book is somewhat rare, and the chapter on ceratiniae is reprinted in Materiaux, xi. (1876), p. I sqq.

The Museum was visited by Ray in 1663 Travels through the Low Countries, i., p. 186, London, 1738, 8vo); by Gilbert Burnet in 1685 Letters cotttaining an account of what seemed most remarkable in Switzerland, Italy, c., p. 122, Amsterdam, 1686); by Misson and his pupil in 1687 A New Voyage to Italy, i., p. 130 sqq.; ii., p. 332); in 1700 by Father Montfaucon, who describes it. The Antiquities of Italy, translated by Henley, p. 294, London, 1725, fol. No part of it was to be seen in 1730. Keysler, Reisen, p. 1020, Hannover, 1751, 4to. See Maffei, Verona illustrata, Verona, 1731-32, folio; 1792-93, 4to; and Blume, Iter Italicum, i., p. 266 (Berlin, 1824).

A part of the Calceolari collection seems to have come into the hands

Another museum at Verona, at this time, belonged to IMapheus Cusanus, an apothecary, "Wherein were shewn many ancient y gyptian idols, taken out of the mummies, divers sorts of petrified shells, petrified cheese, cinnamon, spunge and mushroomes. A jasper stone and an agate having chrystal within them. Stones having upon them the perfect impression or signature of the ribs and whole spines of fishes. A stone called Ocichis mundi, n. d., which when dry shews cloudy and opake, but when put into water, grows clear and transparent."

The museum of Ferrante and Francesco Imperati of Naples was very celebrated in its day, and did much for the advancement of science. It was visited in 1601 by Fabri de Peiresc, who found it well furnished with the rarities of nature, Ferrante seems to have been the first who ascertained the true nature of bronteae and 07nbriae, and showed that the Jew stones were the petrified points of an echinus.

of Mario Sala, an apothecary of Verona, who had a museum in 1663. Ray, ut supra.

Ray, Op. laud., i., p. 186. As to the Ocuhis muiuii, see De Laet, Dc Gemniis et Lapidibus, cap. xviii., p. 69, Lugd. Bat., 1647, 8vo. Dryander enumerates twenty-seven papers on this stone, Catalogus Bibliothecac historico-naturalis Josephi Banks, iv., p. 90.

Barthohnus, Episiolae Medicinalcs, Cent, i., Epist. 49, p. 201, Hag. Com., 1740, i2mo; Happel, Eelatiojics curiosae, iii., p. 136, Hamburg, 1687; Aldrovandi, Musaeum Metallicum, p. 825; Pflaumern, Merciiriiis Italicus, Part ii., p. 65; Major, Bedencken von Kunst- und Naturalien-Kanijiiern, pp. 27, 71, 72, in Valentini, Museum Museorutn, vol. i.

The Museum was the foundation of Ferrante's Natm-al History, Naples, 1599, and of Francesco's work on Fossils, Naples, 1610. There is no foundation for the allegation made by Bartholin that N. A. Stelliola was the real author of the latter.

Gassendi, Vita Peirescii, p. 22, Hag. Com., 1655, 4to.

In 1564 Schloss Amras, near Innsbruck, became the property and favourite residence of the Archduke Ferdinand II. and his first wife, the beautiful Philippine Welser. Here he brought together a rich collection of books and manuscripts, works of art, weapons, antiquities, and curiosities, which attracted sightseers from every part of Europe. Maria Theresa removed the rarer books and the finest of the medals to Vienna, and presented the remainder of the library to the University of Innsbruck. In 1806, on the occasion of the French invasion, the greater part of the armour, art and other valuable objects were taken to Vienna, and now form the Ambras collection (Ambraser Sammlung) in the National Museum. The remains of the collection have been considerably added to in recent years, and the museum is once more open to the public. Misson visited x mras in 1687, and his account indicates that the museum was well and intelligently arranged. The collection of weapons is still one of its features, and seems particularly to have interested Misson. Like all travellers of his day, he is careful to note anything rare or out of the way, and mentions, amongst other weapons, a cross-bow which worked four and thirty bows and

Hirsching, Nachricifen, i., p. 12; iv., p. 256, Erlangen, 1786, 8vo.

Primisser, Die Kaiserlich-Konigliche Ambraser Sammlung, Wien, 1819, 8vo. A second edition was published in 1827, with an account of the ethnographical collections from the South Sea Islands and Greenland in the Imperial Museum.

- Fiihrer diircji die K. K. Ambraser Sai)imhc77g. Wien, 1S79, 1882, and later years, 8vo.

'Misson, A New Voyage to Italy, i., p. iii sqq.; ii., p. 331, London, 1699. This account is repeated by Neickelius, Museographia, p. 20. Keysler, Reisen, p. 25 sqq, Hannover, 1751, 4to.

discharged as many arrows at once; and a piece of the rope with which Judas hanged himself.

Lodovico Settala, a physician of Milan, and his son Manfredo, a Canon of the Cathedral, collected a museum, particularly of what were then known as "artificial curiosities" artificia rariorct), such as medals, intaglios, cameos, chemical preparations, philosophical instruments, and articles of glass and metal. Manfredo Septali," says Sir Andrew Balfour,- "is one of the greatest virtuosi in Italy. His Studie of Books consists of 2 or 3 Roomes. His Galerie of Curiosities of three Roomes. The Curiosities are both Natural and Artificial, of so great a Number and Varietie, that I must not insist upon particulars; but only refer you to the description thereof in Latine by Paulus Maria Tersagus; the Book is in 4to, Dertono, 1664, and bears the name Musaeum Septalianum."" Canon Settala's

The ordinary repeating cross-bow was the so-called Chinese cross-bow (die chinesische Armbrust) which discharged a score of arrows in succession. Demmin, Die Kriegstuaffeji, pp. 102, 900, 908. Gera-Untermhaus, 1891, 8vo.

Gilbert Burnet, Professor of Divinity at Glasgow (1669-1674), afterwards Bishop of Salisbury, when at Basle in 1686 saw a wind-giin that discharged ten shots at once, or could concentrate the force required for ten upon one, a kind of weapon the use of which he thought it the interest of mankind to forbid. Letters, p. 265, Amsterdam, 1686, 8vo, p. 236; Rotterdam, 1687, 8vo.

-Letters Written to a Friend by the Learned and Jiidicious Sir Andreiu Balfour, M. D., p. 245, Edinburgh, 1700, i2mo. It was also visited and described by John Ray in 1663. Travels through the Low Countries, i., p. 209, London, 1738, 8vo.

There is also an Italian translation by Sig. P. F. Scarabelli, Museo b Galeria adimata dal sapere, e dalle studio del Sig. Canonico Manredo Settala., et hora in Italiano dal Sig. P. F. Scarabelli, Tortona, cabinet, says Addison, "is always shown to a stranger among the curiosities of Milan, which I shall not be particular upon, the printed account of it being common enough." Misson's description shows how a museum was visited and what was observed, in the seventeenth century. " Here we observd several sorts of very ingenious machines contrivd for finding out the Perpetual Motion, looking-glasses of all sorts, dials, musical instruments both ancient and modern, some of which were invented by Settala himself; Books, medals, curious keys and locks, seals, rings, pictures, Indian works, mummies, arms, strange habits, lamps, urns, idols, with an infinite number of other sorts of antiquities; Fruits, stones, minerals, animals; a prodigious variety of shells; works in steel, wood, amber and ivory; a great piece of cloth made of the stone Amianthtcs; and without engaging further in those tedious enumerations I promis'd to avoid, all the most rare and curious productions of art and nature, not forofettine Monsters." It was Settala's wish that after his death the museum should be deposited in 1666, 4to. Folding plate and frontispiece. Again, Tortona, 1677, 4to. Ouirini based his treatise, De Testaceis Fossilibiis Musaei Septalliani, Yen., 1676, 4to, on the specimens in the museum.

The collection was visited by Evelyn in 1646, Diary, i., p. 275, London, 1879. See also Happel, Relationes Ctiriosae, iii., p. 133, Hamburg, 1687, 4to.

In Karl W. Hiersemann's Katalog, 223 (Leipzig,, 1899), there are advertised (No. 263) two quarto volumes, containing 138 original water-colour drawings of the more important objects in the Settala collection, of date circa 1670.

"Remarks on Italy," Works, ii., p. 15, London, 1811, 8vo.

"A New Voyage to Italy, ii., p. 220; cf. p. 387, London, 1699, 8vo. Bishop Burnet's account is much the same. He dwells on the monsters, Letters, p. 114, Amsterdam, 1686, i2mo.

the Ambrosian Library, but the arrangement fell through, and the collection was dispersed.

The Senator Ferdinando Cospi of Bologna made a very valuable collection which he gifted to his fellow-citizens as an addition to the museum of Aldrovandi. An excellent catalogue, prepared by Lorenzo Legati, Professor of Greek in the University of Bologna, was published in 1678. It contains a large folding plate showing the arrangement of the museum.

There was great eagferness in France during- the sixteenth and seventeenth centuries to collect coins, medals, and antiquities, and natural objects of all descriptions. Borel and Spon record a vast number of collections, of various kinds, in Paris and other parts of the country, during the earlier part of the seventeenth century f Dr. Martin Lister gives an account of those he found in Paris in 1698; and

Tiraboschi, Storia della Lcttcratura Italiana, viii., p. 140, Milano, 1824. The Duke of Modena had been in treaty for its purchase some years earher at the price of 1000 pistoles. Ray, Travels through the Low Countries, i., p. 202.

Museo Cospiano aijnesso a quello del fanioso Vlisse Aldrovandi, Bologna, 1677, fol. Woodcuts and portrait of Cospi. Tiraboschi, Op. laud., viii., p. 108. This is often treated as a fourteenth volume of the works of Aldrovandi and bound uniformly with them. To this must be added Inventario semplice di tutte le materie, che si trovano nel Mtiseo Cospiaiw. Bologna, 1680, 4to.

See also Neickelius, Museographia, pp. 28, 186, Leipzig, 1727, 4to; Filippo Schiassi, Guida del forestiere al Museo delle Antichita della Regia Universita di Bologna. Bologna, 1814, 8vo.

Supra, p. 21. See also Bonnafte in Gazette des Beaux-Arts, 2 S., i. (1869), pp. 254, 316; xvii. (1878), p. 414; Les collectionneurs de Vancienne France, Paris, 1873, 8vo; Dictionnaire des Amateurs Frafigais aic XVIF Siecle, Paris, 1884, 8vo.

A Journey to Paris in the year i6g8, London 1699, 8vo, reprinted in Pinkerton, Voyages and Travels, vol. iv., p. i. There is an edition by

Neickelius and Kanold bring down the list a few years later. Most of these collections, however, seem to have been comparatively small and to have been soon dispersed. There are detailed catalogues, such as we have of the more important private museums of Italy and Germany, of very few of them.

Bernard Palissy (1510-90), the Huguenot potter, had a remarkable museum of natural objects shells, fossils and minerals and also of enamels and pottery, and gratefully records the gifts of many friends.

Pierre de lEstoile (i546-1611), the diarist, was an enthusiastic collector, and the dangers of the League did not deter him from carrying on his favourite pursuits and steadily adding to his library and cabinet.-

Fabri de Peiresc (1580-1637) of Aix, an exact scholar and profound antiquary, occupied his lifetime in study, in travelling, corresponding with the scholars of Europe and in gathering books, manuscripts, and antiquities and natural curiosities from all parts of the world. These he bestowed with munificent liberality. Though he bought more books than any man of his time, his library was not a large one. As fast as he purchased he made presents to the learned of whatever might be useful in their studies. He dealt in

George Henning, I LD., with notes, London, 1823, but it omits large portions of the text; also a French translation, Paris, 1872, 8vo.

Morley, Palissy the Potter, ii., p. 87, London, 1852, 8vo; p. 251 sqq., London, 1878, 8vo.

Lacroix, XVIP Steele, Sciences, Lettres et Arts, p. 141, Paris, 1882,8vo.

3 Bonnaffe in Gazette des Beaux-Arts, supra, xvii. (1878), p. 421; Les Collectionneurs dc Pa7tcietif! e France, p. 2)71 Paris, 1873, 8vo; Dictionnaire des Amateurs Franqais au XVIP Steele, p. 245, Paris, 1884, Svo.

Gassendi, Vita Peirescii, p. 229 sqq. Hag. Com., 1655, 4to.

the same way with the contents of his museum, and gave coins and antiquities to ever one to whom he thought they would be of use. Athanasius Kircher records with oratitude that, in order to assist him, Peiresc sent him all the Egyptian things in his collection antiquitatuvi gazophylaciiuii) and many others besides. His biography by Gassendi presents a vivid picture of his labours and travels, of the learned men he met or corresponded with, and the museums he visited.- He had agents in all parts of the world on the outlook for manuscripts, antiquities and curiosities. It was one of these agents who, at his expense, unearthed the Arundel marbles, which went astray at Smyrna on their way to France, but were afterwards found and acquired from the finder by the Earl of Arundel. Peiresc sent Theophilus Minutius, a Franciscan friar, on two expeditions to the East, providing him with money and licenses from the Pope and the General of his Order, and through him obtained a great quantity of Samaritan, Coptic, Arabic and Greek manuscripts, coins, roots, seeds and various other objects, including two Egyptian mummies.

Peiresc was a man of sound judgment and considerable observation. He carefully examined an elephant which was brought to Toulon, and had drawings of it made. He satisfied himself that what passed for oiants' teeth and bones were the orinders and bones

The passages are collected by Gassendi, Op. laud., p. 281.

- Illustris Nicolai Claiidii Fabricii de Peiresc Vita., Hag. Com., 1655, 4to, and previously 1651, 4to. Originally published at Paris, 1641, 4to. Translated into English by William Rand, Doctor of Physik, London, 1657, 8vo. Dedicated to John Evelyn. Granger, Biographical History of England., ii., p. 84, London, 8vo, 1779. See Leopold Delisle, Fabri de Peiresc, Toulouse, 1889, 8vo.

of elephants and discredited the Teutobochus myth. He held that fossil shells had been the coverino-s of living animals, and that they and the leaves and wood of trees had been turned into stone by a petrifying- humour which penetrated them. This liquid he thought arose from a lapidific or stone-forming spawn or seed contained in the earth. He believed that the sea had, at one time, covered the highest mountains and that it was still retreating from certain places and encroaching in others. The city of Venice, he said, would one time or other be joined to the continent, seeing that within a definite period the continent had been lengthened 1500 paces or a mile and a half.

The museum was dispersed on Peiresc's death. A portion of it found its way to Paris, and was incorporated with the Cabinet de la Bibliotheque de Sainte Genevieve, where it w as seen by Lister. " Nothing pleased me more," he notes, "than to have seen the remains of the cabinet of the noble Pieresc, the greatest and heartiest Maecenas, to his power, of learned men of any of this age." A considerable part fell to M. Borilly of Aix, secretary of the King's chamber, who had already a considerable collection of all kinds of rarities, amongst which were a meteorite, of 50 lbs. weight.

Gaston, Duke of Orleans (1608-1660), son of Henry IV. of France, and brother of Henrietta

Gassendi, Vita Peitescn, pp. 90, 152, 156. lb., p. 151. A Journey to Paris, p. 123, London, 1699, 8vo.

Borel, Les Antiquites de Castres, p. 138, Paris, 1868, i2mo; Spon, Les Antiquites de la Ville de Lyon, p. 255, Paris, 1857; Lacroix, XVII" Siecle, p. 150; Bonnafife, Diction? taire des Amateurs, p. 32.

Maria, Queen of Charles I., devoted some attention to natural history, established a botanic garden at Blois which for ten years was under the charge of the distinguished Scots naturalist and Royalist refugee, Dr. Robert Morison (1620-1683) and formed a museum in his palace. His gold coins were the commencement of the great Cabinet dtc roi; and a portion of his natural history collections was purchased by Colbert in 1660, and became the foundation of the Cabinet dhistoire 7iatti, relle, which, after being enriched by numberless accessions was, in 1793, transformed into the Museum of Natural History of Paris, Another Frenchman, Paul Contant, Master Apothecary of Poitiers circa 1570-163 2), was an enthusiastic botanist, took long journeys in pursuit of science, and made an interesting collection of plants and their parts, earths, stones, minerals, shells, and fish, of which he published a short catalogue, Exagoge mirabiliuni naturae e Gazophylacio Pauli Contanti, which he dedicates to Sully. He also described various plants and animals in two poems, Second Eden, and Le yardin et Cabinet po tiq ce de Panl Contajit.""

Morison assisted in the preparation of the Hortus Regius Blesenszs, Paris, 1653, fol., which appeared under the authorship of Abel Brunyer. In 1669 he pubhshed Hortus Regius Blesensis anctus. London, 1669, 8vo.

- Bonnaffe, Diction7iaire des Amateurs, p. 35.

Peignot, Dictionnaire raisonne de Bibliologie, i., p. 443. Paris, 1802, Bvo.

See Memoires de PAcadanie des Sciences de Paris, 1753) P- 369; Deleuze, Histoire et description du Museum d histoire naturelle, Paris, 8vo, 2 vols; Centenaire de la fondation du Museum d histoire natureile, Paris, 1893, 4to.

His father, Jacques Contant, had commenced a commentary on Dioscorides, which his son completed. Les Ocuvres de Jacques et

Maistre Pierre Borel of Castres had himself a large collection, of which he published a catalogue in 1645, and an enlarged edition in 1649. It comprised antiquities of all kinds, artificial curiosities, and specimens of natural history. Amongst human rarities, he includes the shoulder-blade of a giant, weighing 35 lbs., 4 palms in height and 7 in width, two giants' teeth half the size of one's fist, and various fragments of Egyptian mummy. He had a piece of a veritable horn of an Ethiopian unicorn, and teeth of fossil unicorns. His birds embraced the bill and wing of the Barnacle goose (les oyes decosse), which he explains spring from the decaying wood of vessels, a piece of which was also in the collection. Amongst the fish was a sea-devil or Galanga, which he gives as an alternative name: and, amongst the leaves of plants, the "herb divine" or tea which, infused in wine and drunk, enables

Paul Contant pere et fils. Poictiers, 1628, fol., 7 plates and engraved title-page.

Our own Cowley, it will be remembered, also wrote a botanical poem, although in Latin; Plantarinn libri duo, Lond., 1662, 8vo; enlarged to six books in 1668, and translated into English by Nahum Tate, London, 1705, i2mo. For other poems on botanical subjects, see Dryander, Catalogus Bibliotjiecae historico-naturalis Josepjii Banks, iii., p. 191.

"Catalogues de choses rares qui sont dans le Cabinet de Maistre Pierre Borel, Medecin de Castres au haute Languedoc, Edition 2 aug-mentee de beaucoup," in Les Antiginfez, Raretez. de Castres, pp. 132-149, Castres, 1649; pp. 146-165, Paris, 1868.

2 Supra, p. 47.

That is, of some kind of fossil ivory. Supra, p. 43.

As to the Barnacle goose, see supra, p. 73. He describes the arbor conchifera in his Historiaruni et Observationum medicophysicarum Centuriae IV., Obs. 96, p. 351, Paris, 1656, 8vo.

one to do without sleep for a long time, without suffering inconvenience In 1670 Leonard Bernon, Sieur de Bernonville, a la Rochelle, published a catalogue of curiosities, in his cabinet, brought from the Indies, Egypt, and Ethiopia; which contains an interestinof list of curiosities formine the personal equipment of a savage chief ("diverses curiositez servant a la personne dun General des sauvages"). Amongst them were A trophy of Christians slain in battle and of enemies whom he had eaten. Two halters with which he bound poor Christian prisoners, mocassins, shoes, bows and arrows, and his tobacco pipe "made of marble, very curious."-

Berend Ten Brocke, better known as Bernardus Paludanus (1550-1633), a learned Dutch physician of

Tea was coming into favour at this time. In 1671 Dufour published De Pusage du Caphe, du The et du Chocohit, Lyon, i2mo, which passed through several editions and was translated into Latin by Dr. Jacob Spon, and into English by John Chamberlayn, London, 1685, i2mo.

Sibbald states that tea restores the appetite and prevents drowsiness. " About twelve leaves are thrown into six ounces of boiling water; the pot is then removed from the fire, a little sugar is added and the tincture is sipped." Atictarium Musaei Balfouriani, p. 105. " It causeth wakefulness, so that whole nights may be spent in study without hurt to the body, because it binds the mouth of the stomach, thereby restraining those vapours which, ascending, would cause sleep." Salmon, New Dispensatory p. 108. Others were, however, ready to cry out against it, and as early as 1665 Professor Simon Paulli of Copenhagen wrote Co7)wicntarius de abusu Tabaci et herbae Thee, Argent., 1665, 4to. Some curious information on the subject will be found in Alston, Lectures on the Materia Aledica, ii., p. 233 sgq.; Hoffmann, Clavis pharmaceutical p. 556.

Recueil des pieces ciirieuses apporiees des Indes, degypte " dethiopie qui se trouvent dans le Cabinet de Leonard Bernon, Sieur de Berno7iville, a la Rochelle. Paris, 1670, Svo, 15 pp.

Enkhuizen, had a famous collection of rarities em Wunder-Kainmer).

In the old world or new, what wonderous thing, Did art to light or nature lately bring, This Paludanus house doth show a rare Proof of the owner's soveraign wit and care.-

The museum was visited in 1592 by Frederick, Duke of Wiirtemberg- "the Jarmane Duke" of The Merry Wives of Windsor when on his way to England. In 1651 it was purchased by Adam Olearius (the Latinised form of Oelschlager), the celebrated traveller and orientalist, for Frederick III., Duke of Schleswig-Holstein-Gottorp, and added to the collection at Gottorp. Olearius prepared a catalogue which was published in 1666, and was long used by collectors as a convenient hand-book. The whole of the Gottorp collection ultimately found its way to St. Petersburg, and was absorbed in the Imperial collection.

Sachse de Lewenheimb, Gaimnarologia, p. 50, Francof., 1665, 8vo; Major, See-Farth, p. 107, Hamburg, 1683, i2mo; Neickelius, Mtiseo-graphia, p. 195, Leipzig, 1727; Jacobus Kok, Vaderlandsch Woorden-bock, xxiii., p. 320, Amst., 1790, Svo.

2 Powell, H. tinane Industry, p. 188, London, 1661, i2mo. The original lines are quoted by Gotfried Hegenitius Ifineraftiwi Frisio-Hollandicimi, p. 30, Lugd. Bat., 1667, originally published 1630), who gives as their author Tobias Schultze van Schwensche Bregoshutz. He also gives others by the learned lawyer, Privy Councillor Hippolyt von Colli, otherwise a Collibus or a Colle.

3 Jacob Rathgeb, Warhaffte Bescreibung z-weyer Raisen; with Index rerum. nati-iralium a B. Paludano. couectaritm. Tubingen, 1603, and again 1604, 4to.

Neickelius, Museographia, p. 197. He also acquired the Foucault collection of coins.

Gottorffische Kunst-Kammer, Schlesswig, 1666, 4to, and again in three parts, lb., 1674, 4to. See Zeitscjirift fiir Mtcseologie, 1800, No. 20.

Johann Bauhin (1541-1613), the great botanist, physician to Duke Ulrich of Wi-irtemberg and his successors, made a large collection of the fossil shells and other objects of interest to be found in the neighbourhood of the baths of Boll, and published an account of them in 1598.

P elix Plater of Basle (1536-1614) had one of the most notable museums of the period, which remained in possession of his family for many years. It contained curiosities of all kinds, works of art in gold and silver, pictures and portraits of eminent men, and a cabinet of coins, Greek, Roman, and modern. Its strong point was the natural histor) section, which was rich in specimens from all the three kingdoms, and had a particular interest as containing the collections of Conrad Gesner.- When Skippon visited it with Ray in 1663, he describes the specimens as "somewhat negflected," although "in Ljood order." He adds, "The doctor's son, who shewed us them.

See Book IV. of his Historiae novi et admirabilis Fontis Balneique Bollensis ifi Dvcaiv Wirtembergico ad acidulas Goepingenses Montisb., 1598, 4to, illustrated with woodcuts. Amongst them are some wonderful representations of belemnites. The book was republished under the title De aquis medicatis? tova Methodus, Montisb., 1612. The part treating of stones, fossils, and natural productions is given as a separate treatise with separate pagination. A German translation of the original was published at Stuttgart, 1602, 410.

Miescher, Die nudizinische Facultdt in Basely P- 52, Basel, i860, 4to; Adam, Vitae mediconim Germanoriini, p. 430, Haidelb., 1620, 8vo; Monconys, Journal des voyages. Part ii., p. 310, Lyon, 1666; Sachse von Lowenheim, Responsoria Disseriaiio, p. 83, in Major, Dissertatio epistolica de Cancris et Serpentibus petrefactis, Jenae, 1664, 8vo. Ray, Travels through the Low Countries, i., p. 85. His museum is also referred to by Bauhin, Op. laud., "Thesaurum habes multarum rerum exoticarum amplissimum artificiosissimaque methodo digestum."

brought us a book wherein we w rote our names, and then gave a golden ducat, it being covetously expected of us." Plater was a sound botanist, and made observations in all branches of Natural History. It was in 1584, when on a professional visit, of several months' duration to Lucerne, being in search of curiosities, that the bones of the oriant, to which reference has already been made, were shown to him in the Court House. He is a fluent and lucid writer. His statements of the cases he deals with in his three books of Observations, the symptoms, remedies applied and their effects, are as precisely set out as in the pages of a modern medical journal. His descriptions of certain mental and psychological conditions are very instructive, and when dealing with deformities, he gives an account of various dwarfs and giants in the ordinary sense that he had met with in practice.

Basil Besler of Nuremberg (1561-1629), an excellent botanist, was also a collector and the author of a beautiful work, Fasciculus rariorum et aspectu dig-7ior 11771 varii generis quae collegit et stiis i77tpensis

Journey in Churchill, Collection of Voyages and Travels, vi., p. 460, London, 1752, fol.

"Supra, p. 46.

Observationum medicalium libri tres, Basil., 1641, and again 1680, 8vo.

Sir William Hamilton quotes Lectures on Metaphysics, i., p. 336) a curious instance of the activity of the mind while the body is asleep which his father Thomas Plater, the printer of Basle, met with Observa-tiones,. 12, ed. 1641; p. 11, ed. 1680).

Plater gives a number of instances of longevity (p. 233, ed. 1641; p. 221, ed. 1680); amongst others of his maternal grandfather, Johann Summer-matter. On a copy of the 1680 edition in the Library of the University of St. Andrews, which formerly belonged to Professor Thomas Simson, he has noted the case of Nicholas Vilant, grandfather of Dr. William Vilant, Principal of the New College, St. Andrews.

aeri ad viva7)i incidi ciiravit Basiliiis Besler His nephew, Michael Rupert (1607-1661), continued to add to the museum and pubhshed a further account of it." One of the objects he figures (pi. 31) as dtus inaxillaris lapideits seems to be the tooth of a fossil hippopotamus.

Jan Smet van der Ketten of Nymegen, an eminent antiquary, began to form a collection of coins and of Roman and other antiquities in 1618. It passed to his son, the pastor of Alkmaar, who added to it and published an illustrated account of the whole in 1678. The coins were sold to the Elector Palatine, John William (1690-1716), for 20,000 florins, for the electoral museum at Heidelberg.

The first museum at Heidelberg was founded by Carl Ludewig (Elector, 1632-80), grandson of our James I. and brother of " Rupert of the Rhine," who purchased a cabinet of coins and other antiquities in Italy, and various curiosities and rarities, and appointed his librarian, Lorenz Beger (1653-1705), keeper. On the death of the next Elector in 1685, the whole collection passed by bequest to the "Great Elector"

Nuremberg, 1616, and continuation, 1622, 4to, with 24 plates.

- Gazophylacium reriim nattcraiiuin, Lipsiae, 1642, fol., 24 plates; and Leipzig, 1733, with 35 plates. Johann Heinrich Lochner published Rariora Miisei Besleriaiii. aejieis tabulis incisa. Nuremberg, 1716, fol., with 40 plates and portrait, which had been prepared by his father, Michael Lochner von Hummelstein. See Nichols, Literary Illustrations of the Eighteenth Ceiitiiry i., pp. 358, 363.

Antiqtiitates Neoinagenses, Nov. Bat., 1678, 4to. It was a new edition of the father's work. Thesaurus antiquarius Sinetiatiiis, Amstd., 1658, i2mo.

See also Nicholas Chevalier's Recherches ciirieuses. Utrecht, 1709, fol. Supra, p. 37.

loO MUSEUM OF HEIDELBERG of Brandenburg, and was transferred to Berlin. Beger accompanied it, and was put in charge of the cabinet which Friedrich W ilhelm was forming. The two collections he described in the stately folios above mentioned, which still remain useful books of reference in the coin room. A less known work of Beger is a defence of polygamy, which he wrote at the request of his patron, Carl Ludewig, who, having quarrelled with his wife and married another, required a piece justificative Ray visited Heidelberg in 1663, before this domestic rupture occurred. The Elector, he says, spoke six languages perfectly, and was greatly beloved of his subjects. Ray and his fellow-travellers were invited to dinner, and "after dinner his highness was pleased to call us into his closet and shew us many curiosities, among others (i) a purse made of alumen pltcmosiim, which we saw put into a pan of burning charcoal, till it was thoroughly ignite, and yet when taken out and cool, we could not perceive that it had received any harm at all from the fire. (2) Two unicorns horns, each eight or ten foot long, wreathed and hollow to the top. (3) The imperial crown and globe of Rupe 'tus Imp. (4) An excellent and well-digested collection of ancient and modern coins and medals of all sorts, in which the Prince himself is very knowing." Ray mentions that they also saw the great church

Supra, p. 34. The Thesaurus ex thesauro Palatino selectus was published at Heidelberg in 1685, fol.

This he wrote under the name Dapifmeus Arcuarius and published in 1679, 4to, without place or printer's name.

Ray, Travels through the Low Countries, i., p. 71, London, 1738, 8vo.

LOSS OF THE UNIVERSITY LIBRARY loI where the famous Hbrary was kept. It will be remembered that, after the battle of Prague and the defeat of the Elector Friedrich, the "Winter King," Tilly took Heidelbero- in 1622, and havincr on behalf of Maxi-milian of Bavaria presented the University library to Pope Gregory XV., the whole of the books and manuscripts were carried to Rome, and added to the Vatican library. Napoleon Bonaparte in turn removed the best of the Vatican manuscripts to Paris in 1797. After his fall the general question of the restoration of collections arose, and was decided in favour of the despoiled proprietors. Heidelberg got whatever parts of the library were to be found in Paris. The principle was extended to what was still in Rome, and in 1816 all the German manuscripts which had formerly belonged to the University were restored.

Very little of the Palatinate museum is now at Berlin, the greater part having been transferred to Dresden in the time of King Friedrich Wilhelm I.-

According to Lord Fountainhall, the Bodleian library was exceeded by the Vatican only by the augmentation the latter got by that of Heidelberg. Journals p. 169, Edinburgh, 1900, 8vo (Scottish History Society).

Leone AUacci, better known as Leo Allatius, afterwards librarian of the Vatican, was entrusted with the duty of transferring the library to Rome, and wrote Tra7isporto dclla biblioteca Palaiina da Heidelberg a Roma.

Klemm, Geschichte der Sammlungeji fiir Wissoischaft und Kiinst ifi Deutschland, pp. 83, 120, 206, 282, 305, Zerbst, 1837, 8vo.

The Novum Organmn was given to the world in 1625, and the Nfew Atlantis in 1627; in 1657 the Accademia del Cimento was founded at Florence; the Royal Society of London received its charter in 1660, and the Academie des Sciences of Paris was established in 1666. At the same time Journals devoted to science were set on foot; the Journal des Scavans was commenced in 1665, and in 1670 the Miscellanea C criosa of the German Academy of Natiwae Curiosi, which had been founded" by Johann Laurenz Bausch of Altdorf (1605-1665), in 1652. These agencies exercised much influence; they aroused a spirit of inquiry; quickened observa- 1 The transactions of the Academia Caesarea Naturae Curiosorum appeared under the title Miscellanea Curlosa, 1670-1705, 32 vols.;

Ephenierides, 1712-1722, 5 vols.; Acta and Noza Acta, I72)7i QQ-i and latterly Leopoldina. See Morhof, Polyhistor, ii., p. 139, Liibeck, 1732, 4to.

- It had no home. In 1687 it was taken under the patronage of the Emperor Leopold, from whom it took the title Leopoldine Academy.

3 Bausch had a museum, which he mentions in his De Uiiicornu fossili Schediasma, printed with Fehr, Anchora Sacra, pp. 173, 183.

tion; taught accuracy; provided new and improved means of communicatino- discoveries, and discussed and criticised opinions.

The Copenhagen Museum, which has done so much in recent times to advance archaeological science, had its beginning in the seventeenth century and even earlier. The principal collections were made under King Christian V. (1670-99), and his son and successor Frederick IV. When the Earl of Carlisle visited Copenhagen in 1664 as ambassador-extraordinary of Charles II. he was shown "the Rarities also in the King's Pallace, which were several very curious pieces of Mechanicks, besides many Curiosities brought from the remotest countries. The Rareties were disposed in five or six several appartements on one floor, and indeed were the only observable things almost he saw in that Pallace. Amongst other things, in one of these appartements, he had the sight of an excellent piece of Art, which was called a little ship ready rigged, whose mast, ladders, sails, and cannon were all of Ivory."- The museum was famous for its cabinet of coins, and, besides many other interesting objects, contained a number of articles from Greenland, such

John Ludovic Hannemann of Kiel gives a most enthusiastic account of the Royal Society of London and of its methods in the Dedication addressed to Thomas Bartholin (1619-1680), the anatomist and antiquary of Copenhagen, of his E. xercitatio de vero et genuino sangiiificaiidi orga7io, Kiel, 1675, 4to.

A Relation of the three Embassies. performed by the Right Honble. the Earle of Carlisle iti the years 1663 and 1664, p. 410, London, 1669, 8vo. The author was Guy Miege, Under-Secretary to Lord Carlisle.

It was also described by Dr. William Oliver in the Philosophical Transactions, xxiii. (1702-3), pp. 1400-1410.

as were to be found in many museums of the period, and other ethnographical material." In one of the rooms, says Dr. Oliver, "there is nothing but the garments, arms and utensils of Indians, Turks, and Greenlanders, and other barbarous nations; which for their number and variety entertain the eye with a very agreeable pleasure."

In 1696 Holger Jacobaeus (1650-1701), a pupil of Steno, and son-in-law of Thomas Bartholin, professor of medicine at Copenhagen, published a sumptuous catalogue of the whole collection, which was followed in three years by a supplement, and was edited and improved by Johan Lorentsen or Lauerentzen in 1710.

One of the most celebrated collections of the seventeenth century was that of Ole or Olaf Worm 1588-1654), a Danish physician from whom the ossicula Wormtana, the supernumerary bones of the skull, have their name who may be considered the founder of what has now become the science

E. g. Museo Cospiano, p. 297.

2 These are again described by Valentini in bis Museum Museorum., ii., p. 130, chapter xxiv., "Concerning wild men such as Hottentots, Greenlanders, and the like."

3 Op. laud., p. 1404.

Museum Regium., Hafniae, 1696-99, fol., 2 vols., with 37 plates.

Noticed in Memoirs of Literature., iv., p. 139, London, 1714, 4to. See also Valentini, Museum Museorutn, ii. Appendix iii., p. 8; Regenfuss, Choix de coquillages et de crustacees, Copenh., 1758, fol., French and German; and The King of Denmark's Collection of Shells a? id Petrifactions, with Descriptions by Regenfuss, with plates, in some copies coloured from the originals. Copenh., 1758, fol. The introduction, p. I sqq., contains a bibhography of works on natural history, including the catalogues of various museums.

To this was added in 1726 an alphabetical Index in two parts. It is more of a precis than an index.

of prehistoric archaeology. A tabular view of his museum drawn up by Georg Seger appeared in 1653, and a more complete account prepared by himself was published after his death by his son, Willum Worm. The Mtisaeum Wormiaimm was not a mere inventory, but was a descriptive catalogue, and for more than a century held its place as a recognised text-book of archaeology; and, with other works of the same class, such as Mercati's Metallotheca and Aldrovandi's Ahisaeum Metallictcm, is still valuable as a summary of the scientific opinion of the times on archaeology and natural history, and a practical

Pope takes Worm as the type of what he chose to think an antiquary was:

But who is he, in closet close y-pent,
Of sober face, with learned dust besprent?
Right well mine eyes arede the myster wight,
On parchment scraps y-fed and Wormius hight.
To future ages may thy dulness last,
As thou preserv'st the dulness of the past.
The Duttciad, iii. 185.

See Granger, Biographical History of England, ii., p. 433, London, 1779, 8vo.

In the first edition the fourth Hne read,

"That wonnes in haulkes and hemes, and H ne hight," which evidently alkided to the antiquary Thomas Hearne. Pope protested that this was not so, and next that " Wormius" was purely fictitious, but res ipsa loquitur.

-Synopsis niethodica Rarioruin. in Musaeo Olai Wormii. Hafniae, 1653 and 1658, 4to.

Seger (1629-1678) was a German, but studied under Thomas Bartholin, of Copenhagen, whose Historiariwi anatomicarum Rariora he translated into German. Francof., 1657, 8vo.

Musaeum Wormianiim, Lugd. Bat. (L. U. Elzevir), 1655, fol., with plates. Some copies have Amsterdam as place of publication.

There was also a small hand catalogue, Catalogtis Musaei Wormiani, published at Copenhagen in 1642 and 1645 in i2mo.

exposition of the scope and aims of the museology of the seventeenth century.

Athanasius Kircher, S. J. (1602-1680), bequeathed to the Jesuit College at Rome the splendid museum of antiquities, philosophical instruments, and other objects, which he had brought together. It has since received many additions, and is one of the great museums of the world, notable for its collection of aes grave It was first described by Sepi in 1678, and next by Buonanni (1638-1725) in 1709, and often subsequently.- " Father Kircher," says Sir Robert Southwell 1635-1702), 'is my particular friend, and I visit him and his gallery frequently. Certainly he is a person of vast parts and of as great industry. He is likewise one of the most naked and good men that I have seen, and is very easy to communicate whatever he knows; doing it, as it were, by a maxim he has. On the other side, he is reputed very credulous, apt to put in print any strange, if plausible story, that is brought unto him." It was Kircher who found in Noah's 1 The aes grave was described by Giuseppe Marchi, S. J., Rome, 1839, 4to, with Atlas of 40 plates.

2 Sir Andrew Balfour visited Rome between 1651 and 1665; see Sibbald, Memoria Balfouriana, p. 94, Edinburgh, 1699. All that he says of the Roman College is that " there is a famous Shop and Laboratorie for Pharmacie, as also a Garden." Letters, p. 134. This is probably explained by what Misson writes in 1688: " Father Kircher's Cabinet, in the Roman College, was formerly one of the most curious in Europe, but it has been very much mangld and dismemberd: yet there remains still a considerable collection of natural rarities, with several mechanical engines." A New Voyage to Italy, ii., p. 117, London, 1699, O-Keysler gives a long account of it in 1729, Reisen, p. 485 sqq.

Letter, 30th May, 1661, Robert Boyle's Works, vi., p. 299, London, 1772, 4to.

ark the first museum of natural history. He was sound, however, on the subject of perpetual motion and machines to exhibit it.

John Tradescant (d. 1638) and his son of the same name (d. 1662) were two of the earliest English naturalists and collectors. Their museum attracted much attention and is often alluded to by contemporary writers; . Nature's wliinisey that outvies Tradescant and his ark of novelties."

In 1656 the younger Tradescant published Mitsaeum

Koehler, Amueisimg fiir Reisende gelehrte, p. 217, Frankf., 1762; p. 728, Magdeb., 1810; Kircher, Area Noe, Amst., 1675, fo'- - Motus perpetui differentia experimenta in suo Musaeo exhibebit Kircherus, quibus motum perpetuum non tarn asseverat sed reprobat." De Sepibus, Romani Collegii S. J. Musaeum, p, 56, Amst., 1678. Evelyn, writing in 1644, says Father Kircher took him to his own study," where with

Dutch patience he shewd us his perpetual motions, catoptrics, magnetical experiments, modells, and a thousand other crotchets and devices." Diary, i., p. 125. As to these, see Dircks, Perpetuum Mobile, 2nd Series, p. 17 sqq., London, 1870, 8vo.

Memoirs of Dr. Stukeley, iii., p. 201 (Surtees Society, No. Ixxx.).-

As to the Tradescants, see The Tatler, i., pp. 388, 435; vi., p. 34, ed. Nichols, Lond., 1786; Gx ng x, Biographical History of England, ii., p. 370, London, 1779, 8vo; Pulteney, Sketches of the Progress of Botany, i., p. 175 sqq., London, 1790, 8vo; The Philosophical Tra? tsactions, vol. xlvi., p. 160; Ixiii., p. 82; Weld, History of the Royal Society, i., p. 187, London, 1848; P. B. Duncan, A Catalogue 0 the Ashmolean Museum, p. iv., Oxford, 1836, 8vo; Parker, The Ashmolean Museum. A Lecture, p. 27, Oxford, 1870, 8vo; Hamel, Tradescant der aeltere in Russland, St. Petersburg, 1847, 4to; N. and Q., ist S., iii., pp. 353, 391, 393, 469; v., pp. 367, 385, 474-

Cleveland, Poems, p. 55 (London, 1687). In the Epistle Dedicatory reference is made to John Tradeskant as a collector of curiosities "minims of art and nature."

The ark in Lambeth was well known. Evelyn, Dia? y, ii., p. 94, London, 1879; Powell, Humane Indjistry, p. 187, London, 1661, 8vo;

Tradescantianuni; or, A Collection of Rarities preserved at South Lambeth neer London This was a bare list, partly in English and partly in Latin, of the objects which father and son had accumulated during many years. The museum, which was considered to be the most extensive in Europe at the time, contained a vast quantity of material natural history specimens and specimens of industrial art, ethnographical, anthropological and archaeological objects, coins and curios but was of little scientific value for want of proper arrangement. It was acquired in 1659 by Elias Ashmole and incorporated with his own collection. The whole passed by gift to the University of Oxford in 1682, and was the foundation of the great Ashmolean Museum. " On

Kippis, Biographia Britannica, iv., p. 347. If we are to rely on Thomas Flalman, it does not seem to have been particularly accessible. Thus John Tradeskin starves our greedy eyes By boxing up his new found Rarities. Flatman's Poems, p. 147, London, 1682; Nichols, Illustrations of the Literary Histo7y of the Eigliteenth Century, iv. 626.

London, 1656, i2mo, with portraits of father and son, by Hollar. At the end there is a list of donors to the museum, which fills five pages.

Tradescant's house and garden at Lambeth were latterly occupied by William Heseltine, the friend of Horace Smith. Beavan, James and Horace Smith, p. 125. London, 1899.

2 The deed remained in Mrs. Tradescant's hands, and after her husband's death Ashmole instituted a suit in Chancery to compel the widow to transfer the collection to him. Mrs. Tradescant replied to the bill, denying that such a conveyance had ever been executed, and cited her husband's Will, of a later date than the alleged conveyance, in which the collection was left to her during life, with power to bequeath it to O. xford or Cambridge University. The Lord Chancellor (Clarendon), however, gave judgment in 1664 in favour of Ashmole, subject to the widow's life interest. N. and Q., ist S., v., p. 385.

When Ashmole transferred his collection to the University of the fifteenth day of May (Thursday), 1679, the first stone of that stately fabric, afterwards called Ashmole's Musaeum, was laid on the west side of the theatre, and being finished by the beginning of March, 1682, were put therein, on the 20th of the same month, about 12 cart loads of rarities sent to Oxon by Mr. Ashmole; which, being fixed in their proper places by Rob. Plot, LL. D., who before had been intrusted with the custody of the said musaeum, were first of all publicly viewed on the 21st day of May following by his royal highness James Duke of York, his royal consort Josepha Maria, princess Anne and their attendants, and on the 24th of the same month by the doctors and masters of the university."

How unsatisfactory the classification of the day was may be judged by Plot's method of dealing with formed-stones, or as we now term them fossils. He adhered to

Oxford he removed everything that might connect the name of either of the Tradescants with it. " The name of Tradescant was unjustly sunk in that of Ashmole." Pulteney, Sketches of the Progress of Botany, i., p. 179. London, 1790, 8vo.

A portion of the collection remained with the widow in 1712, Thoresby Diary, W., p. 108.

Wood, Athenae Oxonienses, iv., 358 (ed. Bliss). By a fire in his chambers in the Middle Temple in 1678, Ashmole lost his library and a large collection of coins and medals. lb.; Evelyn, Diary, iii., p. 442; Family Correspondence of the Family of Hatton, i., p. 171 (Camden Society, 1878).

The museum is described by Thoresby in 1684, Diary, i., pp. 173, 303; ii., p. 427. London, 1830, 8vo.

There is an account of the Ashmolean Museum by Llewellyn Jewitt in The Art fourtial, xi., N. S. (1872), pp. 177, 213. See also Duncan and Parker, supra, p. 107, note, and another lecture by Parker, The Ashmolean Mitsetini. The Additions made to it in the Season 1870-71, Oxford, 1871.

the old view of the origin of such stones, and maintained the doctrine of the plastic power of nature, which, he explains, operates through certain salts, it being the undoubted prerogative of the saline principle to give bodies their figure, as well as solidity and duration. The astroites and the bronteae, he thinks, were formed by an antimonial salt, the belemnites by a nitrous salt, and the ammonites by the joint operation of two salts. He accordingly classifies formed-stones or fossils according as they resemble plants, fishes, shells or the lower animals, or some part of them or some part of man; with a result that is surprising, as he duly catalogues stone horse-heads and bulls' hearts, and various parts of man stone brains, stone eyes, stone thighs, and so on.- A stone, in the form of a button-mould, found near a gfigfantic thig h bone and tooth in Cornwall, he suggests, had belonged to the owner of the bone. He has, however, the merit of having pointed out that stone axes and similar utensils were the actual tools of the early inhabitants of the country, and appeals to a hafted modern example in the museum as showing how they might be fastened to a helve," His successor as keeper of

The Natural History of Oxfordshire being an Essay towards the Natural History of B. nglaiid, chapter v., p. 112 sqq.; cf. p. 33, Oxford, 1705, fol., 2nd ed. As to his collections on which he founded these works, see Evelyn, Diaty, ii., p. 311. London, 1879.

Bartholin gives a long list of petrified portions of the human body. Epistolae Medicinales, Cent, iii., Ep. viii., p. 31, Hag. Com., 1740; and many are referred to by Briickmann, Epistolae Itinerariae, 11, 36, 37, Cent. i. See also Valentini, Museum Museorurn, ii., pp. 19, 27; Koehler, At77veisung fiir Reisende gclehrte p. 251, Frankf., 1762, 8vo, p. 817, Magdeb., 1810, 8vo.

2 The Natural History of Staffordshire p. 397. O. xford, 1686, fol.

the museum was Edward Lhuyd (1660-1709), the Celtic philologist, who published a copious catalogue of the English fossils in the collection in 1699 As regards their origin, he supported the doctrine that fossils were produced from the semina of fishes and other creatures, raised by vapours from the sea, which, tailing with the rain, were carried into the inner parts of the earth.

John Ray (1628-1705), the botanist, made a collection of natural curiosities which he presented to his friend and neighbour, Mr. Samuel Dale, author of the Pharmacologia, to whom they were delivered about a week before his death. Ray had sounder views than Plot regarding petrified shells and figured stones, which he held to be the remains of once-oro-anised bodies.

Kippis refers to the museum of John James Swam-merdam, " apothecary at Lambeth," but this is a mistake. Swammerdam was a Dutchman, and his collection was at Amsterdam, and was visited by Dr. Edward Brown in 1668. A sale catalogue was prepared after his death, which shows that the collection was a large and varied one. One-third of the whole consisted of artificial curiosities, another third of coins, and the remainder of fossils, vegetable and animal specimens.

Michael Bernhard Valentini (1657-1729), Professor

Lithophylacii Britannici Ichnographia. London, 1699, 8vo.-Ray, Travels through the Low Countries (in 1663), i., pp. 96 sqq. 252, 267. London, 1738, 8vo.

Biographia Britannica iv., 347.

Travels p. 100, London, 1685, fol.

Catalogus musei tjistructissuni, e. xhibeits copiosam supeuectilem varia- at Giessen, and a Fellow of the Royal Society of London, to whom frequent reference has been made, was himself a collector, and published in his Museum Mnseoruni 2. catalogue of what he calls the " Re-positorium Valentinianum." It comprised natural history specimens arranged according to the mineral, vegetable, and animal kingdoms; things sacred and superstitious; artificial rarities; philosophical, mathematical, anatomical, surgical, and chemical apparatus; coins and medals.

Franz Ernst Bruckmann of Wolfenbiittel (1697-1753), who, like Valentini, wrote much about other people's collections, found time during a busy life to form a large museum of his own, which he has described in his curious Epistolae Itinei ariae dedicated to Sir Hans Sloane and the Royal Society. He had large collections illustrative of natural history, botany, and mineralogy; many antiquities and other artficial rarities, and a great assemblage of Curiosa mathematico-arithmetica. Amongst the latter was a field glass, which he calls a Polemoscope, otherwise ruvi 7-eruin exoticaruiii tarn naturalium qiiam arte factariim quas collegit Joi. Jac. Siuammerdam (Dutch and Latin), 1679, S O) PP- I43-

See also Le Cabhiet de Mr. Swanunerdam, doctciir en Medecine, on Catalogue de toiites sortes dhtsectes et de diverses preparations anato-7niques que Pon petit dire etre tin supplement tres considerable de PHistoire naturclle des Afii7naux, n. p., n. d., but apparently published at Amsterdam.

Vol. ii., Appendix xxiii., pp. 100-108.

Epistolae 39-47, 57-6o, 64, 65, and 81-84, Cent. i.; Epistola 50, Cent. ii.

Centuria i. was published Wolfenbiittel, 1742; Centuria ii., 1749; and Centuria iii., 1750-53, all in 4to. The Epistles seem to have been originally published separately, and each has an original title-page of earlier date than the complete collection.

Kriegs-Perspectiv or Bataillen-Ktuker; two magic lanterns with two hundred shdes; and a catoptric camera, with four plain mirrors placed parallel and opposite, in which was represented the marriage at Cana; the figures were of wax, and moved to the sound of music, gesticulating with their hands, arms, and eyes, as if engaged in conversation; and many other optical toys. Amongst the aerometric objects was the still familiar hygrometer in the form of a tiny house, with a boy and girl that indicated fine or bad weather according as the one or the other came out or went in, which he calls Hamburgische Wetter-Machine or Wetter-Hdusgenr His anatomical appliances included glass eyes and a human figure of wood, prepared by Dr. Friedrich Hoffmann of Halle, which could be taken to pieces so as to show the arrangement of the internal parts. The artificial curiosities were very numerous, and of such a miscellaneous description that they must have brought I any visitor who tried to view them into a state of! complete distraction. There w ere Turkish and Tartar j weapons; a crucifixion in various coloured amber; wax fruits and figures; Indian reed pens and China ink; Chinese paper, wood pulp paper, and cotton paper; tobacco boxes and snuff boxes; puzzle purses

See alentini, Museum Museorutn, ii., Part iii., pp. 60, no.

-See also Valentini, Museum Museorutn, ii., Part iii., pp. 25, in. At p. 19 he describes the Magdeburg Wetter-Mdnnchen.

See also Epistola 32, Cent. i. Lister describes the perfection of the artificial eyes made in Paris. A Journey to Paris, p. 144, London, 1699, 8vo.

There were similar exhibits in the museum of Albert Ritter of Ilfeld. Briickmann, Epistola Itineraria, 32, Cent. i.; and in Dr. Kahn's Anatomical Museum, Catalogue, p. 31, London, 1851.

and puzzle boxes; tea and coffee cups; games and tops; a silver coin which, when put into the fire, exhibits the sign which appeared in the clouds to Constantine the Great, with the words, In hoc signo vinces; bread of all kinds; febrifuges; shoes; knives and chop-sticks; a small cart or carriole, in which one was wheeled about the garden, and which at the same time weeded, hoed, and rolled the walks and alleys, and gathered up the rubbish; a pedometer; a hand warmer, such as is nowadays extensively advertised under the name of Instra; a magnetic ring or Avicenna's fortune, which when carried on the finger attracts the poison of malignant diseases and becomes black; so long as the wearer is in sound health the ring retains its brioht Qolden colour, if he turns ill it loses its brightness and becomes tarnished; a witch's-dollar, Hexen-Thaler, made of a mixture of the seven metals, and inscribed with magical characters; a talisman, of lead covered with Arabic letters, which was used as an amulet by being placed in burning soda.

The museum had a section devoted to ecclesiastical objects Curiosa ecclesiae Romano-Cat holicae). Apparently, however, it was not intended to illustrate Christian antiquities or ecclesiastical art, but rather to gratify the love of the marvellous. There were It is also described and figured in Epistola Ilinefaria, 32, Cent, i., in which he describes the museum of Albert Ritter. This coin when hung round the neck rendered the weaier proof against bullets and all weapons. There was a similar coin in Kilter's collection. Briickmann gives several references to writers on this curious subject; amongst others to Happel, Relationes Curiosae, iv., pp. 291, 534.

2 Beckmann, History of Inventions, i., p. 5; Nicolai, Reise, i., Beilage i, Berlin, 1783, 8vo.

a great number of charms and amulets; a crystal of red glass, containing St. John's Gospel, which was hung upon infants to preserve them from poison; Spanish weather-crosses, which were believed to ward off thunder and storms, and other metal crosses; vertigo-crosses, made of glass of various colours, which prevented giddiness; a cross of horn which had been touched by the Pope, and was therefore a remedy for all ailments; Indulgence pence; St. Benedict's pence; a perfume plant, whose smoke puts to flight spectres and witches; various relics of saints; raw silk, white and red, consecrated in St. Stephen's Cathedral, Vienna, and good against erysipelas; earth from St. Ulric's grave, near Augsburg, which keeps away mice. A portable altar, with two wings, figures in the list, probably on account of its small size. One of the largest private museums of the seventeenth century was that of Albert Seba (1665-1736), Commencing life as a druggist in Amsterdam, he entered the service of the Dutch East India Company, and acquired great wealth. His early studies had given him a taste for natural history, and j he employed his large fortune in forming a collection of the most interesting objects in the animal, vege- , table, and mineral kingdoms. When Peter the Great visited Amsterdam, in 1716, he purchased the museum

He again refers to St. Benedict's pence, which were a preservative against magical practices, in Epistola Itineraria, i8, Cent. i.

He treats at length of St. Ulric's Earth in Epistola IHneraria, 6, Cent. i.

In Epistola 8, Cent, i., he mentions the portable altar of the Emperor Henr) at Quedlinburg.

and removed it to St. Petersburg; but Seba immediately undertook the collection of another, which soon surpassed every other in Europe. It was, however, dispersed on his death in 1736. He began a description of this museum, one volume of which was published during his lifetime and three more after his death.

Another celebrated museum at Amsterdam belonged to the great anatomist, Frederik Ruysch (1638-1731), which " in the extent, variety, and arrangement of its contents, became ultimately the most magnificent that any private individual had ever accumulated, and was the resort of visitors of every description. Generals, ambassadors, princes, and even kings, were happy in the opportunity of examining it."" Peter the Great, when in Holland in 1698, often dined with Ruysch that he might have an opportunity of examining his cabinet, and on his next visit to Holland he purchased

See Bacmeister, Essai siir la bibliotjieqiie et le cabi7iet de Curiositez et dhistoire naturelle de TAca, d niie des Sciences de S. Petersboia-g p. 149. Petersb., 1776, 8vo.

- Locupletissimi reriun? iaturalmm thesauri accurata Descriptio et iconibus Expressio, per universam physices historiam. Amst., 1734-65, 4 vols. fol. A French translation accompanies the Latin text, and in some copies a Dutch translation is substituted for the French. A copy was advertised by B. J. White in 1795 Catalogue,

No. 37, p, 3, London, 1795), iri which the plates were coloured by J. Fortuyn, at Leyden, soon after the publication of the work, from the specimens themselves in Seba's museum.

The plates were reprinted at Paris in 1827, and a new tey. t was promised, but was not issued. The plates, says Cuvier, are excellent, but the text,5 of no authority whatever, being written without accuracy or judgment. Cuvier, The Animal Kingdotn, by Griffith, vol. xvi. (Index), p. 321. London, 1835.

Chalmers, Ge? ieral Biographical Dictionary, s. v. Ruysch. It was visited by Dr. Edward Brown in 1668. Travels, p. 100, London, 1685, fol.

it for 30,000 florins, and sent it to St. Petersburg in 1717. Like Seba, Ruysch, although an octogenarian, immediately set about the formation of a new collection, which was ultimately acquired by the King of Poland for 20,000 florins." He published a catalogue of the original collection in 1691and of part of the second in 1710. To this there is prefixed a long poem in Latin, descriptive of the museum, by Lambert Bidloo, with a Dutch translation, and a shorter Dutch poem by Hermann Schyn. After Ruysch's death an auction catalogue of the whole of this collection was issued.

The Academy of Naturae Ciiriosi was for long-anxious to establish a library and museum similar to those of the Royal Society of London, but w ant of funds prevented the execution of the plan for many years. Johann Jakob Baier (1677-1735) of Altdorf, the fifth President, who had spent much time and money in forming a private collection, vigorously supported the scheme, fixed upon Nuremberg as the

Scheltema, Afiecdotes historiques siir Picrre-le-Gnmd et sur ses voyages en Hollande, p. 127, Lausanne, 1842, 8vo; Bacmeister, Op. laud., p. isosqg.

Van der Aa, Biographisch Woordetiboek der Nederlanden, s. v. Ruysch.

Catalogus rariorum quae in Museo Ruyschiano asservantur appended to his Observationum anaiomico-chirurgicarum C z rza, Amstelod., 1691, 4to.

Thesaurus aninialiuiii primus., Amstel., 1710, 4to Latin and Dutch with plates. A synopsis of the contents of the whole museum is given by Valentini, Museum Museorum, ii. Appendix xviii., p. 59.

Catalogus Musaei Ruyschiani, Amstel. 1731, 8vo, 94 pp. See also J. F. Schreiber, Historia vitae et ineritorum Frederici u uysck, p. jj, Amstel, 1732, 4to. James Petiver acknowledges his indebtedness to Ruysch for various reptiles, insects, etc.

He describes his library and museum in his Sciagrapkia Musei sui, Norimbergae, 1730, 4to. Infra., p. 219.

most central place for the institution, and made some progress in obtaining books and specimens. After his death its quarters were changed to Erfurt, and accommodation for it was found in the convent of the Augustinian monks. The museum contained anatomical and pathological preparations, coins and medals, minerals, petrifactions and shells. The collection seems never to have been very extensive, and was in 1805 transferred to the University of Erfurt.

Dr. John Woodward (1665-1728), with unwearied industry during forty years, and at great expense, formed a very extensive museum of minerals, fossils, and shells, both English and foreign. It ranked with Sloane's, and was well known at the time.

A verier monster, than on Afric's shore
The sun eer got, or sumy Nikis bore.

Or Sloane or Woodward's wondrous shelves contain.

The foreign fossils w ere sold after his death, but the greater part of the English ones he bequeathed to the University of Cambridge, together with a sum of money for the endowment of a professorship for the study of geology. The collection was remarkable for

Biichner, Acadeniiae. Naturae Curiosoruin Historia, p. 565 sqq. Halae Iagd., 1755, 4to, with a View of the Hall. Hirsching, Nachricjiten von sejiensiuurdigen Gcmcilde. Kunst- und Naiuralien-Kabineten. in Teutschland, iii. 22; vi. 91.

-An attanpt toivards a Natural History of the Fossils of England, in a Catalogue of the English Fossils in the Collection of f. Woodward, M. D., part i., tome i., London, 1729, 8vo, pp. xvi., 243, dealing with 1574 specimens; part ii., pp. 115; tome ii., London, 1728, contains Additional English Native Fossils, pp. no. This is followed by Catalogue of the Foreign Fossils, part i., pp. 52, and part ii., pp. 33, and Ati Addition, pp. 21, and another Addition, pp. 15.

Pope, Satires of Dr. Donne versified, iw 28.

its extent and variety, and is particularly worthy of note as having been made with the express object of determining- the true nature of petrified bodies. His views regarding the relative positions of the various strata of the earth's crust were accurate, and he clearly saw that water had played an important part in their formation, and that what is now dry land had formerly been submerged. This submersion he assumed was the Noachian deluge, which implied a very short period of time, so that in accounting for geological phenomena he had to attribute to it extraordinary powers. Its waters, he maintained, had an almost universal solvent power, by which rocks and mountains were melted down, and were thus able to admit foreign bodies, such as shells, into their interior, and so themselves became rock.- Woodward had also "a curious collection of Roman antiquities, not only of urns, but gems, signets, rings, keys, stylus scriptorius, res turpiculae, ivory pins, brass

Dr. Woodward's views are alluded to in a satirical broadside ballad of the period Tauronomachm relating to the quarrel between him and Dr. Mead, in which he appears under the title Onos.

First Onos there of great Renown,
A famd Empirick of the Town,
Noted for skill in occult Arts
And Sciences

He, by Deduction long and sage, Teaches, How with impetuous Rage Th Abyss, deserting dark Abode, From subterranean Caverns flowd, And dissipating all the World Into a Hodge-Podge Deluge hurld.

Both Doctors are alluded to in another contemporary broadside, The Drury Lane Monster, in which Dr. Mead is described as, A famous Physician as ever was seen, WTiio once had a Patient and she was a queen.

Jibidae, etc.,"- and a very extensive library, all of which were sold in 1728.

One of his specimens gave rise to a storm of controversy and many personalities. This was a small but curious iron shield of a round form, which he had acquired at the sale of Mr. Conyer's museum about 1693. The latter had purchased it of a brazier, who bought it amongst some brass and iron fraoments which came out of the armoury in the Tower of London near the end of Charles II."s reign. When it passed into Woodward's possession, it became an object of interest to antiquaries. He had several casts of it taken, and had it engraved at Amsterdam in 1705. On the concave side were represented, in the upper part, the ruins of Rome when burnt by the Gauls; and below, the weighing out of the gold to purchase their retreat, together with the arrival of Camillus and the flight of the Gauls; and in the centre a grotesque mask with horns very large and prominent. Antiquaries could not agree as to its age. The Dutch thought that it was an antique; the French that it was modern. Henry Dodwell wrote a dissertation upon it, in which he fixed its date as the time of Nero, and suggested that it had come out of

Thoresby's Diary, i., p. 340. London, 1830, 8vo.

A catalogue of the library, antiquities, etc., of the late learned Dr. Woodward. By Mr. Christopher Batenian, bookseller, aitd Mr. John Cooper. London 1728, 8 o. The catalogue of the library contains 4756 numbers.

The University of Cambridge, in order to make their collection complete, purchased two of the cabinets, ordered to be sold, at the price of 500.

See inf7-a, p. 134.

Biographia Britannica, vi. 4330, London, 1766, fol.

some public collection such as the Shield Walk, Whitehall. Theophilus Downes took a different view, and would not allow that it was ancient. Ainsworth abridged Dodwell's paper, and inserted it at the end of the Museum Woodwardianum, and re-edited and improved it in 1734.

Woodward was not popular with his contemporaries, and some of those whom he had offended took "all occasions to vex him, which they thought might be done to purpose by decrying the antiquity of this monument." Amono-st these " ino-enious o-entlemen " was Pope, who ridiculed both him and the shield. In the Memoirs of Martinus Scriblerus he figures as Cornelius, "a grave and learned gentleman, by profession an antiquary," who had chosen his wife because on the father's side she was related to Cardan, and to Aldrovandi on the mother's. He was fond of an antique buckler which he held as a most authentic relic, and, remembering that the cradle of Hercules had been a shield, determined that the infant Martinus should be cradled in his own. The

De parmn equestri Woodwardiana Disscrtatio, published by Hearne, Oxonii, 1713, 8vo. See N cho s, Afiecdofcs 0 Afr. Boiuyer, p. 109, London, 1782, 4to; Illustrations of the Literary History of the Eightec7ith Century iv., pp. 100-102.

-De Clipeo Caiiiili aittiquo. Disscrtatio, Lond., 1734, 4to.

Woodward was evidently of a somewhat jealous and petulant temperament. See Letter by Sir Hans Sloane in Nichols, Literary Illustrations of the Eighteenth Cefitury, i., p. 272. Thoresby, Correspondence, i., p. 409. Sloane mentions that Woodward's collection was a very fine one. Sir John Clerk of Penicuik says "he himself was the greatest curiosity of the whole collection," Memoirs of Dr. Stukcley, i., p. 213; Metnoirs of Sir John Clerk, p. 127.

Thoresby, Correspondence, ii., p. 108.

housemaid, " concernd for the reputation of her own cleanliness, and her young master's honour, scoured it as clean as her And-irons," to the inexpressible grief of Cornelius. In the Epistle to Addison, Pope reverts to the subject:

Poor Vadius, long with learned spleen devourd, Can taste no pleasure since his Shield was scourd.

At Woodward's sale the shield was purchased by Colonel Richard King, one of his executors, for oo, and at the sale of his effects in 1768 it was sold to Dr. Wilkinson for forty guineas.

A physician in Glasgow got a similar shield from Spain in 1737.

Dr. Richard Mead (1673-1754) spent three years at the University of Utrecht, under the great classical scholar and antiquary, Graevius, and probably imbibed from him a taste for classical learning and classical antiquities, which he cultivated during the rest of his long life. From Utrecht he passed to Leyden and became a pupil of Paul Hermann (1646-1695), Professor of Botany. Hermann had lived for several years in the East Indies, and had made a large collection of oriental plants, animals, and other objects which he used in illustration of his lectures. How far the influence of Hermann, and a residence in Leydipn, with its great museums, stimulated the collecting spirit, it is impossible to say, but both Mead and his fellow-student, Hermann Boerhaave (1668-1738), became

Biographia Britanntca, ict supra; Gough, British Topography, i., p. 720, London, 1780. Memoirs of Dr. Stukeley, ill., p. 411 (Surtees Society, No. Ixxx.). 3 See post, p. 146.

collectors and formed museums. Mead was a successful physician, and the wealth which he acquired enabled him to indulge his tastes. His spacious house in Great Ormond Street "became a repository of all that was curious in nature or in art, to which his extensive correspondence with the Learned in all parts of Europe not a little contributed." His collections were always available for the use of students, and were freely open to the public.

Egyptian mummies were still rarities, and the hieroglyphics on their cases had not ceased to puzzle scholars. Mead was the fortunate possessor of a mummy, and Alexander Gordon Jonathan Oldbuck's Sandy Gordon endeavoured to solve the mystery by a comparative study of this and all the other mummies in England, which do not seem to have exceeded three.

Maty, Memoirs of the Life of Richard Mead, M. D., p. 51, London, 1755, 8vo. Prefixed is a view of the Library and Museum; Nichols, Anecdotes of William Botuyer, pp. 255, 550, London, 1782, 4to.

-An Essay toward explaining the ant lent Hieroglyphical Figures on the Egyptian Mummy in the Museum of Doctor Mead, London, 1737, fol.

Gordon pubhshed 25 plates of all the mummies and other Egyptian antiquities in England, as also this Essay and another on the mummy belonging to Captain William Lethieullier, London, 1737, fol. He intended to publish similar essays explanatory of the other plates, but no more appeared. Two plates of the Lethieullier mummy had been previously engraved by G. Vertue, London, 1724, fol.

Mead's mummy and Gordon's book are referred to in Koehler, Anwei-sung fiir Reisende gelehrte, ip. 219, Frankf, 1762, 8vo; p. 736, Magd., 1810, 8vo.

The mummy was purchased at Dr. Mead's sale by Dr. John Hunter for thirteen guineas, and its remains are now in the museum of the Royal College of Physicians. The Royal Society's mummy was opened in 1763 and caused the death of Dr. Hadley, Gough, British Topography, i., p. 662.

Mead's various collections were brouoht to sale after his death, and realised upwards of; i6,000. The library, which was particularly rich in rare and curious editions of the classics, produced over 5000. His coins and medals brought nearly 2000, and his antiquities 3246.

Another London collection of repute was that of John Kemp (1665-1717). Its foundation was one which had been formed a number of years before by Jean Gailliard, a Frenchman, who had been governor to George, first Lord Carteret, to whom he sold it for an annuity of 200. After Lord Carteret's death, in 1695, Kemp purchased the museum from his representatives and added largely to it. The objects, says a writer of the day, "are neatly dispos'd in excellent order in a square room, tho' at your entrance you would not imagine to find such treasure there."

Ralph Thoresby, who visited it in January, 1709, found much to interest him, "I visited Mr, Kempe, who showed me his noble collection of Greek and Roman medals, several of the laroe medallions in

Nichols, Anecdotes of Mr. Bowyer, pp. 252-255; Museum Afeadiaman, London, 1755, 8vo. This is in two parts. The first (pp. 210) is of the coins. The second (pp. 213) embraces antiquities, gems and objects of natural history. A month later there was a second sale of the general antiquities. A Catalogue of the. Collection of valuable geiiis bronzes., marble and other busts and antiquities of the late Doctor ij i London, 1755, 8vo.

There were separate sales and catalogues of the library, the prints and drawings and the pictures.

- Nichols, Anecdotes of Mr. Bowyer, p. 108; Literary Anecdotes of the Eighteenth Century, v., pp. 249, 519; Literary Illustrations, iv., p. 432.

A Compleat Volume of the Memoirs for the Curious, ii., p. 259, London, 1710, 4to; Gough, British Topography, i., p. 761, London, 1780, 4to.

A Compleat Volume of the Memoirs for the Curious, ii., p. 260.

silver, and others larger in copper, valued at vast sums of monies; he had also two entire mummies (in their wooden chests, shaped with a human head, c.), one of which has the Egyptian hieroglyphics painted upon the swathing-bands; he had fragments of another and gave me a piece, which seems converted into a dark coloured rosin or gum by the embalming, which has penetrated the very bones, which are not only outwardly but quite through of a black colour, as is evident per a piece he gave me; but what 1 was most surprised with was his closet of the ancient deities, lares, lamps, and other Roman vases, some of which were Monsieur Spon's, and are described in print, others not yet; being the noblest collection I ever beheld of this kind. The Duke of Buckinoham had

O a design upon them, but not yielding to the price, Mr. Kempe advanced; io and procured the treasure, and has wrote over thai part of the museum Hie sitis Lmibus laetor " Three years later on a second visit he found that it had been considerably added to.

With a view of keeping his collection together, Kemp directed in his will that it should be offered, together with his library, to Robert, first Earl of Oxford, or his son Edward, Lord Harley, for 2000. The offer was declined, and the museum was brought to sale in 1721, when Mead was an extensive purchaser.- Some objects fell to Ebenezer Mussel, who was subsequently a considerable purchaser at the

Diary, ii., pp. 31, 112.

2 Note on a copy of the Momnnenta Vetustatis Kempiana, London, 1719-20, 8vo, in the library of the Royal Medical and Chirurgical Society of London.

Mead sale, and were again dispersed at the sale of his own curiosities in 1765. An elaborate catalogue of Kemp's collection was prepared by Robert Ainsworth (1660-1743), the author of the well-known Latin Dictionary, who was a hunter after antiquities and ofot tooether a small museum.

One of the most industrious collectors of the period was Ralph Thoresby (1658-1725), the historian of Leeds. Another was William Stukeley (1687-1768), the antiquary. Both kept diaries and preserved their correspondence. These have been published and give much interesting information regarding collectors and collectino-in Eng-land in the first half of the eighteenth century.

Infra, p. 184.

"Monumenta Vetustatis Kempiana, London, 1719-20, 8vo, in two parts.

3 Nichols, Anecdotes of Mr. Bowyer, pp. 108-no; Literary Anecdotes of the Eighteenth Century, v., p. 248.

Thoresby, Diary, London, 1830, 2 vols., 8vo; Letters of Emijieiit Me7i addressed to R. T., lb., 1832, 2 vols., 8vo; Stukeley, Family Memoirs, 1882-87, 3 vols., 8vo (Surtees Society), Infra, p. 183.

Robert Hubert alias Forges "Gent, and sworn servant to his Majesty," had a collection " of many natural rarities " which he had collected ' with great industry, cost, and thirty years' travel in foraign countries." He withdrew it from England during the troubles of the Commonwealth period, and exhibited it at Leipzig in 1651, and thereafter at Hamburg, and printed a catalogue in German for the use of visitors." Amongst those "whose love of virtue, learning, and of the admirable works of

A change of name was often a necessity in those times. Courtine adopting the name of Charleton infra, p. 129) is another example. Carte, the historian, lived in France under the name of Phillips. Maty, Memoirs of the Life of Richard Mead, M. D., p. 39, London, 1755, 8vo. We have William Hubord, alias Lowden, a plotter in Westmoreland in 1663. Cale7idar of State Papers, Domestic, 1665-66, P- 377-

Sachse de Lewenheimb, Gammarologia, p. 53, Francof., 1665, 8vo. He gives some further particulars in Major, Dissertatio Epistolica de Cancris et Serpentibus, pp. 63, 85, Jenae, 1664, 8vo; amongst others, that the collection originally belonged to King Charles I. See also Major, See-Farth, p. 109, Hamburg, 1683. In the printed Catalogue Charles I. heads the list of donors.

God in natural rarities," had been shewed " by their bountiful addingr of somethino-to the encrease of the fore-mentioned collection," were " Gaston, Duke of Orleans, Dr. Housewetel, Physitian to the King of Sweden and chief Physitian in Hamburg," Doctor Towers of Hamburgh, and Dr. Bezler, Chief Physitian in Nuremberg. After the Restoration Hubert brought it back to England, and in 1664 exhibited it "at the place called the Musick House, at the Miter, near the west end of St. Paul's Church."" It was considered a good collection at the time, but now would be thouo-ht to have little scientific value. Amongst the specimens from the animal kingdom were "a rib of a Triton or Mereman, taken by Captain Finny upon the shoals of Brasil, five hundred leagues from the Maine"; " the head and beak of a true Griffin "; "a very perfect great and true Remora of India, whose property is to hinder or stay ships as they swim (if we will believe Heathen philosophers)."

A Catalogue of Natural Rarities, London, 1665, i2mo.

' A Catalogue of Natural Rarities, London, 1664, and again in 1665, i2mo. The two editions differ slightly. I have quoted from both. There is another catalogue, A Catalogue of part of the Rarities collected by R. H. alias Forges, Gent, London, n. d., 8vo, mentioned in Catalogus Bidliotiecae Harleianae,. 13,398. London, 1743, 8vo. Aga. ss z, illio-graphia zoolo iae et geologiae, s. v. Forges, London, 1848-54, 8vo.

As to this collection, see The Tatler, vi., p. 33, ed. Nichols, London, 1786. Kippis, Biographia Britannica, iv., p. 347, London, 1789, fol.; Weld, History of the Royal Society, i., p. 188.

The Remora is the sucking-fish echefieis) of which the ancients related the most wonderful stories (Pliny, Histojia Naturalis, ix. 41 (25), xxxii. i), faithfully repeated, with additions, until comparatively recent times. It is figured and described by Briickmann, Epistola Itineraria, 50, Cent, i., and by Ignazio Bracci, Reinorae pisciculi Effigies, Romae, 1643, fol.

Besides "divers stones of strange shapes and regular forms," he had a considerable assortment of, what was then a favourite exhibit, "natural landskips in stone." Amongst them "a white stone that represents a tree, as if it was made by art with a pen "; "a stone with the natural land-skip of a castle on a hill, a town at the bottom, and a pathway between, very pleasant to behold." Hubert mentions that he had an Arcuata coccmea, a sort of sea-curlew, 'given me together with the full relation of it, by the learned Dr. Charlton, one of the King's Majestis Physitians in ordinary, and excellently knowing in Natural Rarities," and " a great Crocodile given by noble Squire Courtine, a lover of vertue and ingenuity."

Squire Courtine was William Courten (1642-1702), better known as William Charleton, a name which he assumed and under which he lived for many years. His collection Evelyn declared to be one of the largest and most perfect he had seen, and cost;! 8ooo."" Petiver alludes to it as " the incomparable Museum of that most curious preserver of both natural and artificial rarities, and my worthy friend

For instance, Briickmann, Epistolae Itinerariae, 25, 50, Cent. i. Grew, Musaeiim Regalis Societatis, p. 311, London, 1681, fol. In the Copenhagen museum they had " a piece of marble with a natural representation of a Crucifix on its outside, mightily valued by the Lutherans." The Philosophical Transactions, xxiii. (1702-3), p. 1412.

-Evelyn, Diary, iii., pp. 29, 86, 99, 442, London, 1879; Numismata, pp. 246, 251, 282, London, 1697; Thoresby, Diary, i., p. 299; ii., p. 250, London, 1830, 8vo; Brown, Travels, p. 102, London, 1685, fol- M. de la Combe de Vrigny Travels through Denmark and sotne parts of Germany, p. 7, London, 1707, 8vo; Neickelius, Museographia, p. 67, Leipzig, 1727, 4to; Cramer's Introduction to Rumph, Amboinische Raritdten-Kammer, p. vii., Wien, 1766, fol.

Mr. William Charleton in the Middle Temple." It was bequeathed on his death in 1702 to Sir Hans Sloane; but was in confusion when it came into his possession. It now forms part of the British Museum. Dr. Charleton (1619-1707) was the well-known physician, and author of the Chorea Giganturn in which, supported by arguments supplied by Ole Worm, he essays to prove that Stonehenge was erected by the Danes, and which was the occasion of Dryden's spirited Epistle:

Stonehenge, once thought a temple, you have found A throne, where Kings, our earthly gods, were crownd; " Tiere by their wondring subjects they were seen, Joyd with their stature and their princely mien.

Shortly after its incorporation the Royal Society, on the initiative of Daniel Colwal, began to form a museum of curiosities at Gresham College. " Those of the Society that are now in London," writes Henry Oldenburg, " do endeavour to get a good collection of natural and artificial curiosities for the Society's reposi-

The Philosophical Tratisacfiotis, xxi. (1699), p. 295.

-Letter by John Calder, 1788, in Nichols, Literary Illustrations of the Eighteenth Century, viii., p. 265; Jb. i., p. 800; Kippis, Biographia Britannica, iv., p. 334 sgq.; The Taller, vi., pp. 476, 488-502, ed. Nichols, London, 1786; Weld, History of the Royal Society, L, p. 452; Chambers, Edinburgh Journal, xv. (1851), p. 310; Edwards, Memoirs of Libraries, i., p. 440, London, 1859, 8vo; Lives of the Founders of the British Museum, p. 248 sqq., London, 1870, 8vo.

Thoresby, Correspo? ide? tce, i., p. 409. London, 1832, 8vo.

Gentleman s Magazitie, vol. 86, pt. ii. (1816), p. 395; Dryden, Works, ed. Scott, xi. p. 12, Edinb., 1821, 8vo.

Weld, History of the Royal Society, i., p. 190.

London, 1663, 4to. See Bartholin, Epistolae Medidnales, Cent, iv., Epist. 92, pp. 479, 480. Hag. Com., 1740, i2mo.

tory; and they hope to make shortly an acquest of a very good stock of that kind, which will look as somethinor towards a foundation." This was a collection 'which had belonged to Mr. Hubbard," which was purchased with; ioo presented by Mr. Colwal. Many additions were made, and the museum soon became one of the attractions of London; " Inquire at Gresham Colledge for Dr. Pope," says Sir Andrew Balfour, " that by his means you may see a verie fine collection of naturall rarities kept in that Colledge." In 1678 Nehemiah Grew (1628-1711), the vegetable anatomist and physiologist, was requested to prepare a descriptive catalogue of the collection, which was published three years afterwards, and w hich passed throuqfh several editions. The Catalosfue was founded on several lectures read by the author before the Royal

Robert Boyle, Works, vi., p. 215. London, 1772, 4to.

Weld, History 0the Royal Society, i., p. 186, London, 1848, 8vo.

Colwal himself is said to have been a collector. Granger, Biographical History of England, iii., p. 402, London, 1779, 8vo.

Letters written to a Friend by the Learned and Jttdicioies Sir Andrew Balfour, M. D., p. 4. Edinburgh, 1700, i2mo. The letter in question was written about 1668.

A Catalogue and description of the natural and artificial rarities belonging to the Royal Society and preserved at Creshatn College. London, 1681, fol., with engravings, prepared at the expense of Daniel Colwal, the founder of the museum. Valentini,

Museujn Museorum, ii. Appendix, p. 19, gives a short account of the collection founded on the Acta Lipsiensia of 1681-1686.

Sir Hans Sloane wrote, "An account of a China Cabinet, filled with several instruments, fruits, etc., used in China; sent to the Royal Society by Mr. Buckly, Chief Surgeon at Fort St. George." The Philosophical Transactions, xx. (1698), pp. 390, 461; xxi. (1699), pp. 44, 70.

Society in 1676. The collection itself was ultimately-transferred to the British Museum

There seems little doubt that the stock which formed the foundation of the Royal Society's Museum was that of Robert Hubert alias Forges. Hubert's collection was for sale at the time; and a comparison of his catalogue with that of Grew seems to settle the question. Take but a few examples. The first entry in the former is "A Giants Thigh-bone, more than four feet in length, found in Syria. Grew describes it, "The leg bone of an Elephant. It was brought out of Syria for the Thigh-bone of a Giant." Hubert had the horns of a hare which had belonged to the Prince Electors of Saxony, and a rhinoceros' horn which was given to him by the Duke of Holstein. Both objects appear 1 Flower, "The Museum of the Royal College of Surgeons, England," in Transactions of the International Medical Congress, 7 Sess., i., p. 133, London, 1881; Essays on Musetans, p. 76.

2The purchase was made in February, 166, and Hubert's museum was on exhibition in 1664 and 1665 supra, p. 127). According to Oldys, " this collection, or a great part of it, was purchased by Sir Hans Sloane;" (Hawkins, History of Music, iv., p. 379, London, 1776, 4to). But I think part, at any rate, went to the Royal Society. There was no Mr. Hubbard, a collector, so far as I have been able to ascertain, and I take it that Hubbard is a mistake for Hubert.

Sir Hans Sloane's part of the museum seems to have come by way of Mr. Courten The Tatler, vi., p. 34, ed. Nichols, London, 1786). Allibone, Dictionary of Englisji Literature, i., p. 909, London, 1859, 8vo, says that the collection was destroyed in the great fire of 1666, but there seems to be no authority for the statement.

A Catalogue of many Rarities, p. 68, London, 1665, l2mo.

Hares' horns were great curiosities. King James L of England had one of the horns. The horned hare was found in Saxony. Mtcseum Wonnianiim, p. 321; Keysler, Reisen, p. 1309, Hannover, 1751, 4to.

in Grew's catalogue, with the same note of former ownership. Grew seems to have been puzzled by the horns of the hare, for he adds, "so I find them inscribed." The flamingo i phaenicopter) which he describes was, he says, "Given by Thomas Povey, Esq." Hubert's specimen was "given by the ingenious lover of rarities, Mr, Povey, treasurer to His Hignesse the Duke of Yorke." Hubert had a leg of a dodo, which duly figures in the Royal Society's collection. They were likewise indebted to him for the leg and t. g of the cassow ary. Besides the objects catalogued, Hubert mentions that he had forty chests or boxes furnished with many hundred rarities.

As an assistant in the great work of collecting, mention should be made of Thomas Willisel, a Northamptonshire man, who " was employed by the Royal Society in the search of natural rarities, both animals, plants, and minerals; for which purposes he was the fittest man in England, both for his skill and industry. He gave great assistance to Ray and other botanists in collecting specimens for them," He served as a foot-soldier in the army of Oliver Cromwell. " Lying at St, James's (a garrison then, I thinke), he happened," writes Aubrey, "to go along with some simplers.- He liked it so well that he desired to goe with them as often as they went, and tooke such a fancy to it that in a short time he

Pulteney, Sketches of the Progress of Botany, i., pp. 348, 349. Ray, Travels throug i the Low Countries, i., p. 98.

A "simpler" is what Ray supra, p. 81) terms an "herbarist." Dr. Adam Littleton in his Latin Dictionary explains Herbarius as " an herbarist or simpler; he that has knowledge of herbs, plants, etc."

became a good botanist. He was a lusty fellow, and had an admirable sight, which is of great use for a simpler; was as hardy as a Highlander; all the clothes on his back not worth ten groates, an excellent marksman, and would maintain himselfe with his dog and his gun and his fishing-line. The botanists of London did much encourage him, and employed him all over England, Scotland, and good part of Ireland, if not all; where he made brave discoveries, for which his name will ever be remembered in herballs. If he saw a strange fowle or bird, or a fish, he would have it and case it." Some of his collections were in Sir Hans Sloane's Herbarium and so found their way to the British Museum.

John Conyers, by profession an apothecary in Shoe Lane, and by taste an antiquary, had a museum of rarities which he had collected during thirty years. In 1691 he had it newly "methodized," and made "a Proposal to the publick of exposing his collections to such as shall be curious to see them." The Athenian Society " for the resolving all nice and curious questions" was consulted upon the proposal, and after viewing the collection and shortly describing it, pronounced this somewhat enigmatical

Aubrey, The Natural History of Wiltshire, ed. Britton, p. 48, note, London, 1847, 4to. (The Wiltshire Topographical Society.) 2 He was also inventor of an improved Hygroscope, an improved Pump, and an improved Speaking-Trumpet. The Philosophical Transactions, xi. (1676), No. 129, p. 715, xii. (1677-78); No. 136, p. 888; No. 141, p. 1027. Sloane MS. 958, contains a number of observations by Conyers from 1673 to 1690. See also Harleian MS. 5953, f. 112. He mentions finding of the tooth and bone of an elephant, supposed to have been " slain in the battle between ye Romans and ye Britains." Cf. supra, p. 50.

opinion: " Now of what use a carefull and observant view of these things may be to the Divine, the Naturalist, Physician, Antiquary, Historian, or indeed any person of Curiosity will not be hard to determine." It was sold apparently about two years later." James Petiver (d. 1718), apothecary to the Charterhouse, an excellent botanist and entomologist, corresponded with naturalists all over the world, and formed a large miscellaneous museum, which he described in various publications between 1695 and 1717. On his

The Athenian Merairy, vol. iv., No. i6, 2ist November, 1691. Of Conyers himself, see Nichols, Literary Anecdotes of the Eighteenth Century, i., p. 535.

There is mention about this time of an exhibition on Ludgate Hill, Where Crocodile, Rhinoceros, and Baboon With other Prodigies are daily shown: which may refer to this collection. State Poems Cojitifiucd, p. 162, in Poems on Affairs of State, vol. i., London, 1710, 8vo.

2 Nichols, Literary Illtistratioiis of the Eighteenth Century, iv., p. 101; Supra, p. 120.

Sloane, A Voyage to the Islands of Madeira. and famaica, ii., p. iv., London, 1725, fol.; Pulteney, rz i- of the Progress of Botany, ii., p. 31. There are a great many notices of Petiver in the first volume of Nichols, Literary Illustrations of the Eighteenth Century.

He occasionally got specimens from Scotland, e. g. " Muscus Scoticus corallio incrustatus. Got in a fresh River near Clacmannan on Forth within a few miles of Stirling; procurd me thence by my Curious and Worthy Friend, Mr. James Hamilton, Surgeon in Edinburgh." Gazo-phylacii Naturae et Artis Decas Priina, Tab. x. No. 10, p. 16, Londini, 1702.

At the end of the Museum Petiverianum, infra, he returns thanks for specimens to many friends. Amongst them are No. 13, Mr. James Hamilton, Surgeon in Edinburgh; and No. 26, Mr. James Sutherland, Superintendent of the Physick Garden at Edinburgh. Itfra, p. 159.

'Museum Petiverianum, London, 1695-1703, 8vo; in ten centuries, each describing one hundred plants, animals, or fossils. Petiveriana, London, 1716-17, fol. See also A Compleat Volume of the Memoirs for the Curious, p. 222, London, 1710, 4to; Valentini, Museum Museorum, ii., Appendix xiv., pp. 43-52; The Philosophical Transactions, xx. (1698), death Sir Hans Sloane purchased the collection together with his books and manuscripts all of which subsequently passed to the British Museum. The Herbarium has recently been transferred from Montague House to the Natural History Museum at South Kensington.- One of the orreatest collectors whom the world has ever seen was Sir Hans Sloane (1660-1751), the celebrated physician, President of the College of Physicians and of the Royal Society," and a contemporary of Dr. Mead. He early commenced to form a museum, and continued to add to it without intermission until the close of his long life. In 1687 he made a voyage to Jamaica, and is said to have been the first man of learning whom the love of science alone led to that, then distant, part of the orlobe. He brouo-ht home with him not fewer than 800 different species of plants, and this was the first laro e accession to his collection. Amongst other important acquisitions which he made in later years were the Charleton or Courten and Petiver collections, which have already been mentioned, and those of Dr. Christopher Merret

PP- 313, 393; xxi. (1699), PP- 289, 295; xxiii. (1702-3), p. 1411 sqq.; xxvii. (1710-12), p. 142 sqq.

Petiver also published Brief Directions for the easie making and preserving Collections of all Natural Curiosities, n. d.

1 Sloane, tit supra; Pulteney, Op. laud., ii., p. 78; Nichols, Illustrations of the Literary History of the Eighteenth Century, i., p. 276. Edwards, Lives of the Founders of the British Museum, p. 290. London, 1870, 8vo.

2 See Briickmann, Epistola Itineraria, 64, Cent. i.; Memoirs of Dr. Stukeley, i. pp. 65, 125 (Surtees Society, No. Ixxiii.).

(1614-1695) of Dr. Leonard Plukenet (1642-1706), a friend of Courten, and of Rev. Adam Buddie, Reader at Gray's Inn, which consisted chiefly of botanical specimens or other objects of natural history. Pope, speaking- of the connoisseur or agent, mentions the principal collectors of the day:

He buys for Topham, Drawings and Designs, For Fountain Statues, and for Pembroke Coins; Rare monkish Manuscripts for Hearne alone, And Books for Mead, and Rarities for Sloane.

The arrangement of his treasures cost Sloane much time and trouble. In 1725 he had 5497 specimens of earths, bitumens, metals, minerals, stones, and fossils; 804 corals; 8226 vegetable and vegetable substances; 200 large volumes of dried samples of plants; 3824 insects; 3753 shells; 1939 echini, Crustacea, fishes, and the like; 568 birds and 185 eggs; 1194 quadrupeds and their parts; 345 vipers

Sloane, A Voyage to the Islands of Madeira. and amazca, ii., p. ii., London, 1725, fol.

-Pulteney, Sketches of the Progress of Botany, ii., p. 28.

Nichols, Literary Illustrations of the Eighteenth Century, i., pp. 269, 282, 364.

Pope, Moral Essays, Ep. iv., 7. " Rarities " became " Butterflies " in the later editions. In these editions the name of Sir Andrew Fountain (1676-1763) was dropped out. He was a well-known antiquary and virtuoso. " By his skill and judgment he furnished the most considerable cabinets of this kingdom, to his own no small emolument." Nichols, Literary Anecdotes, v., p. 253, "Walked with Mr. G. Plaxton to the ingenious Sir Andrew Fountain's, who showed me several admirable curiosities and antiquities from Ireland, both Roman, Danish, and Irish, of copper and other metals," Thoresby, Diary, ii., p. 28. Of Lord Pembroke's coins Thoresby says, "It is incomparably the best collection in the nation, if not in the universe," Op. laud., ii., p. 35. As to the catalogue of this collection see supra, p. 15.

and serpents; 507 Jimviana 1169 miscellaneous objects, both natural and artificial; 302 things relating to the customs of ancient times, or antiquities, urns, instruments, etc.; and 81 large seals; 319 pictures, many relating to natural history; 54 mathematical instruments; 441 "large vessels, handles, and other things made of agats, jaspers, cornelians, christals, besides many camei and seals, excisa and incisa; 20,228 coins and medals, ancient and modern; 136 books in miniature or colours, with drawings of plants, etc., and all sorts of natural and artificial curiosities; 580 books of prints; 2666 volumes of manuscripts, the greater part of them relating to physick and natural history, travels, etc." In all he had 53,018 separate specimens, which by 1733 had increased to 69,352, and went on increasing for the next twenty years. He was equally industrious in collecting a library relating to the medical art, natural history, chemistry, anatomy, etc., which contained 40,000 printed volumes and 4100 mss. In 1740 he resigned the presidentship of the Royal Society, which he had held since 1727, and next year removed his

This is his own account in the Introduction to vol. ii. oi A Voyage to the Islands of Madeira. and Jainaica London, 1725, fol.

Maitland, History of Lofidon, ii., p. 1287, London, 1772, fol.

The museum as it stood in 1748 is described in Tie Getitlema-n's Magazine, xviii. (1748), p. 301. See also John Ragford's account, lb. (1816), part ii., p. 395. The number of articles in 1753 is given in Edwards' Lives of the Founders of the British Museum., p. 303, London, 1870, 8vo. See also Wendeborn, Zustand des Staats, der Religion, der Gelehrsamkeit und der Kunst in Grosbfitannieft, vol. ii., p. 162, Berlin, 1785-88, 8vo. English translation, i., p. 317, London, 1791, 8vo, but this is an abridgment and does not give the particulars in the original.

library and museum to Chelsea, where he died nth January, 1753. museum and library had cost upwards of 50,000, and its value, according to his own and other accounts, was 80,000. By his Will he bequeathed the whole to the nation on condition that 20,000 should be paid to his family. The document is an interestino- one:

Whereas from my youth I have been a great observer and admirer of the wonderful power, wisdom, and contrivance of the Almighty God, appearing in the works of his creation, and have gathered together. books, both printed and manuscript,. natural and artificial curiosities, precious stones,. dried plants,. and the like,. amounting in the whole to a very great sum of money: Now, desiring very much that these things, tending many ways to the manifestation of the glory of God, the confutation of atheism and its consequences, the use and improvement of the arts and sciences, and benefit of mankind, may remain together and not be separated, and that chiefly in and about the city of London, where they may, by the great confluence of people, be of most use. Do hereby request that. (my) trustees. do make their humble application to Parliament. to pay.; 2o, oco. unto my executors. in consideration of the said collection (it not being, as I apprehend and believe, a fourth of the real and intrinsic value), and also to obtain. sufficient and effectual powers. for the preserving and continuing my said collection, in such manner as they shall think most likely to answer the public benefit by me intended.

The gift was accepted, and in 1753 an Act (26 Geo. II., c. 22) was passed for the purchase of the Sloane library and museum and of the Harley col- 1 Letter by Horace Walpole, who was one of his trustees, to Sir Horace Mann, 14th February, 1753. Walpole, Letters ed. Cunningham, vol. vii., p. 320, London, 1857, 8vo.

lection of charters and manuscripts, which was in the market at the time, for uniting them with the Cotton Library, and for providing one "general repository " for these and any other additions that might thereafter be made. The Act authorised the raising of the funds required by means of a lottery, and fully 95,000 was obtained. Of this, 20,000 went to the two daughters of Sir Hans Sloane, Mrs. Stanley and Lady Cadogan;; i i0,000 to the Duchess of Portland, heiress of the second Earl of Oxford; 10,000 for the purchase of Montagu House; 13,000 for altering and repairing it; and 30,000 was set aside as a capital fund, the interest of which, it was hoped, would meet salaries and cost of maintenance. The three collections thus acquired and housed became the British Museum, which was opened to the public on Monday, the 15th of January, 1759, and is now one of the greatest museums and libraries of the world.

While the Harleian manuscripts were secured for the nation, it is to be rei retted that the o'reat Harleian Library had been allowed to be dispersed a few years earlier. It was purchased, in 1742, by Tom Osborne, the bookseller, for 13,000, a sum which is said to have represented less than the price of the bindings, and was sold off in detail. Grateful to the deceased Earl of Oxford for many favours, Osborne determined to issue a sale catalogue that would be a monument to his memory, and employed Samuel Johnson to assist in its preparation. " Hie artiuni liberalium disciplin-

Oldys, in Brydges, Censttra Literaria, i., p. 438, London, 1805, 8vo.

artmiqiie aniatoribus offertur catalogiis; tanquam perefdie qiiidam literariitm Musei Harleiani momi,-mefttum."

The first donor to the new establishment was Colonel William Lethieulher, who bequeathed to the museum a collection of English and Egyptian antiquities and a very perfect mummy, which had been described by Gordon. A committee of the trustees waited upon the Colonel's executors upon 23rd February, 1756, to return thanks for the legacy, when Pitt Lethieulher, the Colonel's nephew, presented them with several antiquities which he had himself collected during his residence in Cairo.

Gustavus Brander (i 720-1787), a wealthy London merchant, employed his leisure and his means in making various collections, and amongst others a collection of fossils found in the cliffs about Christ-church and the west of Hampshire. These he presented to the British Museum, and a description of them prepared by Daniel Charles Solander, the keeper of the printed books, was published in 1766

The catalogue, Catalogus Biblioihecae Harleianae London, 1743-45, is in five volumes and contains 36,690 lots, representing probably 100,000 to 150,000 volumes, in addition to 251 volumes of books of prints and 36 lots of drawings. Gough states British Topography, i., p. 658) that the last three volumes were only shop catalogues, in which the unsold articles are repeated. This may be true to some extent, but they likewise contain a great quantity of books which are not in the first or second volumes.

2 Supra, p. 123.

: ho 's,, Anecdotes of Mr. Bcwyer, pp. 108, 548; Literary Attecdotes of the Eighteenth Century, v. p. 372.

Fossilia Hantonieiisia colleeta, et in Musaeo Britatinico deposita, a Gustavo Brander, London, 1766, 4to, with plates; London, 1829, 410; Nichols, Op. Laud., vi., p. 260; Edwards, Lives of the Founders of the British Museum, pp. 22, 401, London, 1870, 8vo.

In 1764 and 1765 a collection of birds, insects, and other objects was exhibited at Spring- Gardens, and was ultimately absorbed by the Museum.

But the first large and comprehensive addition to the archaeological department was that made in 1772 by the purchase by means of a Parliamentary grant of the museum of antiquities which had been formed during seven years' researches in Italy by Sir William Hamilton, British Ambassador at Naples.-

One of the most eminent of the benefactors of the British Museum was Sir Joseph Banks (1743-1820), who, like Sir Hans Sloane, occupied the chair of the Royal Society for a long series of years. Like Sloane, he made a voyage in early life for the study of natural history and for collecting and describing specimens. He continued to collect during the remainder of his lone life, but as a rule limited himself to what he acquired personally and did not ransack the market or buy up whole museums as Sloane did Much of his time and energy were given to the formation of his library. His opinion was that private collectors

A Catalogue of Birds, Insects, etc., now exhibiting at Spring Gardens. London, 1764 and 1765, i2mo.

2 Edwards, Lives of the Founders of the British Museum, p. 247 sqq. London, 1870, 8vo.

Dr. Samuel Johnson had some thoughts of being a member of this expedition, "I see but at a small distance. So it was not worth my while to go to see birds fly, which I should not have seen fly; and fishes swim, which I should not have seen swim," Boswell, Life of Johnson, ed. Croker, iii., p. 172, London, 1859, 8vo.

He bought Dr. William Fothergill's natural history collections after his death in 1780, but the Doctor had by his will ordered that they should be offered to him at a valuation. Nichols, Op. laud., ix., p. 740.

should "confine their libraries to one individual branch of human knowledge, by which means a great number of particular collections, each complete in its kind, would quickly be brought forward, and the purposes of instruction be more easily attained, than whilst the rage of indiscriminate collection subsisted, and the number of competitors for the same book precluded the possibility of completion."- Acting upon this rule he confined himself to books relating to natural history, with the result that his collection is one of the most complete ever brought together by one man. It was under the charge first of Dr. Solander, and subsequently of Jonas Dryander (i748-1810), Librarian of the Linnaean Society, who prepared an accurate and valuable catalogue of its contents.- Sir Joseph left the library and all his collections to the British Museum. The library is still kept in a room by itself, and contains probably more books relating to museums than any other existing collection.

As originally organised, the British Museum was divided into three departments: (i) manuscripts, medals, and coins, 2) Natural and artificial productions, and (3) Printed books.

Nicolai, Das Gelehrte England, English Preface by George Forster, Berlin, 1791, 8vo., quoted in Brjdges, Censiira Literaria ii., p. 248, London, 1806, 8vo.

- Catalogus Bibliothecae hislorico-naturalis, Josephi Banks, Baronetti, London, 1796-1800, 8vo, 5 vols.; Nichols, Op. land., ix., p. 43.

Edwards, Op. laud., p. 507.

The General Contents of the British Museum, London, 1761, 8vo; Letters on the British Museion, London, By A. Thomson 1767, i2mo.

In 1802 the great collection of Egyptian antiquities acquired under the Capitulation of Alexandria passed into the museum. This was followed in 1805 by the purchase of the Towneley marbles and terracottas, and of the bronzes, coins, gems and drawings in 1814. These acquisitions rendered it necessary to create a new department, that of Antiquities and Art, to which were united the Prints and Drawings as well as the Medals and Coins. Botany was added, as a fifth department, in 1S27. after the bequest of Sir Joseph Banks' collections. In 1837 the Prints and Drawings were separated from the department of Antiquities and became an independent department. At the same time the department of Natural History was divided into two, one of Geology, including Palaeontology- and Mineralogy, the other of Zoolocf-. In 18 7 Mineralocry was constituted a separate department. In 1S61 the department of Antiquities was subdivided into (i) Greek and Roman Antiquities, (2) Coins and IMedals, (3) Egyptian and Assyrian Antiquities; and in 1866 the British and Mediaeval Antiquities were formed into a separate department along with the Ethnographical collections. Between

1880 and 18S3 the Natural History collections were transferred to the new Natural Historv Museum in Cromwell Road.

The greater number of the old museums were what are now known as general collections, but there were also many special museums. Anatomical and pathological preparations were recognised as necessary for the intelligent study of the structure, physiology, and diseases of the human body, and Leyden, Amsterdam, and Cassel were long famous for their collections. The Gottorp Museum was to a considerable extent ethnographical, as was likewise that

As to the Leyden Museum, see pp. 29, 190, 209.

As to the Amsterdam Anatomical Museum, see Valentini, Musewn Museorujti, ii., Appendix xv., p. 52; Ausfuhrlicfie Beschreibung der Nie-derlande, p. 309.

The Cassel Museum, which is now a large and excellent general collection, is known as the Museum Fridericiamutn; Stoltz, Beschreibung des Kurfurstlidien Museu? ns zu Cassel Cassel, 1832, 8vo; Valentini, Op. laud., ii., Appendix v., p. 14.

Theodore Kirkring of Hamburg (+1693) made a large anatomical collection, which was acquired by Anthony Verbrocht of Hamburg, on whose death, about 1727, it was catalogued and advertised for sale, but was bought in by the town. Ripke, Dissertatio historico-litteraria de meritis Hamburgensium in Hisioriam naiuralem, p. 30, Hamb., 1791, 4to.; Neickelius, Museographia,. 199; Kirkring, Spicilegium anatomi-cwn, Amsl, 1670, 4to.

Olearius, Gottorffische Kunst-Kammer, p. 3 sqq. Schlesswig, 1674, 4to. K of Lorenz Hofmann of Halle. Friedrich the Great was amongst the first to appreciate the value of such a collection, and despatched first Polemann, and after his death, Cleyer to the East to collect arms, clothing, utensils, and the like for the Berlin Museum. Augustus II., Elector of Saxony and King of Poland, in 1731 sent Professor Johann Ernest Hebenstreit, with four companions and an artist, to collect specimens for the Dresden Museum and for his zoological garden. The collections of Johann Georg Kisner of Frankfort and G. F. Richter of Jena were com. posed largely of fossils. Hermann Boerhaave (1668-1738) had a museum of chemical and pharmaceutical preparations. Many collections were principally illustrative of natural history, as for instance those of Johann 1 GATMATOi'TAAKIOX, sive Thesaurus variarum Rerum antiquarum et exoticarum tarn naturalium quam artificialium collectus. Latin and Germ. Halae, 1625, 8vo.

Klemm, Geschichie der Sajfimlungen fiir Wissenschaft und Kunst in Deutschland, p. 206, Zerbst, p. 1837.

Gundling, Historic der Gelahrheit, i., p. 590, iv., p. 5280, Franckf., 1734-37, 4to, 5 vol.

On his return Hebenstreit gave an account of the Roman remains in Africa, Oratio de antiquitatibus Romanisper Africanis exstantibus, Leipzig,

Catalogus figuratorutn fossilitwi in Museolo D. Kisneri Francofurti 1711, in Valentini, Museum Museorum, ii., Appendix xiii.

Petiver dedicates his 48th Table to Kisner.

Museum Richterianum continens fossilia, anijnalia, vegetabilia, marina cum comment. Jo. Ernesti Hebenstreitii. Lips., 1743, fol., with figures.

Museum Boerhavianum. Lugd. Bat, 1739, 8vo. This was a sale catalogue drawn up after his death. The chemical preparations all made by Boerhaave's own hand comprise 422 lots. There were 215 lots of dried or preserved specimens of natural history and 54 lots of physical instruments and rarities.

Conrad Ratzel of Halberstadt, Gottfried Nicolai of Wittenberg, and Christopher Gottwaldt of Danzig (1636-1700), which last ultimately found its way to the Academy of Sciences of St. Petersburg. Georg Eberhard Rumph (1634-1706), an enlightened merchant at Amboyna, in the Dutch service a member of the Academy of Nahirae Curiosi, in which he took the title " Plinius Indicus," made an excellent collection of shells. The States of Holland presented a fine collection to Charles II., but it was soon dissipated and lost. Nicolao Gualtieri (1688-1744), of Florence, previously a physician at Pisa, made another, and Signor Micconi of Genoa had one

Valentini, Op. land., ii., Appendix xix.

lb., Appendix xxi.; Neickelius, Museographia, p. 131; and Christian Wurlitz, Museum Curiosum, Wittenberg, 1710, 4to.

Bacmeister, Op. laud., p. 150; Nouvelle Bios, raphie generale, s. v. Gottwald; Musaeum Gott-ivaldianutn sive Catalogus rerum rariarum,. collectarmn a D. Christophero Gottivaldio patre et D. Joh. Christoph. Goilivaldio Jilio Dditizig, 1714, 8vo. A sale catalogue. The collection was principally natural history specimens; but there was also a considerable number of artificial curiosities, antiquities, and works of art; amongst others, "Reliquiae tunicae S. Catherinae Bononiensis"; Musei Gotiuialdiani testaceorum, siellarutn marinaruin et coralliorum Tabulae. Norimb., 1782, fol., with plates, ed. by J. S. Schroter.

Thesaurus Imaginum pisciu? n testaceorutn cochlearu7ii, Lugd. Bat., 1711, fol., with 60 plates; first published, DAmbonische Rariteit Kamer, Amst., 1705, fol., and again Latin and Dutch, 1741, fol., 7 vols.; translated into German under the title Amboinische Raritdten-Katmner, by P. L. S. Miiller, with additions by J. H. Chemnitz, and an Introduction by J. A. Cramer. Wien, 1766, fol., with 33 plates.

Granger, History of England, iii., p. 402. London, 1779, vo; Lister, A Journey to Paris., ed. Henning, p. 82. London, 1823, 8vo.

Index testarum conchyliorum quae adservantur in Musaeo Nicolai Gualtieri J et methodice distributae exhibentur tabulis aeneis ex., Florent., 1742, fol., with portrait. The figures, says Cuvier, are numerous and exact.

of the best in Italy; and cabinets of shells were common elsewhere." Dru Drury (1725-1803) brought together a remarkably fine collection of insects, which was of material service in the advancement of entomology.

The university of Giessen had a collection of philosophical and scientific instruments; there was another large and well arranged one at St. Petersburg. Similar collections were formed by Henry Johann Bytemeister of Helmstadt, "Johann Jakob Spener of Halle and by the astronomer, Professor Erhard Weigel of Jena (1625-1699). The last was included amongst the seven wonders of the town.

Ara, Caput, Draco, Mons, Pons, Vulpecula Turris, Weigeliana domus, septem miracula Jenae.

Addison, "Remarks on Italy," Works, ii., p. 6. London, 1811, 8vo.

2 M. de la Combe de Vrigny who accompanied Mr. Vernon on his embassy to Denmark in 1702, mentions the Cabinet of shells of M. de la Faille, bailiff of Delft as particularly interesting. Travels through Denmark and some parts of Germany, p. 6. London, 1707, 8vo.

A notice of various collections of shells and other objects of natural history, principally in Denmark, will be found in Regenfuss, Choix de Coqiiiuages et de crustacees, p. vi. sqq. Copenhag., 1758, fol.

See Saint-Fond, Travels in England, Scotland, and the Hebrides, i., p. 123, London, 1799, 8vo.

Valentini, Op. laud., vol. ii., Appendix xvi., p. 56.

Museum Imperiale Petropolitanum, vol. ii., pt. i., pp. 3-72. Petrop., 1741, 8vo.

Bibliothecae Appendix, sive Catalogus Apparatus curiosorum arti-ficialium et Tiat-uraliu7n. Helmstadt, 1731, 8vo; 1735, 4 0-

This collection also contained natural and artificial curiosities. He figures a beautiful perforated stone hammer and a stone chisel (Tab. xvi. 219) as " lapides ceraunii seu fulminares nigri," p. 47.

"Museum Spenerianiwi. Lips., 1693, Svo.

8 Valentini, Op. laud. Appendix xvii., p. 58.

Neickelius, Museographia, p. 57. These verses are explained by Keysler, Reisen, p. 1344, Hannover, 1751,4to; Nicolai, Reiscdurch Deutsch-

A considerable portion of Dr. Bargrave's museum consisted of philosophical instruments and toys, and Briickmann, as has been mentioned, had a large number of the same kind of things. Johann Hubner of Hamburg formed a collection of maps, charts, and astronomical instruments.

The nature of such collections is well described by Kinderling, and may be seen in the present Mathematisch-Physikalischer Salon at Dresden, which was part of the original Kunst-Kammer, and is still very much what it was in the early part of the eighteenth century. There is a similar but recent collection in the Germanic museum at Nuremberg, which is more instructive, as it forms one section of an organized whole. A room, in the Imperial Art-History Museum at Vienna, is devoted to such objects, many of them from the Schloss Amras and from the Imperial Schatz-Kammer, admirably shown and excellently arranged."

There is a collection of surgical instruments in the Nuremberg; there is another and more extensive land iind Sciiveiz, i., p. 58, Berlin, 1783. Keysler mentions in 1730 that Weigel's instruments had gone to ruin.

Pope Alexander the Seventh and the College of Cardinals. luith a Catalogue of Dr. Bargrave's Museimi, 1867, 4to. Camden Society, No. xcii.

"Supra, p. 112.

Museum Geographicuni Hamburg, 1726, 8vo.

Koehler, Aniveisung mit nutzen zu reiscn, edited by Kinderling, pp. 837-845, Alagdeb., 1810, 8vo.

Drechsler, Katalog der Sammlung des K. JMathematisch-Physikali-schen Salon. Dresden, 1874, i2mo.

Filhrer durch die Sammlung der Kunstindustrielle7i Gegenstdnde, p. 14 sqq. Wien, 1891, 8vo.

The best collection is probably that in the ictoria and Albert (late South Kensington) Museum.

one in the Museum of the Royal College of Surgeons, London, and others in various anatomical museums.

A collection of arms and armour was considered especially appropriate in royal palaces and in the castles of wealthy nobles. It was regarded as a symbol of rank and power, and was particularly attractive at a time when almost every gentleman was a soldier. Such objects were gradually introduced into ordinary museums, and are now an essential feature of every historical museum and of every collection of industrial art. There are large and instructive collections in London and Paris, Madrid and Venice, Stockholm and Copenhagen, Berlin and Dresden, Vienna and Buda Pesth, Moscow and St. Petersburg, and in nearly every important museum in Europe.

1 Weltmann, Le tresor de Moscou Oroujeynaja Palatd). Moscou, 1861, 8vo.

-At Zarskoje-Selo. Described by Gille, Musee de Tzarskoe-Selo, St. Petersbourg, 1835-53,50!. 3 vol.; K mratx r, Arsenal de Tsarskoe-Selo, lb. 1869, fol.

See Demmin, Die Kriegstvaffeti, Introduction, Gera-Untermhaus, 1891, 8vo; Guide des amateuis d Amies et Armures anciennes, Paris, 1869, 8vo.

Amongst early Scottish collectors were Timothy Pont, the topographer, and Robert Maule, Commissary of St. Andrews, but by far the most celebrated were the illustrious brothers Sir James Balfour 1600-1657) and Sir Andrew Balfour (1630-1694). Sir James, " with unweared industry and at great expense," says his biographer, " collected a library filled with the choicest books in every branch of literature, but more especially in those which illustrate the history of Scotland, antiquities and heraldry. And seeinof that thinofs and events involved in obscurity are often illustrated by ancient coins, rings, collars, bracelets, seals, and other remains of a former age, he carefully collected this precious antiquarian material, and arranged it in cabinets tit loczilis) as a supplement to his library. The Romans had long been settled in this northern part of Britain, which now comprehends the Kingdom of Scotland, and for protecting the Provincials against the Scots and Picts had constructed walls and many camps, and had left some buildings in which were inscribed stones; these he was assiduous in investigating and in recording the inscriptions. He likewise cultivated Natural History. He wrote on gems and prepared an alphabetical treatise in the Scots tongue containing the description, names, virtues, qualities, of every kind with the places where they are found. He also compiled an account in Latin of the frauds practised in preparing imitations of precious stones."

Sir Andrew, after completing his education, went to London where he lived for some time, and then spent fifteen years in travel abroad. Returning to Scotland about 1667 he brought with him the best library, particularly in medicine and natural history, that had appeared in Scotland; as also a series of medals and a collection of arms, costume, and ornaments, mathematical, philosophical and surgical instruments, a complete cabinet with all the simples of the materia medica and some compositions in pharmacy; and large collections of fossils, plants, and animals. He continued to add to the museum during the rest of his life. On his death it passed into the hands of Sir Robert Sibbald, while the library was sold.

Sibbald, Metnoria Balfouriana, pp. 33, 34, 45. Edinburgh, 1699, i2mo; Michael Balfour, Preface, p. 11, to Letters written to a Friend by the Learned a7id Judicious Sir Andrew Balfour, M. D., Edinburgh, 1700, i2mo.

Sibbald, Op. laud., pp. 63-67; Walker, "Memoirs of Sir Andrew Balfour," in Essays on Natural History, p. 353, London, 8vo; Letters by Sir Andrew Balfour, pp. iii. iv.; Remains of Sir Robert Sibbald, p. 21, Edinburgh, 1837.

Auctarium musaei Balfouriani e musaeo Sibbaldiano, Pref Edin-burgi, 1697, i2mo; Walker, Essays, p. 362.

Sir Robert Sibbald (1641-1722) was an industrious naturalist and antiquary, and a diligent collector, and was the first to give a systematic account of the natural history of Scotland Imitating the recent example of Ashmole in gifting his collection to the University of Oxford, Sibbald, in 1697, presented Balfour's collection to the University of Edinburgh that it might be open to the public, and in the hope that it would receive numerous additions and be the means of creating a general interest in natural history in Scotland. In order that the museum might be as complete as possible he added a large number of additional specimens from his own collection, which he described in a catalogue or handbook for the use of students. The volume is instructive as indicating the scope and character of the science of the day, and is interesting on account of the local information it contains and the number of Scottish words and quaint expressions which it preserves. Defoe mentions that the collection was placed in the upper Common Hall of the old College on the south side of the Cowgate. He calls it "a curious and noble museum"; and says that "it contains a vast treasure of curiosities of art and nature, domestic and foreign, from almost all parts of the world; and is greatly valued by the Virtuosos, containing some rarities that are not to

His Scotia illustrata sive Prodromus historiae yiaturalis was published at Edinburgh in 1684 in folio. See also The Philosophical Transactions, xxii. (1700), p. 693. J. K. Cramer in his Introduction to Rumph, Amboinische Raritciten-Kaminer, p. ix., Wien, 1766, fol.

"Auctarium musaei Balfouriani e Mnsaeo Sibbaldiano. Edinburgi, 1697, i2mo.

be found either in those of the Royal Society at London, or the Ashmolean at Oxford." So little, however, did the University appreciate the treasures which had been entrusted to its care that it allowed the collection to be made away with, and in less than a century from the date of the gift not a vestige of it remained," a fate which likewise nearly overtook Ashmole's collection. In 1753 the greatest rarity the University of Edinburgh possessed was a crooked transparent horn, eleven inches in length, which had been removed from the head of a woman in 1672, a kind of curiosity which possessed great attractions for the collectors of the seventeenth century.

A Tour thro' the whole Island of Great Britain by a Gentleman (1727), iv., p. 79, London, 1753, 8vo; The Gentle? nan's Magazine, xv. (1745), p. 687.

Memorial to the Lord Advocate for the Society of Scottish Antiquaries (1783), p. 4. Reprinted by Smellie, in Account of the institution and progress of the Society of Antiquaries of Scotland, part ii., p. 27.

In a printed letter by the Earl of Buchan and the Secretary to the members of the Society of Antiquaries it is said: The University " seem to be ashamed that the Society has already been entrusted with a more valuable collection of natural objects, than the

University have allowed to perish since the days of James VI., the founder of their incorporation."

Gough, British Topography, ii., p. 629. London, 1780, 4to.

Maitland, The History of Edinhirgh, p. 371. Edinburgh, 1753, fol.

Thomas Kirk saw it in 1677, Thoresby's Correspondence, ii., p. 418. Thoresby himself saw it in 1681, Diary, i., p. 102; and it is also mentioned in the Catalogue of the Rarities in his Museum, p. 2, reprint in the Ducatus Leodiensis, 1816, fol. Sir Robert Sibbald refers to it, and had it copied and engraved by John Adair. It was removed on 14th May, 1671, by Arthur Temple, a well-known surgeon in Edinburgh. Sibbald, Prodrofnus naturalis historiae Scotiae, Part ii., lib. 2, p. 60. Edinburgh, 1683, fol.

George Buchanan's skull was another of the attractions. Memoirs of Dr. Stukeley, i., p. 316; iii., p. 416 (Surtees Society, No. Ixxx.).

Worm, Danicorum Monujnentorum Libri sex, p. 364. Hafniae, 1643, fo'- Bartholinus, De Unicornu, p. i sqq., Amstd., 1678, who refers

When Pennant visited Edinburgh in 1772 he found the museum "totally empty, for such," he adds "has been the negligence of past times, that scarce a specimen of the noble collection deposited in it by Sir Andrew Balfour is to be met with, any more than the great additions made to it by Sir Robert Sibbald." John Macky, on the other hand, states that in 1723 Sir Andrew Balfour's museum was in the Hall of the College of Physicians in the Cowgate, while in the University library there were only a few natural curiosities, but he evidently confuses the collections.- In 1764 the Incorporation of Surgeons proposed to transfer their library and collection of natural curiosities to the University of Edinburgh, as an addition to the library and the inconsiderable museum to numerous examples. See also his Epistolae Medicinalcs, i., p. 95. Hag. Com., 1740. Such curiosities are still in repute with the crowd. In Dr. Kahn's Anatomical Museum there was shown a horn ten inches long which had been extracted from the forehead of a woman, 80 years of age, and who lived seven years afterwards. Catalogue of Dr. Kahn's Anatomical Museum, p. 25, London, 1851, and various other editions.

Tour in Scotland in 1772, Part ii., p. 246, London, 1776, 410.

A Journey through Scotland, pp. 68, 70. The Physicians had a meeting-house and some property near the Cowgate Port. Arnot, History of Edinburgh, p. 322. The old University buildings were a little to the south of the Cowgate, and Macky probably confounded them. Defoe's precise statement at the very time at which Macky was writing shows that the latter was in error. A Tour thrd the whole Island of Great Britain by a Gentleman, iv., p. 79, 5th ed., originally published in 1727.

Wallace mentions that a Finnish boat, with the oar and dart for striking the fish, was preserved in 1693 "in the Physicians' Hall," Edinburgh (Wallace, Description of the Isles of Orkney, p. 34, ed. Small, Edinburgh, 1883, 8vo), so that the Physicians had some sort of a collection.

which Still belonged to the University. The gift was accepted, and next year the old library was fitted up "as a museum for natural curiosities." In 1766 the Earl of Buchan presented another collection of natural objects to the University for the purpose of supplementing this new museum f and when Dr. Robert Ramsay was shortly afterwards appointed Regius Professor of Natural History and Keeper of the Museum, the Town Council confirmed the appointment on condition that he " deliver to the clerk a full list or inventory of all the curiosities or rarities belonging to the University." The fitting up of the new museum completed the ruin of the Balfour collection. Part of it existed in 1750, and was, Professor Walker tells us, the first thing that inspired him with a love for Natural History; but when the rearrangement of 1765 was carried out, "it was dislodged from the hall where it had long been kept; was thrown aside; and exposed as lumber; was further dilapidated, and at length almost completely demolished."

The Earl of Buchan's collection shared the fate

Dunbar, History of the University of Edinburgh, ii., pp. 433. 434, 435; Session Papers in Magistrates of Edinburgh v. University of Edinburgh, Revised Answers for the University, p. 88, reprinted 15th January, 1829. The case is reported 7 S., p. 255.

Defoe speaks of their "chamber of rarities, in which there are several skeletons of uncommon creatures, a mumy and many other curiosities." A Tour thrd the whole of Great Bj-itain, iv., p. J7, London, 1755, 8vo, originally published in 1727; Maitland also mentions it. History of Edinburgh, p. 182.

2 Smellie, Account of the Society of Antiquaries of Scotland, p. 95, Edinburgh, 1782, 4to.

Dunbar, Op. laud., ii., p. 440.

Essays, pp. 353, 365, London, 1812, 8vo.

of Balfour's, and by 1783 had wholly disappeared. Pennant states in 1769 that by Dr. Ramsay's assiduity " the museum bids fair to become a most instructive repository of the naturalia of these Kingdoms." This probably refers to his private collection, as in 1772 he records that the " University museum is at present totally empty." When John Walker (1731-1803) became professor in 1779 he commenced the formation of a museum for teachingr purposes, and included in it a few objects which still remained from Balfour's collection. M. Faujas Saint-Fond, who visited it in 1784, describes it as excellently arranged, and on that account more interesting- than the British Museum. On Walker's death, in 1803, the museum was claimed by his representatives as his private property, removed from the precincts of the University, and sold. The University, however, possessed a few cases containing specimens of birds, serpents and minerals, and some ethnological objects; but whether any part

Smellie, Account of the Society of Antiqiiaries of Scotland, p. 95. Smellie presented the inventories to the Society.

Tour in Scotland in jydg, p. 55, 2nd ed. London, 1772, 8vo. The passage quoted does not appear in the later collected edition of the Tours, e. g. London, 1776, 4to, which bears to be the fourth edition; or in the fifth, London, 1790.

Tour in Scotland in 1772, Part ii., p. 246, London, 776, 4to.

While holding the professorship of Natural History, Walker was a parish minister and was Moderator of the General Assembly in 1790. In 1765 the University of Glasgow conferred upon him the degree of M. D., and in the same year the University of Edinburgh gave him that of D. D.

Walker, Essays, p. 353; Arnot, History of Edinburgh, p. 405, Edinburgh, 1788, 4to.

Travels in England and Scotlaftd, ii., p. 228, London, 1799, o. The date is fixed, vol. i., p. 249 n.

of Sir Robert Sibbald's gift was amongst these does not appear. Walker was succeeded, in 1804, by Robert Jameson (1774-1854), who placed his own collection in the University Museum, and made great exertions to add to it." It was enriched by the bequest of the collection of minerals made by Dr. Thompson, of Palermo, and by the gift of the similar collection made b the great geologist, Dr. James Hutton (1726-1797). The latter had not been unpacked in 1845, seems doubtful whether it is now extant. In 1807 Professor Jameson suggested that an application should be made to the King for an Order directing the officers of the Navy to forward to the museum such specimens of Natural History as they could obtain. The request was granted, and by this means a vast quantity of valuable material was obtained. In 1819, on the dispersion of the great collection of William Bullock, known as the London Museum, a large number of specimens were purchased by the Senatus Academicus, and at the same time the entire collection of M. Dufresne, of Paris, was acquired, the total expenditure being 3000. The museum was, however, for long badly managed. The Scottish Universities Commissioners of 1826

Report of the Scottish Universities Commission of 1826; Visitation at Edinburgh, Appendix, p. 48.

2 It was evidently popular in 1813. A Walk through Auld and New Reekie in the year 181 j, by John Millar, pp. 16, 17, Edinburgh, 1829, 8vo.

3 Report of the Universities Commission of 1826; Visitation at Edinburgh, Appendix, p. 48; Report relative to the University of Edinburgh, p. 90.

New Statistical Account, i., p. 682. According to the Dictionary of National Biography, s. v. " Hutton," the collection cannot now be traced.

reported that, although it was practically a national institution supported by public funds, the majority of the students were excluded from it, and scientific men were only allowed to use it under very stringent and restrictive regulations.

In 1854 the Town Council of Edinburgh, as patrons of the University, transferred the museum to the Science and Art Department of the Board of Trade, and in 1857, along with that department, it was placed under the charge of the Committee of Council on Education. There were afterwards added an Industrial Museum, and a library of reference and in 1864 its title became, The Edinburgh Science and Art Museum. It stands alongside the University buildings, so that it is to all intents a University Museum maintained at public expense. The annual charge is upwards of 13,000, over and above the use and maintenance of buildings.

Besides books and manuscripts, the Faculty of Advocates began shortly after the establishment of their library in 1682 to collect antiquities. In 1707 they purchased from James Sutherland, the keeper of the Edinburgh Botanic Garden, a large and valuable

General Report, p. 95 sqq.

2 Gentleman's Magazine, xli., N. S. (1854), p. 605; xliii. (1855), p. 394.

He was a well-known collector. Supra, p. 135, note 4.) He sent Edward Lhuyd a number of coins and a stone, found in the north of Scotland, which smelt strongly of violets. Another of these he sent to Mr. Charleton and a third to the Ashmolean

Museum. Thoresby, Correspondence, ii., p. 416. Such stones Lapides odorati) were in much request amongst collectors, and are often mentioned by the old writers, and are discussed at length by Briickmann, Episiola Itineraria, 13, Cent. i. The smell came from " the corrected vitriol of the stone," Keysler, Reisen, p. 104, Hannover, 1751, 4to.; i., p. 119, London, 1756.

collection of Greek, Roman, Scottish, Saxon, and English coins and medals, Inscribed stones from the Roman Wall and other antiquities were, from time to time, presented to the curators for deposit in the library as partaking of the character of a national institution.

Towards the end of the seventeenth century the University of Glasgow received by donation many Roman altars, legionary stones, and other monuments; and during the eighteenth century several additional Roman stones and other objects of interest were added to the collection. Writing in 1732 Horsley says, "The two principal collections in Scotland are those of the University of Glasgow and of Baron Clerk; for I do not know of three inscriptions together in any other place in Scotland." By his Will, dated in 1781, Dr. William Hunter bequeathed to the University his splendid museum valued at 65,000. It was

Edward Lhuyd in The Philosophical Transactiotts xxvm., 1713, p. 100; Maitland, The History of Edinburgh, p. 417. Edinburgh, 1753, fol. Sibbald, Collections Concertiing the Roman Ports, Preface (Edinburgh, 1711); Memoirs of Dr. Stukeley, i., p. 317; iii., p. 416. The coins are described by Gordon, Itinerariiim Septentrionale, p. 119 sqq.

Dr. Thomas Reid, when describing the University in 1794, says, "In an adjoining apartment the College has placed a number of milestones altars, and other remains of antiquity, which have been discovered in the ancient Roman Wall between the Forth and Clyde." Works, ed. Hamilton, p. 738; Old Statistical Account, xxi., Appendix, p. 48.

Britannia Romana, p. 181. London, 1732, fol.

In 1781 Dr. William Hunter presented a considerable number of coins to the Museum of the Society of Antiquaries of Scotland. Smellie, Account of the Society, p. 62. Edinburgh, 1782, 4to. Dr. Hunter was M. D. of the University of Glasgow, and an honorary member of the Faculty of Physicians and Surgeons of Glasgow.

removed to Glasgow in 1807, "" considerable additions have since been made to it.

John Anderson (i726-1796), Professor of Natural Philosophy in the University of Glasgow, formed a considerable collection of natural history specimens and physical apparatus. The Rev. John Lettice, who visited Glasgow in 1792, was struck by its excellence, and assuming that it belonged to the University calls it the " repository of their philosophical apparatus and natural history." " I have seen no repository of this kind," he says, " in any university, either at home or abroad, more abundantly furnished with mathematical, mechanical, and optical instruments, and every sort of machinery or model requisite for the illustration of science; nor any so agreeably and conveniently arranged, as this in the college of Glasgow. It is, indeed, a splendid collection; and few perhaps have been rendered more successfully subservient to the purposes, for which they were designed." On the Professor's death, it was transferred to the Institution which he founded, and to which his name was

Ma. wma. n, Excursion to the Highlands of Scotia? id, p. no, London, 1805, 8vo. Hughson, London, iv., p. 331. London, 1807, 8vo. DArchenholz, Picture of England, ii., p. 219. Captain James Laskey, A General Account of the Hiinterian Museum, Glasgow. Glasgow, 1813, 8vo. P. S. A. Sco., xxii. (1888), p. 349. A short but good account by Professor John Young appeared in The Glasgow University Magazine, February, 1889.

Catalogue of Anatoniical preparations in the Hunteriaji Museum. Glasgow, 1840, 8vo. The preface bears date ist Nov., 1841. Catalogue of anatomical and pathological preparations of Dr. William Hunter in the Hunterian Museum, University of Glasgow. By John H. Teacher, Glasgow, 1900, 2 vols., 8vo. This is an admirable catalogue.

"A Tour through various Parts of Scotland, p. 61. London, 1794, 8vo.

Garnett, Tour itt Scotland, ii., p. 196. London, 1800, 410.

given. It was added to from time to time, and a short account of it, prepared by Dr. John Scouler (1804-1871), was pubhshed in 1831, When this Institution was merged in the Glasgow and West of Scotland Technical College, in 1887, the natural history and general specimens were presented to the Hunterian Museum, and the remainder was retained as the nucleus of a mineralogical and geological collection to be used for teaching purposes in the new College. This technical museum is being organised and extended, and will soon be a valuable educational instrument.

Repeated efforts were made by the Faculty of Physicians and Surgeons of Glasgow during the eighteenth and nineteenth centuries to form a museum, but these invariably resulted in failure. The collection of "rarities" in natural history to which occasional references are made in the Minutes of last century appears to have left no trace in the present century. In 1823, and again ten years later, movements towards the institution of a pathological museum resulted in the formation of a considerable nucleus of such a collection. In the former year a sum was voted for the museum, and in the latter proposals were made for the erection of a suitable building, but the scheme eventually came to nothing, and in 1852 the entire collection was handed over to the Pathological Museum of the Royal Infirmary. Of that museum a catalogue

Accomit of the Andersonian Museum, Glasgow. Glasgow, 1831, 8vo.

2 Duncan, Memorials of the Faculty of Physicians and Surgeons of Glasgow, p. 215. Glasgow, 1896, 4to.

has been published. In the Western Infirmary, Glasgow, there is an excellent Pathological Museum, of which a catalogue is in preparation and is expected to be published presently.

Dr. Peter Wright (d, 1819), five times President of the Faculty of Physicians and Surgeons, one of the Trustees, and the first President of the Ander-sonian Institution, Mr. Gilbert Hamilton and Mr. Alexander Brown, of Glasgow, were collectors, and made various gifts to the museum of the Society of Antiquaries of Scotland,

Many objects of curiosity were acquired by Marischal College, Aberdeen, during the seventeenth and eighteenth centuries, which were deposited in the College library. The collection gradually grew and included natural history objects, coins, and medals. In 1764 it was proposed to provide a separate apartment for it, but this was not done until 1786. The collection of philosophical instruments was in 1798 considered one of the best in the kingdom; and was supplemented by models of the most useful machines

Catalogue of the Pathological Micseum of the Glasgow Royal Infirmary edited by Joseph Coats, Glasgow, 1872, 8vo; again edited by David Foulis, Glasgow, 1878, Svo.

Stuart, Essays on Scottish Antiquities p. 31, Aberdeen, 1846, 4to. Old Statistical Accounts, xxi., Appendix, p. 131; Gough, British Topography, ii., p. 628.

In Marischal College the teaching of Civil and Natural History was in 1827 entrusted to one professor. He dealt with both in one course, and his teaching embraced in one session the history of the Egyptians, Phoenicians, Greeks, Persians, and Romans; Mineralogy and Zoology; Chemistry, Electricity, Galvanism, and Magnetism, Light and Heat. Report of the Universities Commission of 1826, Visitation at Aberdeen, Marischal College, pp. 22 sqq., 40 sqq.

in the various arts and manufactures, acquired out of a grant made during several years by the Board of Trustees for promoting Fisheries and Manufactures in Scotland.

There was a separate museum in King's College, Aberdeen, which was much increased by the exertions of Professor William Ogilvie (i 736-1819), and his own valuable collection of Greek coins was ultimately transferred to it. In i860 King's College and Marischal College were united, when the Natural History section of Kino's Colleo e was transferred to the museum in Marischal College, and the remainder became the Archaeological Museum of King's College.

There seems to have been no attempt to form a museum in the University of St. Andrews until comparatively recently, and it was only in embryo in 1827. The Literary and Philosophical Society of St. Andrews, soon after its foundation in 1838, began to form a collection, and this together with various departmental museums belonging to the University are deposited in a suite of rooms in the University buildings. The archaeological collection is illustrative of the neighbourhood, and contains a number of objects ot

Douglas, General Description of the East Coast of Scotland, p. 198, Paisley, 1782, 8vo; Ogilvie, Birthright in Land, with Biographical Notes by D. C. Macdo7iald, p. 239. London, 1891, 8vo.

- P. S. A. Scot., xxii. (1888), p. 356. Catalogue of Antiquities in the Archaeological Museum, King's College. Aberdeen, 1887, 8vo.

Report of the Scottish Universities' Commission of 1826, Visitation at St. Andrews, p. 19, and Evidence of Dr. Chalmers, p. 68, and of John MVicar, pp. 183, 184. Report of the Commissioners, p. 28.

In 1782 the skeleton of the college carrier and a few objects of a similar character were preserved in the library. Douglas, General Description of the East Coast of Scotland, p. 31. Paisley, 1782, 8vo.

much interest. The natural history museum is of considerable extent, and there are excellent collections of fossils and geological specimens, a number of ethnological objects, and a well-arranged osteo-logical collection

Robert Wodrow 1679-1734), the minister of Eastwood, had some taste for natural science, and although unwearied in gathering materials for his History of the Singtlla7 Sufferings of the Church of Scotland, found time to collect a small museum of antiquities and fossils, the use of which he gave to Sir Robert Sibbald. Writing to Sibbald, he says, "If there are any of your Roman curiositys that are perfectly doubles, or any natural products that you have doubles of, it would be a new obligation to send some of them to augment my small collection."- The collection was dispersed on his death."

"Report of the Si. Aftdrezvs University Commissioners p. 19, London, 1845, fol.; Roger, History of St. Andrews, p. 119, 2nd ed., Edinb., 1849, 8vo; P. S. A. Scot., xxii. (1888), p. 345.

-23rd November, 1710, Remai? is of Sir Robert Sibbald, pp. 21-40. Wodrow Correspondence, i., pp. 32, 171; ii., pp. 289, 344; iii., p. no.

George Crawfurd, in his General Description of the Shire of Renfrew (Edinburgh, 1711, fol.), mentions "several curiosities observed by Mr. Robert Wodrow." There is a letter from Professor Robert Simson, 6th August, 1725, to Wodrow introducing Gordon, the author of the Itiner-arium Septe7tt7ionale, and referring to this collection. Gordon himself mentions it, Itinerariicm Septe? itrionale, p. 118. Maidment, Analecta Scotica, ii., p. 220. Edinburgh, 1837.

Memoir of Wodrow by Dr. Robert Burns, prefixed to his edition of Wodrow's History, i., p. iii. Glasgow, 1829, 8vo, 4 vol.

Dr. Stevenson Macgill, his successor in the parish of Eastwood, states Old Statistical Account, xviii., p. 211) that Wodrow "was among the first who attended to natural history in this country; and he left behind him a small Museum of fossils, chiefly collected from his own parish, and also a collection of medals."

The study of natural science was just commencing in Glasgow at this time. Caleb Threlkeld (1676-1728), the author of the tirst treatise on the plants of Ireland, commenced Master of Arts in the University of Glasgow in 1698, and it was probably when a student there that he first beo-an to interest himself in the study of botany. In 1704 part of the College Yards was laid out as a Physic or Botanical Garden,- and John Marshall, surgeon in Glasgow, was appointed teacher or professor of botany. It was through his opportunities for study in this garden that Robert Simson, the mathematician, became a learned botanist; and it was there that Charles Alston (1683-1760), whose work on the Matejia Medica has been repeatedly quoted in these pages, acquired his first knowledge of the science of botany which he afterwards so successfully cultivated.

Amongst other private museums in Scotland, the most extensive was the collection of antiquities made by Sir John Clerk, of Penicuick (1684-1755), better

Pulteney, Sketcjies of the Progress of Botany, ii., p. 196. Cf. Mitnivienia Universitatis Glasguensis, iii., p. 159. Glasg., 1854, 4to.

Muniinenta Universitatis Glasguensis, iii., pp. 512, 514.

In the librar of the University of Glasgow (of which Wodrow was keeper for several years), there are copies of Gesner, De reruvi fossiliuvi lapidujii et ge i? iaruvi Liber supra, p. 25), and of Boetius, Geminarum cf lapidutn Hisioria supra, p. 26), presented by him in the same year, 1704.

3 In his Testament (recorded 27th November, 1719, Commissariot of Glasgow) he is styled " Professor of Botanie in the University of Glasgow."

He commenced M. A. in the University of Glasgow in 1717 and M. D. in 1719, Munitmnta, iii., pp. 173, 305. He had gone to Leyden in 1716, but e-idently returned to Glasgow next year to take his degree. In 1720 he began to lecture in Edinburgrh.

known as Baron Clerk. Somewhat later Mr, James Macgolian, of Edinburgh, made a similar collection which was described by Pennant in 1772.

The most important museum of archaeology in Scotland is that collected by the Society of Antiquaries, which is now national property. The Society was founded in 1780 on the initiative of the Earl of Buchan. One of its objects was the formation of a museum, which, it was intended, should embrace not onl) antiquities but also specimens of the natural productions of Scotland. Many donations were received, and the museum quickly took shape. In 1782 the Society applied for a Royal Charter of in-corporation. The application was most strenuously opposed by all the vested interests of Edinburgh by the University, the Faculty of Advocates, and the Philosophical Soci-ety but the opposition, which was evidently prompted by jealousy, fortunately failed. It was supported on various flimsy grounds, one of which was the in-advisability of sanctioning the formation of a museum. The opponents apparently despaired of being able to extinguish the Society, but endeavoured to supersede it by suggesting the incorporation of another upon a more extensive plan, to embrace literature and science, and to be called " The Royal Society of Scotland."

Mn 1857 Clerk's inscribed Roman stones were presented to the National Museum. P. S. A. Sco., iii., p. 37. It is to be regretted that they were not added to the collection in Glasgow, which would then have approached completeness.

2 Tour in Scotland in 1J72, Part ii., p. 241. London, 1776, 4to.

Gough also refers to the collection of John Cay, Deputy Secretary of Excise at Edinburgh. British Topography, ii., pp. 628, 744. He was grandson of Robert Cay, the Antiquary, often mentioned in Stukeley's correspondence.

Dealing with the question of museums, the University of Edinburgh, headed by Principal Robertson, the historian, say " The library of the Faculty of Advocates has been during a century the repository of every thing that tends to illustrate the history, the antiquities, and the laws of this country. The collection is very considerable, though still far from being complete. By its situation it is easily accessible to the Courts of Justice, and to the practitioners at the bar. It is humbly submitted, whether an attempt to form a new and rival collection be a measure prudent, expedient, and of advantage to the public. The musaeum of the University of Edinburgh contains those objects of natural history which are exhibited by the professor of that branch of science to his students, and are illustrated by him in the course of his lectures. It appears to the Senatus Academicus that the establishment of another Musaeum would not only interrupt the communication of many specimens and objects which would otherwise have been deposited in the Museum of the University, but may induce and enable the Society of Antiquaries to institute a lectureship of natural history, in opposition to the professorship in the University." After detailing their scheme for the Royal Society which they advocated they next propose " that whatever collections of antiquities, records, MSS., etc., shall be acquired by this Royal Society shall be deposited in the library of the Faculty of Advocates, and all the objects of natural history acquired by it shall be deposited in the Musaeum of the University of Edinburgh, so as both may be most accessible to the members of the Society, to the public, and of most general utility." The Lord-Advocate Henry Dundas, to whom the petition for the Charter had been referred, was not to be duped by such arguments, and, appreciating the aims of the

Society, recommended that the Charter should be granted, and it passed accordingly in May, 1783.

The museum has now been transferred, under certain conditions, to the Government, and receives an annual grant in aid.

In 1784 the Literary and Antiquarian Society of Perth was established after the pattern of that of Edinburgh, and the formation of a museum was commenced. It contains a considerable number of objects of various kinds, but it is not very extensive, and has not had the good fortune, like that of Edinburgh, to have been taken over and maintained by the State.

Memorial for the Principal and Professors of the University of Edinburgh. Reprinted by William Smellie, Account of the Institution and Progress of the Society of Antiquaries in Scotla7id, part ii., p. 13. Edinburgh, 1784, 4to. Smellie (1740-95) was superintendent of the Society's museum.

Transactions of the Literary and Anfiquaria? i Society of Perth. Perth, 1827, 4to. This volume contains a catalogue of the contents of the museum at that date. See further P. S. A. Scot., xxii., p. 337; Nature, xlvi. (1892), p. 472; Museums Association, Proceedings at Seventh Meeting, ed. by Howarth and Platnauer, p. 43. London, 1896, 8vo; Sir William Henry Flower, Address at the Opening of Perth Museum, 29th November, 1895. Garnett, Tour in Scotland, ii., p. 104. London, 1800, 4to.

It is unnecessary, for the present purpose, to trace the history of other museums. Dealing in curiosities had become a recog nized callino", Collections continued to be formed both by private persons and public bodies in England and on the Continent, and many of great extent and value were made. They could be counted by the score in Rome, and in every important town in Italy,- Holland, France, and Germany there were numerous collections. " I am now makino- a collec-tion of natural rarities," says Robert Hooke in 1666, "and hope within a short time to get as good

Evelyn, Diary, i., p. 51; Nuniismata, p. 199.

Giovanni Ciampolini was a noted dealer in antiquities in the time of Pope Leo X., and was a friend of Politian.

Philippe Sylvestre Du Four (1622-1687), druggist in Lyons and friend of Dr. Jacob Spon, was an antiquary and collected on his o vn account, but he was always prepared to sell his pieces as readily as his drugs when opportunity occurred. At least, so says Niceron, Mcmoires pojir servir a Vhistoire des homines illustres, vol. xvi., p. 362.

Kanold prints a catalogue of antiquities for sale by Matthaeus Bayer of Ulm. Neickelius, Museographia, p. 70.

For example, Misson, A New Voyage in Italy, ii., p. 368, London, 1699; and Spon, supra, p. 21. See Bonnafte, Les Collectioneurs de rancienne Rome, Paris, 1867, 8vo.

as any have been yet made in the world." " I am extremely glad you tell me you intend to collect Natural Curiosities," writes Sir Hans Sloane to a correspondent. " I have," says another, just back from India, "collected innumerable Specimens of Plants. I have likewise made a good Collection of Insects, Fishes, etc., which are partly dried and partly preserved in spirits. Of Shells I have a good store, many of them very fine; and have not neglected antiquities, but have collected a great number of Pagods, Amulets, and other curiosities of the kind, which the country afforded."- John Evelyn, as Beck-mann subsequently did, included amongst inventors, " the diligent and curious collectors of both artificial and natural curiosities, types, models, machines, c." Every traveller visited the principal collections, and many of them have left a record of what they saw.

So popular had such collections become in the eighteenth century that a museum of curiosities was thought an attraction in a London coffee house. One of the sights of London during the eighteenth century was the repertory of curiosities in Don Saltero's Coffee House in Cheyne Row, Chelsea. It was established in 1690, and sold off in 1799. The founder was James Salter, an old servant of Sir Hans Sloane, who helped him with the collection. ' From Putney we returned to Chelsea to see Mr. Salter's Collection of Curiosities,

Robert Boyle, Works, vi., p. 505. London, 1772, 4to.

Nichols, Literary Illustraiions of the Eighteenth Century, i., pp. 270, 314-

"Xiimis7nata, p. 282, London, 1697, fol.

Don Saltero appears frequently in the pages of The Tatler. In Number 34 he and his coffee-house are described by Steele.

which is really surprising considering his circumstances as a coffee-man; but several persons of distinction have been benefactors." There was a printed Catalogue which was sold to visitors, and passed through about fifty editions.

"Monsters of all sorts here are seen,

Strange things in nature as they grow so, Some relics of the Sheba queen,

And fragments of the famous Bob Crusoe."

This success led to imitation. Ralph Thoresby records that in 1714 Mr. Miers, who kept a coffeehouse which was frequented by Sir Hans Sloane and other learned men, " hath a handsome collection of curiosities in the room where the virtuosi meet."

Another London attraction in the middle of the eighteenth century was Adams's museum at the Royal Swan in Kingsland Road. It was shown in three rooms, in an entry or passage and a long room at the back. There were no less than 567 numbers comprising a most miscellaneous lot of things, most of them rubbish, many of them fictitious or absurd, but all appealing to popular curiosity: Charles of Swede-land's boots; Harry the Sth's spurs; tobacco stopper made from the royal oak King Charles was hid in at Boscobello Grove in Staffordshire; Vicar of Bray's clogs; caps, gloves, and shoes from Hudson's Bay; Mandarin's hubble-bubble from Gambroon in Persia; Chinese chop-sticks; Star and Garter made of Indian arrows, with a George in the middle; a corn-mill in a bottle, that goes without wind, water, or clock work;

Thoresby, Diary, ii., p. 376.- Op. laud., ii., p. 229.

thunderbolt stones, and many relics of the risings of of 1715 and 1745.1

Another popular collection was that of James Cox in Spring Gardens, Charing Cross. It consisted of mechanical contrivances, waterfalls, Asiatic temples, jewellery, and curiosities in richly decorated rooms, and was for some time a fashionable resort- " I promised precisely at twelve to call on Lady Frolic, to take a turn in Kensington Gardens, to see both the exhibitions, the staind glass, dwarf, giant, and Cox's museum." When the attendance began to fall off. Cox applied to Parliament and was successful in obtaining an Act authorising him to dispose of it "by way of chance." It is alluded to by Foote. "His father," says the incoherent Mr. Aircastle, "keeps a pastry cook's shop in Spring-gardens, just where Cox's museum is by the by, they tell me, Cox will get devilish rich by his lottery."' So it was generally thought.

Hubert's museum and that of John Conyers,

A Catalogue of the Rarities to be seen at Adams's at the Royal Swan in Kingsland Road, leading from Shoreditch Church. London, 1756, 8vo. The third edition.

A descriptive Catalogue of the several superb attd magnifcent pieces of jnechanism and jexvellery exhibited iii the Museum at Spring Gardens, Chari? ig Cross. London, 1772,410.

The Museum is well described in Miss Burney's Eveliria, Letter xix.

DArchenholz, Picture of England, i., p. 106 sqq. London, 1789.

3Mrs. Simony, in Foote's "The Cozeners," Works, ii., p. 157, infra.

13 Geo. III., c. 41. The contents are scheduled to the Act.

Foote, op. laud., ii., p. 195. London, 1799, Svo.

"In the debate on Sir Ashton Lever's Bill, i? if?-a, p. 176, it was said that both Cox's lottery and that of the Messrs. Adam for the disposal of their Adelphi Buildings had been frauds on the public. The Gefttleman's Magazine, liv. (1784), p. 705. As to the Adelphi lottery, see lb., xliv., p. 138.

although of a superior kind to any of these, were also open to the public, and seem to have been formed for the purpose of exhibition. Others followed their example. Richard Greene (i 716-1793), surgeon and apothecary in Lichfield, began collecting curiosities about 1740, and continued to do so with unremitting zeal until his death, nearly fifty years later. His museum was shewn to the public gratuitously. It was visited by Dr. Johnson in 1774, and again in 1776 along w ith Boswell, who describes it as " truly a wonderful collection both of antiquities and natural curiosities and ingenious works of art."" A descriptive catalogue was published in 1773 and passed through several editions. In that year the collection contained coins and medals, Christian antiquities, and natural history specimens. In later years there were added many ethnographical objects from the South Seas, books and manuscripts, arms and armour. After Greene's death the collection was broken up; first the fossils were sold in 1799 to Sir John St. Aubyn, and next year the arms and armour to William Bullock; and

There is an account of Greene and his museum in Nichols Illustrations of the Literary History of the Eighteenth Century, vi., p. 318-326; see also Literary Anecdotes of the Eighteeiith Century, ix., p. 380. The museum is shortly described, and a plan of part of it is given in The Gentleman s Magazine, Iviii., part ii. (1788), p. 847.

-Life of fohnson, ed. Croker, vi., p. 98, London, 1859. Johnson said of it, "Sir, I should as soon have thought of building a man-of-war as of collecting such a museum."

The New and Accurate Survey of the Lichfield Museum, 3rd edition, Lichfield, 1786, extends to 84 pages.

Amongst the specimens was "the tusk of an Elephant dug out of a gravel pit near Stratford-upon-Avon six feet beneath the surface of the ground."

afterwards nearly the whole of the remainder to Walter Honeywood Yate, of Bronsberrow, who printed a catalogue of it in 1801 This part was ultimately acquired by Richard Wright, of Lichfield, Greene's grandson, but was finally dispersed on his death in 1821.

Sir Ashton Lever (i 729-1788) early in life became a collector of natural history specimens, and began the formation of a museum at his house, Alkrington Hall, near Manchester. In this he was assisted by James Douglas, the antiquary, author of Nenia Britannica. In later years he added ethnographical objects, coins, medals and casts, and all kinds of curiosities. In 1775, "flattered by his great success," he removed the museum to London, styled it Holophusikon, and exhibited it in Leicester House, Leicester Square, " not doubting but he would make it, by its pre-eminence over all other collections, a national honour." He entered upon the undertaking "with a determined spirit," and "secured every capital article that offered itself." By selecting out of some hundred thousand specimens, he formed a " collection of subjects of natural history and of art superior to

A concise. Catalogtie of. the. curiosities in the Museum of W. H. v., 8vo. 1801.

-Described in Tie Ge? itleviatis Magazine, xliii. (1773), p. 219; and in

Wendeborn, Der Zustand des Staats, der Religion, der Gelehrsatnkeit und der Kunst iti Grosbritannien, ii., p. 142. Berlin, 1785, 8vo. English abridged translation, i., pp. 323, 350, London, 1791, 8vo. See also

Compayiioti to the Museum late Sir A. Lever's, London, 1790, 8vo; I Shaw, Micsei Leveriani Explicatio (Latin and English), London, 1792-96, n 2 vols., 4to, with 72 coloured plates; Skelton, Engraved Illustrations of Meyric s collectioti of Ancient Armour, contains several of the general I objects from Lever's museum in addition to the armour, 1830, 2 vols., fol.

anything of the kind in Europe." Whether this be so or not, it was evidently an attractive show, as one httle lad of ten was so carried away with excitement that he addressed a set of verses to Sir Ashton, which were printed in the Gentle-mans Magazine:

View there an urn which Roman ashes bore, And habits once that foreign nations wore, Birds and wild beasts from Afric's burning sand, And curious fossils rangd in order stand.-

The collection had cost him 53,000, which made so serious an inroad on his fortune, that he became anxious to dispose of it, and offered it to the Trustees of the British Museum for a moderate sum, but they declined to purchase it. Dr. Johnson was in favour of the acquisition by the nation both of it and of the Houghton collection of pictures belonging to Lord Oxford, which was likewise for sale at this time. The Government allowed the pictures to slip through their fingers, and they are now one of the principal ornaments of the Hermitaoe Museum in St. Peters-burg. In 1783 Sir Ashton petitioned Parliament for an Act to authorize him to dispose of his museum by way of chance. The petition was referred to a committee, who reported favourably,

Preamble to the Act 24, Geo. iii., Sess. 2, cap. 22; House of Commons Journals xxxix. (1783-84), p. 161. Duncan, Catalojriie of the Ashmolean MKseum, p. iii. Oxford, 1836, 8vo.

= xlix. (1779), P- 319-

The Gentlemaiis Magazine, Iii. (1783), p. 919.

Boswell, Life of fohnson, ed. Croker, ix., p. 337, London, 1859.

H. of C. Journals, xxxix., p. 161.

Next session an enabling Bill was introduced, and after some discussion was passed. A lottery was then an accepted method of raising money, and, as we have seen, it was by this means that money was obtained for establishing the British Museum and for paying for the collections out of which it grew. Sir Ashton's Act"- allowed him to sell 36,000 tickets at a guinea apiece, but of these only 8000 were applied for by the public. The museum fell to Mr. James Parkinson, a holder of two tickets, who exhibited it in the Rotunda near the Surrey end of Blackfriars Bridge. It was very popular for some years. " The trouble to obtain a sight of the British Museum," says an American writer, "renders it of less value to the public than a private collection belonging to Mr. Parkinson, called the Leverian Museum." In the course of time it was neglected and was sold off in 1806. A few of the objects are now in the Hunterian Museum, Glasgow.

Gcntlemaiis Magazine, liii. (1783), 919; liv., (1784), 622, 705.

24 Geo. iii., 2 Sess., c. 24, "An Act for enabling Sir Ashton Lever to dispose of his Museum as no s' exhibited at Leicester House by way of chance."

The contents of the museum are scheduled to the Act.

"Nichols, Literary Illustratiotis of the Eighteenth Century, vii., p. 469; Hughson, London, iv., p. 329. London, 1807, 8vo.

See the Advertisement in Thornbury, Old and Netv London, vi., p. 382.

"Peale, Discourse on the Science of Nature, p. 20. Philadelphia, 1800, 8vo.

Catalogue of the Leverian Museum, London, 1806, 4to, pp. 410. There is a copy in the British Museum, with the prices and the purchasers' names.

Part of the ethnographical collection was purchased for the Vienna museum. Klemm, Geschichte der Sainmlungen fiir IVissenschaft und Kunst in Deutschland, p. 299, Zerbst, 1837, 8vo.

William Bullock, a goldsmith in Liverpool, in early-life began to form a museum. In 1800 he bought the greater part of the arms and armour from Greene's Museum, the remainder being acquired for the collection in the Tower of London. He likewise made considerable purchases at the sale of Sir Ashton Lever's Museum. In 1805 he opened the " Liverpool Museum" at 22 Piccadilly, in the room originally occupied by Astley for his evening performance.- In 1808 he had the Egyptian Hall erected for him, transferred his collection to it and opened it to the public as the London Museum, which soon became one of the most attractive sights in London. By 1810 it had cost him 22,000, and in the next year he spent on it 8000 more. In 1819 he sold off the whole, and commenced an extensive scheme of travel extending over several years. During this time he formed a Mexican collection, which he exhibited at the Egyptian Hall in 1824. The University of

A Companio7i to the Liverpool Museum. 6th edition. Hull, 1808, 8vo. A seventh edition was published in 1809.

- Timbs, Cu7iosities of London, p. 266. London, 1855, 8vo.

A Compa7iion to Mr. Bullocks museum. now open for public inspection in the Great Room No. 22 Piccadilly, London, 8th edition. London, 1810, 8vo. This is called the eighth edition, being a continuation in a new form of the original Liverpool Companion. A seventeenth edition was published in 1816.

Catalogue of the Roman Gallery of A itiquities and Works of Art and the London Museum of Natural History. at the Egyptia7i Hall. which will be sold by auction. London, 1819, 4to.

The whole collection was first oftered to the British Government for 50,000; but, the age of lotteries having passed, they declined to purchase.

A large portion of the ethnographical section went to the Berlin museum. Klemm, Geschichte der Sammlungen fiir IVissenschaft und Kunst in Deutschland, p. 210, Zerbst, 1837, 8vo.

Edinburgh, as already mentioned, purchased a considerable portion of the original collection. The armour which Bullock had acquired from Greene's Museum was purchased by Sir Samuel Meyrick (1783-1848), and in 1871 was sold with the rest of Sir Samuel's magnificent collection to M. Frederic Spitzer, of Paris. In 1893 the Spitzer collection was in turn disposed of by auction.

Charles Wilson Peale (i 741-1827), the portrait painter of Philadelphia, was one of the first to form a museum in the United States. He was much interested in Natural History, delivered lectures on the subject, and was indefatigable in collecting material. The foundation of the collection was a few of the bones of a mammoth, which he acquired in 1785. Sixteen years later he obtained the first entire skeleton which had ever been found. Besides specimens of natural history the museum contained wax figures of the different nations of the North American Indians, "dressed in their proper habiliments," a collection of their arms and utensils, other Indian and European curiosities, and casts of ancient gems and statues. For ten years it was kept in the Philosophical Hall, but in 1802 the greater part of it was transferred to the State-House, the use of which was granted by the Legislature of Pennsylvania for its display. There were also some models of machines, and in one of the rooms there was a person "with Hawkins' ingenious Physiognotrace, who draws the Profiles of such as chuse to pay the cost of paper, free of other expence."

Scientific a7td Descriptive Catalogue. Philadelphia, 1796, 8vo; Guide to the Philadelphia Museum., Philadelphia, 1804, 8 o. See also Rembrandt In one of his lectures Peale gives a succinct account of various European museums, and of the uses such institutions are intended to serve.

In 1804 Messrs. Delacoste and Curling exhibited an extensive cabinet of Natural History in New York. Delacoste, who evidently was a precursor of Barnum, solicited subscriptions, and undertook to augment the collections and make it as useful and interestino- as possible. Not to be behind Peale, he bound himself "to travel throuoh the whole continent of North America for the purpose of procuring a skeleton of that anonymous animal called the Mammoth, which has given so much credit to the museum of Philadelphia, and of completing as much as can reasonably be expected the collections of the natural productions of the United States, so that the cabinet of New York might, in an inconsiderable time, rival not only the above-said museum, but all institutions of the kind in other parts."-

Vtaxe, Accoiinf of the Skeleton of the Mammoth, London, 1802, 4to; An historical Disquisition on the Mammoth, London, 1803, 8-o.

He exhumed two specimens, one of hich was erected in his father's museum. The other he brought to London for exhibition.

Discourse itttroductory to a course of Lectures on the Science of Nature luith original Music composed for a7ici sting on the occasion. Philadelphia, 1800, 8vo.

He published an earlier lecture in the same year, Introduction to a course of Lectwes on Natural History. Philadelphia, 1800, 8vo.

- Catalogue of the natural productions and curiosities lohich compose the collection of the Cabinet of Natural History, opetied for fo'thcr exhibition at No. 38 William Street, New York. New York, 1804, 8vo, pp. 87.

The New York Lyceum of Natural History was formed shortly afterwards. See Catalogue of the orga7iic remains and other geological and mineralogical articles cofitained i? i the collection Presented. by S. L. Mitchell. New York, 1826, 8vo, pp. 40.

A FEW private collections, as for instance those of Consul Sherard (1659-1728) John Martyn (1699-1768), and Richard Pulteney (i 730-1801), have been absorbed in public museums, but the greater number have been dispersed, as it comonly fares with such curiosities where the next heire is not a virtuoso." The money represented by a collection was in many cases needed for a widow or children, so that a sale could not be avoided; and pathos may be found in a sale catalogue. jOrgen Hahn, or, as Latinised, Georgius Hannaeus of Copenhagen (163 7-1699), the friend and eulogist of Thomas Bartholin, formed a con-

Described by Thoresby, Diary, ii., p. 374.

-'Letter by Evelyn to Pepys, Diary, iii., p. 443 (London, 1879). " Nonnuuis hujus-modi Thesauris baud raro accidit; ut, quos longus pertinaxque labor una accumulavit, defuncto possessore, brevi distra-hantur." Catalogus Bibliothccae Harleianae, vol. i., Dedication written by Michael Maittaire. London, 1743, Svo.

War was also a disturbing element. Dr. Edward Brown mentions that his father, Sir Thomas Brown, had a piece of unicorn's horn which had formerly been amongst the Duke of Curland's rarities, which were apparently dispersed after he was taken prisoner by Douglas in the wars between Sweden and Poland. Travels, p. 102, London, 1685, fol- 182 SALE OF HAHN AND SCHVNVOET's MUSEUMS siderable museum of natural history. On his death his widow issued, in 1699, a catalogue of the objects " ancient and recent, natural and artificial, home and foreign which are preserved in the museum of the late Professor beati professoris), arranged therein with much labour and no less cost and are to be seen in beautiful order and now, since his death, long for a sympathetic purchaser (curiosum desiderunt emptorem)." The reasons assigned for a sale are sometimes rather far-fetched. Simon Schynvoet (1652-1727), the naturalist and friend of Rumph, was a diligent collector, and by 1698 his museum, or at least the numismatic portion of it, was of sufficient importance to be annexed by Peter the Great. Like his countrymen, Ruysch and Seba, he immediately began again, and at his death left a large collection of shells, fossils, minerals, precious stones, and petrifactions, which passed to his only daughter, as heir-at-law. Her husband, however, not being-a man of science, could make no use of it, and, being of opinion that it would injure the reputation of his late father-in-law if such a collection was practically buried, he resolved to offer it for sale in two parts minerals and shells to some prince or great person. If not sold to such a purchaser by a fixed day, he reserved right to deal with it as he might think proper.

PJiysicotlieca beati Doct. Geojgii Haujiaei. Hafniae, 1699, 4to.

Supra p. 147.

Muntkabinet der Roomsche Keyzers e? i Keyzcrinncn. hi vaarcn beschreven door Abraliam Bogaert. Amst., 1695, 8vo, with 70 plates.

Catalogiis Musaei p7-aestantissimi Fossiliian. Simon Schynvoet, n. p., n. d., 8vo but Amst., 1744. Latin and Dutch.

Catalogue dun tres famcux et ires excellent Cabinet Royal de toutes

Besides those already mentioned, or referred to, the museums of Kirke, Thoresby, and Stukeley, of Edward Harley (i 689-1724), second Earl of Oxford and of his daughter, Lady Margaret Caven-dish-Harley (1715-1785), Duchess of Portland, of sortes des Coqiiilles. assembles. par. Simon Schynvoet, n. p., n. d., 8vo but Amst., 1744. French and Dutch. See Gersaint, Catalogue raisoimc dc Coquilles, p. 40. Paris, 1736, i2mo.

Nichols, Literary Illustrations of the Eighteenth Century, iv., p. 174.

-Musaeum Thoresbyanum (London, 1725, 8vo), reprinted with additions in Ducaius Leodie? isis, 1816, occupying 123 folio pages, followed by A Catalogue and Description of the Natural and Artificial Rarities in this Musaeum, lb., 116 pp., with plate. The Philosophical Transactions, xxiii. (1702-3), p. 1070. Supra, p. 126.

He was much pressed to give part of his collections to the Ashmolean Museum, " but kept off promising till I see how it please God to dispose of me as to marriage, posterity, etc." Diary, ii., p. 429.

The museum was bequeathed to Thoresby's son, Ralph, and after his death what remained of it was sold by auction in London in 1764. See Notes and Queries, ist S., iii., p. 247.

Thomas Hearne, writing in 1726, says, "I am much obliged to you for your information concerning Mr. Thoresby and his curiosities. I wish they may fall into good hands; methinks they might be proper to be joined with Sir Hans Sloane's." Nichols, Literary Illustrations of the Eighteenth Century, i., p. 307.

A Catalogue of the Collection of Coins and Medals, various Antiquities, Fossils, and other Curiosities of William Stukeley. London, 1766, 8vo. Supra, p. 126.

A Catalogue of the Collection of the Right Honourable Edward Earl of Oxford, deceased. London, 1742, 4to. A sale catalogue. The collection consisted of pictures and works of art, and a few Roman and other antiquities. Amongst the latter some British celts, one of them in the mould it was cast in (p. 14). There was a separate catalogue and sale of the coins and medals.

Nichols, Literary Anecdotes of the Eighteenth Century, v., pp. 494, 495. Catalogue of Coins and Medals of a person of distinction. London, n. d. A Catalogue of the Portland Museuin, lately the property of the

Dowager Duchess of Portland. London, 1786, 4to.

Horace Walpole writes, 30th May, 1751: "I have just seen her collection, which is indeed magnificent, chiefly composed of the spoils of her father's

Henry, third Lord Coleraine (i693-1749), Arthur Pond, Ebenezer Miissell John Neilson, George Scott," James West, Richard Bateman, Samueltyssen, George Humphrey of St. Martin's Lane, Dr. Lettsom, the famous Quaker physician, Daniel Boulter of Yarmouth, Rackstrow, and Professor Ramsay of Edinburgh, were sold. Sir John Soane, profiting by the experience of these and of many other eminent collectors, obtained during his lifetime an Act of Parliament for settling and maintaining his museum and works of art.

The extensive museum of Marmaduke Tunstall, and the Arundel collections. The Gems of all sorts are glorious." Letfet's, ed. Cunningham, ii., p. 225. London, 1857, 8vo.

The catalogue was prepared by Rev. John Lightfoot, the author of the "Flora Scotica." Nichols, Literary Anecdotes of the Eighteenth Century, iii., p. 670.

It is said that Linnaeus readjusted his system of Shells after visiting the Duchess' Museum. Laskey, Account of the Hiinterian Mjtseinn, p. 104. Glasgow, 1813, Svo.

Nichols, Literary Illustrations of the Eighteenth Century, iv., p. 432.

Catalogue of the genuine and curious collection of Roinan atid Egyptian antiquities. and other effects of Ebenezer Mussel I, Esq., of Bethnal Green, deceased. London, 1765, 8vo. A sale catalogue. There were separate catalogues and sales of his Coins and Library. The library contained many examples of the presses of Caxton, Pynson, and Wynken de Worde.

-Correspondence of John Ray, p. 482. London, 1848, Svo.

"Catalogue of the Museum of James West. London, 1772, Svo. Two parts. Memoirs of Dr. Stukcley, iii., p. 3 (Surtees Society, No. Ixxx.).

A Catalogue of that much esteemed and truly valuable Museum of the late Hon. Richard Bateman, deceased. London, 1774, Svo.

Fox, Synopsis of the Newcastle Museum, p. 179. Newcastle, 1827, Svo.

"Fox, Op. laud., p. 179,

Catalogue of Rackstro Lfs Museum. London, 1794, Svo.

Descriptioti of the House and Museum. of Sir John Soane, p. loi. London, fol., n. d.

of Wycliffe, was sold on his death in i 790, and purchased by George Allan, of Darlington, who added it to his own collection, and threw the whole open to the public. Mr, Allan died in 1800, when his collection was sold. It was purchased by his son, who retained it until 1822, when he advertised it for sale by auction, but disposed of it privately to the Literary and Philosophical Society of Newcastle-upon-Tyne, and it thus became the foundation of the Newcastle Museum.

The valuable collections of shells and insects made by Dr. John Fothergill (1712-80) were acquired by Dr. William Hunter, and are now in the Hunterian Museum at Glasgow. His series of drawings of rare plants in his famous botanical garden at Upton was purchased after his death for a large sum by the Empress of Russia.

Museums have sometimes suffered from theft. Samuel Stryk (1640-1710) the celebrated jurist, president of the Faculty of Law in the University of Wittemberg, had a collection of coins, which was made away with by his servant, a misfortune which caused him great grief.-

Fox, Synopsis of the Newcastle Museum, Newcastle, 1827, 8vo; Nichols, Literary Anecdotes of tlie Eigjiteejith Century, viii., pp. 366, 752, 753.

-Gundling, Historic der Gelahrheit, iii., p. 4072. Franckfurt, 1734-37, 4to, 5 vol. Gundling has a chapter on Museums, abridged from Bertram, Valentini, Neickelius, Major, Morhof, and Misson.

Two cases of museum theft are reported in December, 1900: the one of Nelson relics from Greenwich Hospital Museum, and the other of old silver from West Ham School and Technical Museum, Stratford.

While an enormous quantity of material was collected, it was only gradually that its real value began to be appreciated, and that it was turned to proper account. The early museums had often certain definite aims, and were intended to be exponents of science; but natural history was hampered by traditional opinions, and physical science was overweighted by metaphysics. Everything was explained, but the explanations had always to be in accord with the accepted doctrines of logic and metaphysics, which had themselves in turn to square with theology. The wonders of nature had an extraordinary fascination for men of science, who were constantly on the outlook for them. Any variation of the ordinary type of a common object was eagerly sought after, and the more extraordinary it was the greater was its attraction. Hence museums had a tendency to represent the abnormal rather than the normal, what was rare rather than what was common. A museum

Leibnitz, for instance, appeals to curiosprum Musea' in his Pro-tbgaea 24.

was a collection of curiosities, and although the word 'curiosity" in its older sense had a broader meaning than at present and as it still has in France,

Thus Addison describes the museums at Florence as "the noblest collections of curiosities to be met with in any part of the whole world." "Remarks on Italy," IVorcs, ii., p. 157, London, 1811, 8vo.

Canon Bargrave says that the seeing of the various collections at Rome " put me likewise into a humour of curiosity, and making this collection insuing." Pot Alexander the Seventji and the College of Cardinals, p. 116, 1867, 4to, Camden Society, No. xcii.

Bishop Burnet entertained Ralph Thoresby " most agreeably with the sight of several valuable curiosities, as the original of Magna Charta of King John." Diary, ii., p. 27. Mr. Wanley, the keeper of the Harleian Library, was "a gentleman of great curiosity." lb., p. 36.

"Mr. Thomas Knowlton was a man of general curiosity and observation; and, amongst other matters, not inattentive to the pursuits of the antiquary." Pulteney, Sketches of the progress of Botany, ii., p. 240.

One of the oldest examples of the use of the word is Curiostifu Urbis Romae regioniim xiv., probably dating somewhere between the fourth and the eighth centuries. See Jordan, Topographie der Stadt Rom itn Alterthiaii, ii., p. 3 sqq., 541 sqq.

Robert Estienne renders Antiquarius, as Ung homme curietilx dauuoir OH scatioir chases antiques. Dictionnarium Latino-Gallicuin, s. v. Paris, 1538, fol.; Les mots Francois. iournez e7i latin pour enfants. Paris, 1544, 4to. Bargrave uses " Antiquarian " for a dealer in curiosities. Op. laud., p. 127; again, "a rare antiquity and curiosity," p. 135.

-In France Curiositc corresponds pretty much to what we call " applied art," ceramics, furniture, and the like. The Catalogue of the Orleans Museum (Orleans, 1851, i2mo) is Explication des Tableaux, Dessins, Sculptures, Antiquites et Curiosites quiy sont exposes."' The old usage was the same, e. g. Gersaint, Catalogue raisojinc de diffcrens effets curieux et rares contenus dans le cabinet de Mr. de la Roque comine Tableaux, Dessins, Estainpes, Bronzes, Porcelaines ancienncs, Diamants, Pierres fines, Pieres gravies, etc. Paris, 1745, i2mo; Catalogue raisonne des diverses curiosites de Mr. Quoit in de POrangere, composees de Tableaux origitt. des tneilleurs Mattres de Flandres, etc. Paris, 1744, 12mo. See Gersaint's remarks in the preface to the latter.

In France the contents of the South Kensington Museum would be described as cu7-iositc's. Edmond Bonnaffe, the originator of the corresponding collection in the Louvre, writes Le Commerce de la curiosite (Paris, 1895, 8vo), and many other works on the same subject. In there was generally implied in it the idea of strangeness or rarity. The object to which it was applied was to be regarded as worthy of being looked at because it was odd or rare. Of Sir Hans Sloane, Edward Young writes: . Sloane, the foremost toyman of his time, His nice ambition lies in curious fancies.

The Ashmolean Museum he terms " Ashmole's baby-house." At Antwerp, says a well-known Scotsman, "I saw the oddest whim of this kind that could be imagind, which was a collection of eggs from the Ostridge down to the Tom Tit." In the Tradescant Museum were pieces of stone from Apollo's Oracle, Diana's tomb, and the like. The same sort of things figure in Valentini's collection. Amongst sacred curiosities he includes a stone from the wall of Damascus; another stone from the same city where St. Paul prayed; a stone from Mount Guarantana where our Saviour was tempted of the devil; wood from an olive tree in the Garden of Gethsemane. Amongst his artificial curiosities he had

Gazette des Beaiix-Arts, 2 S., i. (1869), p. 327, he gives the history of the word. See HIntermediaire des Chercheurs et Curieux, xxvii. (1893), 587. The Germans use the term " Kunstgewerbe," art-industry.

"The downfall of May-Fair has quite sunk the price of this noble creature the elephant, as well as of many other curiosities of nature." Addison, "The Tatler" No. 20, Works, ii., p. 209, London, 1811. Bulph the pilot " had the little finger of a drowned man on his parlour mantelshelf, with other maritime and natural curiosities." See Dickens, Nicholas Nickleby, c. xxiii.

-Young, Love of Fame, Satire iv.

John Macky A Journey through England, p. 260, 2nd ed. London, 1722, 8vo. The owner of this collection was Monsieur Peters. He had also a collection of shells and another of pictures.

a MS. of the Koran; Chinese ink, which was then a great rarity, and various other objects from China; a Turkish tobacco pipe and an English tobacco box with a burning glass; a piece of writing done by a cripple with but one finger on each hand, and a model of a mine cut in wood. Sometimes, when sounder ideas of arrangement began to prevail, such articles were relegated to a special class under the title "fjhola," but such cases are exceptional.

Very considerable numbers of objects, such as are now known as ethnographical exhibits, were to be seen in various museums, but they were brought together not for the purpose of enabling the visitor to study the arts, industries, and instruments of primitive peoples, but to excite in the spectator a feeling of wonder and surprise, in some cases by their rudeness and clumsiness, in others by their finish and elegance. " The older naturalist," says Professor Ferguson, "collected chiefly the exceptional things of nature (the more wonderful, the better for his purpose), w hich he found on record, without question; or. if he questioned, without attempting to substantiate his opinion by a personal observation or experiment. The ordinary phenomena were passed by as of no importance, or as too familiar to deserve notice or to require explanation."

Leyden was one of the most famous schools of ana- alentini, Museum Museoruvt, vol. ii., Appendix xxiii., pp. 103, 104.-This was so in the case of the St. Petersburg Museum. Muscuni imperiale Petropolitaniim, ii., pt. i., p. 127. Petrop., 1741, 8vo. See the Preface to the third part of alentini's book, vol. ii. Trartsactions Archaeol. Soc, Glasgow, ii., p. 11.

tomy of the seventeenth century. "Amongst all the rarities of Leyden," says John Evelyn, "I was much pleased with a sight of their Anatomy schole, theater, and repository adjoyning, which is well furnishd with natural curiosities; skeletons from the whale and eliphant to the fly and spider, which last is a ver) delicate piece of art. Amongst a great variety of other things, I was shewn the knife newly taken out of a drunken Dutchman's guts by an incision in his side, after it had slipped from his fingers into his stomach."- The account of Leyden given by Gotfried Hegenitius half a century earlier is very similar. Balthasar de Monconys (1611-1665) particularly mentions an anatomical preparation made after the method of Lodewijk de Bils. Amongst the considerable things in the university Edward Leigh notes, " the Anatomy-Theatre, where there is mummies of Egypt, the idols of the heathens, birds which came from China and other far countreys." When speaking of the collection of Paludanus,

C. S. Scheffel, Vita Schelhatmneri in Ad G. S. Schelhammcrum Epistolae Selectiores, pp. i8, 19, Wismar., 1727, 8vo.

-Evelyn, Diary, i., p. 24, London, 1879. There was a similar exhibit in the Vienna Museum. Dr. Edward Brown, Travels, p. 149, London, 1685, fol. See also Briickmann, Epistola Itineraria, 23 Cent. i. Dr. William Oliver saw at Konigsberg a knife which had been swallowed by a peasant in 1685 "d cut out. The PJiilosopjiical Transactions, xxiii. (1703), p. 1408.

Itinerarium Frisio-Hollandicmn, p. 61, Lugd. Bat., 1667. The account in Les Delices de la Hollande, p. 51. Amsterd., 1697, i2mo., is also similar.

Journal des Voyages de Monsieur de Monconys, Pte. ii., p. 151. Lyon, 1666.

= A treatise of Religion and Lear? iing and of religious and learned Men, p. 74. London, 1656, fol. Thoresby's account is similar, Diary i., p. 18.

of Enkhuizen, Hegenitius mentions the stellio or newt, which he describes as a fish not unhke a Hzard, and adds that although the skin, which it sheds once a year, is a sovereign remedy against epilepsy, it nevertheless deprives man of its use by swallowing it as soon as it is cast;- and that hence the crime " stellionate " has its name. In short, the first requisite of a museum exhibit was that it should be something rare or costly, which was apt to degenerate into what was bizarre or outlandish.

The more an explanation appealed to the marvellous, the more acceptable it was; and the belief in the miraculous, which had characterized the liddle Ages, had not died out in the seventeenth century. "Piety," says Arnauld, the great Port Royalist, "does not oblioe a man of orood sense to believe all the miracles related in the Golden

Legend, or in Simeon Metaphrastes, since these authors are full of so many fables that we have no ground to be assured of any-

Hegenitius, Op. laud., p. 32.

All the newts treat their cast skin in this manner. See Alfred Brown in Lumsden and Brown, Natural History of Loch Lomond, p. 68. Glasgow, 1895, 8vo.

3There is a long and interesting note in Hoffmani Lexicon Universale, S. V., on the Stellio. See also Agncola, De ajiimafiiidus subterraneis with his De re Metallica, p. 487. Basil., 1657, fol. Theophrastus mentions that the skin of the newt icioxtiln-( ) is good against epilepsy Frag. 175, Opera, p. 460, ed. Trimmer, Paris, 1866, 8vo.

Stellionate in Roman law was applied to a crime which involved fraud and had no special name. Dig., 47. 20. See Pliny, Hist. Nat., 30, 27 (10).

Gundling, Historic der Gelahrheit, i., p. 589. Franckfurt, 1734-37, 4to, 5 vol. At the same time, he says, the objects must not be trifling, like the Judas rope at Amras supra, p. 87).

A wonderful catalogue of wonders collected by Sachse von Lowen-heim is given by him in Major, Dissert alio Epistolica de Cancris, et Serpentibiis petrefactis, p. sqq. Jenae, 1664, 8vo.

thing on their testimony alone. But I maintain that every man of good sense, though he has no piety, ouo-ht to receive as true the miracles which St. Aug-us-tine relates in his Coufess707is. nd in the City of God, as having happened before his eyes, or of which he testifies himself to have had most minute information from the persons themselves to whom these things had happened." It was indeed no longer allowable to ascribe every extraordinary phenomenon to a miracle, but a firm belief in extraordinary and exceptional powers of nature was an easy means of explaining away every difficulty. Take the case of Thomas Bartholin, the elder, (i619-1680) of Copenhagen. He was an excellent anatomist, author of a standard work upon the subject which was translated into English,"- travelled over the greater part of Europe, and corresponded with all the savants of the time. Yet notwithstanding his culture, learning, and experience, his range of view was very narrow. He was oppressed by the traditional science of the day, and found it impossible to form an independent judgment upon the vast array of facts that came before him. He visited Malta in 1644, and seems to have found much that was interesting and instructive in the island, but he records only what is of the nature of the marvel-

The Port-Royal Logic by Baynes, Pt. iv., c. 14, p. 358. Edinburgh, 1854, 8vo.

- Bartholinus Atiatoiny. iti four books and four manuals. biiblished by Nich. Odpeper and Abdiah Cole, Doctor of Physick. London, 1668, fol.

Of Culpepper the Rev. John Ward records: " Nick Culpepper says that a physitian without astrologie is like a pudden without fat." Diary, p. 95. London, 1839, 8vo.

lous and out of the way. The whole land, he says, produces plants that are antidotes against poison liniversa terra alexipharmaca est), which is attributed to the blessing of St. Paul. Earth is dug from a grotto in which St. Paul spent a night, and is used for the cure of many ailments, and yet, strange to say, although this has gone on for centuries the supply never diminishes.

His account is contained in a letter to Joseph Donzelli, Epistolae Medicinales, Cent, i., Epist. 53, p. 223, Hafniae, 1663, and again Hag. Com., 1740, i2mo. See also Hoffmann, Clavis pharmaceutical p. 130. Halae, 1675, 4 0-

"According to popular belief the blessing of St. Patrick conferred similar qualities on the soil of Ireland. There are no serpents in Ireland, says Bartholomew de Glanville De Proprietatibus rerum, lib. xv., c. 80), and the soil is such an antidote to poison that if carried elsewhere and scattered on the ground it kills snakes and toads.

See Reiske, Deglossopetris Luneburgensibus, p. 51. Norimb., 1687, 8vo. Caruana, Monografia critica della Grotta di San Paolo. Malta, 1896. 8vo.

This is also mentioned by Ray, Travels through the Low Countries, i., p. 262. The virtues of Malta earth were recommended in a printed sheet, distributed in the island, which is preserved by Ole Worm Museum lvor7 iianuin, p. 7), to whom it was no doubt sent by Bartholin. It is also given in French and Latin by Reiske. Op. laud., p. 53; in German and Latin by Valentini, Museum Museorum, i., p. 66.

There was a specimen in the Copenhagen Museum and another in the Royal Society's Museum. Nehemiah Grew refers to the Musaeum Calceolarii Stci. 2, p. 130) for a description of its virtues, but seems himself rather sceptical regarding them, Jusaeum Regalis Societatis, p. 347.

It found a place, however, in the pharmacopeia of the day. See, for instance, Catalogus medicamentorum quae in officina Dietriciana sunt, p. 36 (xvii. cent.), MS. in the Germanic Museum at Nuremberg (Room 64). It was esteemed a cordial, a sudorific, and a certain remedy for the bites or stings of venomous animals of all kinds.

In the eighteenth century it was sent from Malta made up in little cakes of the form of segments of a cylinder, stamped with the impression of a Cherubim's head and wings, and with the words Terra sigillata underneath. Hill, History of the Materia Medica, p. 206.

He has no doubts as to fossil man. After referring to the case of Lot's wife, as a crucial example, he goes on to relate that recently a city in Africa, near Tripoli, had been, by the judgment of God, turned into stone, and that a petrified boy had been sent from it to Cardinal Richelieu. As evidence of the truth of this story he adduces a piece of petrified wood which he saw in Abela's museum and which was said to have been brought from the same town. The story is a striking one, and evidently made a deep impression

Fossil man came into great prominence next century on the publication of Scheuchzer's Homo diluvii testis et Qeda-Kovos, Zurich, 1726, 4to. He maintained that a petrifaction found in the quarries at Oeningen, on the lake of Constance, was a petrified man who had been witness of the flood. Cuvier ultimately proved it to be a salamander. The object now is or was in the museum at Harlem.

James Parkinson cites some wonderful stories of fossil men. Organu Remains of a Former World, i., p. 38. Briickmann mentions some examples Epistolae Itinerariae, ii., 35 Cent, i.), but cautiously adds regarding one of them, " haec relatio magnam requirit fidem." In Epistola 55, Cent, i., he relates the story of a monk who, having stolen a chalice and denied it upon oath, was turned into stone.

-The story was again repeated in London in 1728. Kundmann, Rariora naturae et artis, p. 31, Breslau, 1737, fol.

Another petrified child seems to have been one of the sights of Paris. See John Baptist van Helmont, De Lithiasi, p. 25, in his Opuscula medica. Col. Ag., 1644, i2mo. It was purchased by a merchant in Paris, carried to Venice, and sold there in 1653 to Frederick III., King of Denmark, and became one of the most noted objects in the Copenhagen Museum; Jacobaeus, Museum Regium, Sect, i., No. 6, where it is figured; Valentini, Museum Museorum, i., pp. 417,420. Dr. William Oliver was disappointed of seeing the carved cherry-stone, but he saw the stone child and an egg laid by a woman, the size of a hen's egg, and many other things equally strange. The Philosophical Transactiotrs, xxiii. (1703), p. 1401.

Some other wonders of a similar kind are related in The Spottiswoode Miscellany, ii., p. 522. Edinburgh, 1845, 8vo.

Montfaucon saw in the museum of Bernard Tarvisiano, at Venice, " a board petrifyd, with the knots in it, in such manner that it appears to the eye like wood, and is found to be stone by the touch." The Antiquities of Italy, translated by Henley, p. 55. London, 1725, fol.

Upon him, as he refers to it in at least three of his published works; but what surprises the modern reader is that a man of undoubted ability, and one able to form a sound judgment on all ordinary matters should have been so influenced by authority as to surrender his own powers of reasoning and observation. The assumption that nature constantly operated in an exceptional manner and contrary to common experience, and the desire to record instances, are probably the explanation. This tendency is apparent even in his professional papers. He is too fond of monsters and other things strange and unusual; he believes in spells and charms, and pins his faith on peculiar remedies and, in the case of epilepsy, even upon amulets.

But Bartholin was not singular in his attitude. His opinions were those of most of his contemporaries. Johann Daniel Major, to whom reference has fre-

Epistolae Medicinales, ut supra; De Unicornu, p. 371, Amstd., 1678, i2mo; Historiaruni anatoniicaritin Rariora, Cent, ii. Hist. 100, p. 319, Amstd., 1654. The account in the last is the most detailed.

Bartholin's statement is quoted and relied on by Antonius Deusing in Historia foetus extra Uteriim geniti, p. 121. Groningae, 1661, i2mo. This work involved the author in a storm of controversy, carried on, like a Chinese duel, with the most provocative personalities.

'Historianmi atuitonicariein Rariora Cent, iii., Hist. 71, p. 141. His use of a charm to cure epilepsy was adduced by Sir George Mackenzie, when defending a woman charged with the crime of witchcraft, because she had tied a paper with a few words upon it to the wrist of her patient, as showing that there was nothing objectionable in the practice. Pleadings in some Remarkable Cases, p. 192. Edinburgh, 1673, 4to.

Historiarum anatomicarum Rariora, Cent, ii., Hist. 78, p. 278. He frequently reverts to the subject of epilepsy, e. g. Op. laud., pp. 301, 304.

Robert Boyle was a firm believer in the virtues of amulets, and explained their effect by asserting that they emitted effluvia which passed through the skin. Works, ii., p. 171; iv., pp. 767, 768. London, 1772,4to.

quently been made, not only accepted the story of the city turned into stone, but explained how it came about. No petrifaction is possible without a certain predominant presence and activity of salt. Salt is the basis of all combinations and of all changes. If there be an excess of some pure, free, and volatile salt, which is impelled forcibly forwards, it fills up the pores of the first permeable body that it meets, unites with its volatile particles, and the spirits being dispersed, destroys the power of fermentation. Hence the earthy portion of the body being deprived of volatile salt congeals and hardens in virtue of the power of the fixed salts. Sachse von Lowenheim, commenting on this, mentions that during an earthquake in Austria, in 1348, fifty peasants who were milking cows were turned into statues of salt by the earthy spirit which was liberated by the violent commotion.

Everything, it was held, might be changed into stone, as, for instance, the head and legs, even the tongue and heart of man; a hen hatching eggs; a stag with a serpent in its stomach. These were mostly produced by what were known as stone-forming waters, the usara Xiooyova of Gesner, which were to be found in all parts of the world. One of these was the

Dissertaio Episiolica de Cancris et Serpentibus petrefactis pp. 13, 22. Jenae, 1664, 8vo. Lot's wife was, he thinks, transformed in this manner, but the change was effected in a moment.

Major, Op. laud., p. 68. Conrad von Meidenberg, an eminent mathematician, states that he and the Chancellor of Austria saw the statues. Other similar cases are mentioned by J. B. Van Helmont, Op. laud., p. 25,

Kundmann, Op. laud., p. 31 sqq. i treats fully of the subject, and relates many examples. Supra, pp. 62, 72, no.

A long list is given by Sachse von Lowenheim in his Responsoria water of the Rattray Cave, or White Cave of Slains, in Aberdeenshire, which had a European reputation, and is vouched for by Dr. Sylvester Rattray, a Glasgow physician. This water "doth in a short time congele into stone. Here you would take notice of i a story which will convince you of the possibility of this. A Scottish Gentleman, having been in France and there acquainted with another of that country, who (it seemeth) was curious to know the various and (almost) miraculous operations of Nature, did inform him by writing concerning this well and its water. The Frenchman returned this answer, I am sorry, that you should think me such a fool as to believe such a paradox as this is, that water should, in a short time, be converted into stone. Thereupon our countryman fearing least the other should think this a meer fiction, he took the pains to set a glass under the droping water, untill it became full, and then he sent the glass unto him, the water therein contained being converted into a stone. A very increnious argument for convincincr so confident a Gain-sayer." In course of time it was ascertained that the stone-forming power of such waters arose not from a creative spirit, but because they carried lime in solution. Sibbald understood this, and a specimen appeared in his museum as stalactite; but alongside dissertatio de miranda lapidiiin natura with Majors Dissertatio Epistolica de Cancris et Serpentibus peirefactis p. 70 sqq. Jenae, 1664, 8vo.

Aditus novus adoccultas Sympathiae et Antipathiae causas inveniendas p. 52. Glasguae, 1658, i2mo.

"Matthew Mackaile, The Oyly-Well; or a topographico-spagyricall Description of the Oyly- Well at St. Cathrinis-chappel, in the paroch of Libberton p. 136. Edinburgh, 1664, i2mo.

of it he had "the yolk of a stone of the figure of an Holland cheese," "a white pebble resembling a Hen's tog"" " stone resembling a heart," another resembling a human foot, and another resembling the mould of a button. All these were placed under the head "Regular stones." So great was the belief in the creative power of the earth that some writers maintained that the old urns found buried in the soil were products of nature.

Rarities and freaks of nature and art engfagfed the attention of everyone. Amongst the things which Lord Bacon recommends the intelligent traveller to see, are " treasures of jewels and robes; cabinets and rarities." Sir Andrew Balfour directs the Baron of Livingstone, when visiting the Abbey of St. Denis, " to take notice of Charles the Great's Crown, in which there is a Rubie of the Bigness of a Pidgeon's Egg; A large Cup of oriental Aggat, which they count much of; One of the Nails that fixed our Saviour's Bodie to the Cross, sent to Charles the Great by Constantine V., Emper-our of Constantinople; One of the Potts wherein our Saviour changed the water into wine at the

"Auctarium Mtisaci Balfouriani, p. 55 sqq.

Hagendorn in Miscellanea Cnriosa, Ann. iii. (1672), Lipsiae, 1681, 4to; Stieff, De Urnis iti Silesia. Epistola p. 15, Wratislav., 1704, 4to, 5 plates; Reusch, De Tiimulis et Urnis sepnlchralibus in Prussia, p. 45, Regismonti 1724, 4to; Kundmann, Rariora naturae et artis, p. 31 sqq., Klemm, Handbuch d. germ. Alterthumskunde, p. 188.

The popular belief was that they were fashioned in the earth about Whitsuntide or St. John's day by pigmies, and they were in consequence known as Johannis-Topflein. It was thought that milk creamed better in them and that they produced better butter, and hence they were called Milch-Tdpfe. Many other virtues of a like kind were attributed to them Stieff, Op. laud., p. 15; Reusch, Op. laud., pp. 45, 47; Klemm, ut supra.

marriage of Cana in Galilee; The Pucel of Orleans Sword, wherewith she overcame the English; the Lantern that was carried before Judas, when He betrayed our Saviour; and a thousand other things of great value." The slippers of the Virgin Mary used to be one of the sights of Upsala;- part of her skirt; and another of the water pots of Cana are still to be seen in the treasury of the Abbey Church of the old town of Quedlinburg.

The famous Green Vaults of Dresden the Treasury of the Electors and Kings of Saxony founded by the Elector Augustus in 1560, is a survival of the old type of museum, and possesses much of its original character and arrangement. The objects are still arranged according to their substance bronze, silver,

Letters written to a Friend by the learned and judicious Sir Andrew Balfour, M. D., p. 14, Edinburgh, I7cx, i2mo. Evelyn gives a similar list, Diary i., pp. 43-45, London, 1879 5 adds a mirror that belonged to Virgil. See also Montfaucon, The Antiquities of Italy, p. 42.

Bremner, Excursions in Denmark, Norway, and Stueden, ii., p. 304, London, 1840, 8vo.

The water pot is an onyx vase about 18 inches in height, and was brought home from the East by the Empress Theophano (955-991), wife of the Emperor Otto IL, and presented to this church. It is figured and described by Briickmann, Epistola Itineraria 19, Cent. i. The Treasury also contains a number of relics of Mary Magdalene, St. Paul, and others. These e. xcited the curiosity of Bnickmann, who deals with them in the same Epistola and in the Supplement, pp. 11, 12.

More than twenty of these Cana pots were to be seen in various European collections. There was one at Bologna. It is, says Montfaucon, " entirely like the funeral urns discovered lately by Cardinal Bouillon, Dean of the Sacred College, at the gates of Ostia. It is of marble, a foot high, gracd on the outside with foliage." The Antiquities of Italy, translated by Henley, p. 284, London, 1725, fol.

One of the nails that fastened our Saviour to the cross; the knife He used at the Passover feast; and the Virgin Mary's comb, are figured by Valentini, Museufn Museorum, ii. Tab. xxxvii.

gold, ivory, and so on set out on valuable tables or on brackets placed on boards across the great mirrors which line the walls. There are no doubt many beautiful objects in the collection, but they are not brought together to illustrate beauty of design or of workmanship or the development of art. The ivory ship, the tower of Babel, the Court of the Great Moguv and other costly gimcracks, the objects in amber and rock crystal, mother of pearl, coral and ivory, are intended to exhibit the technical skill and patient labour of the craftsman and the wealth and magnificence of his patron, and to impress the imagination of the spectator with feelings of wonder and surprise. The collection as it stands, notwithstanding the costliness of its specimens, is of little educational or scientific value.

The Tradescant Museum was "a collection of rarities." Oldenburg, writing on 3rd March, 166, of a meeting of the Royal Society, says "there were also produced several curiosities to be lodged in our repository; as a great bone petrified; a whole egg in an egg; a stone bottle which seven years ago was filled full with Malaga sack, and well stopped, but is now empty, though said never to have been opened, and the outside is all covered over with a thick mucous coat, having stood in a corner of a wine-celler all that time." Grew described the Museum as a collection "of Natural and Artificial Rarities." Addison, while insisting on the advantage

There is a series of articles on this object in Zeitschriftfur Museo-logie, vol. ii., pp. 99 sqq. Dresden, 1879, 4- Robert Boyle, Works, vi., p. 272. London, 1772, 4to.

to be gained by visiting a well arranged museum ot Roman antiquities, adds, "This would perhaps be much more useful to universities than those collections of whalebone and crocodile skins in which they commonly abound."

Even an antiquary of such eminence as Bernard de Montfaucon hardly rises above the feeling of interested curiosity, and his accounts of the various collections he visited in Italy are entirely wanting in grasp. "On the 6th of July 1698, we went to the Closet of the Renownd Bidelli, well stord with Rarities, Antiquities and Coins. In the Series of Brass Medals of the largest and middle size are some that are very rare." "One day it was our amusement in the afternoon to view the Closet of Septala, where we observd in particular a certain King of France (they call him Charlemaign) cut in a Lapis Lazuli, bearing a scepter in one hand and a sword in the other, surrounded with flower-de-lys's. On another stone is Alexander the Great, with the Horns of Jupiter Ammon.""- The collection of Signer Rugini, of Venice, "abounded in things petrified, wallnuts, eggs in which y yealk rattld, a peare, a piece of beefe with y bones in it, an whole hedgehog, a plaice on a wooden trencher turnd into stone and very perfect, charcoale, a morsel of cork yet retaining its levitie, sponges and a piece of taffety part rolld up, with innumerable more."

"Dialogues on Medals," Works, i., p. 347. London, 1811, 8vo.

Montfaucon, Tte Antiquities of Italy, translated by Henley, pp. 16, 17. London, 1725, fol. Supra, p. 87.

Evelyn, Diary, i., p. 257, London, 1879; see also De Montfaucon, Op. laud., p. 48.

Stone bread Japides paniforntes), stone biscuits, cakes, pancakes (laganites), and stone cheese tyro-7norphites) abounded in every museum; and the most marvellous tales were related of them. Take but one instance. In 1316 a poor woman, with a numerous family, being distressed by hunger, applied to a wealthy sister for bread to save the lives of herself and her perishing children. The sister answered that she had no bread in the house, and adjured God that if there was it might be turned into stone. To the horror of all the bread which she had beside her, and which she denied, immediately became stone. One of these loaves was for long preserved in the Church of St. Peter in Leyden.

In 1791 the British Museum was described as "an Exhibition of a great variety of Antiquities and Natural Curiosities"; while Timbs in 1855 describes the leading curiosities of the several collections." In 1847 Mr. Albert Way entitles the Catalogue which he prepared for the Society of Antiquaries, "Catalogue of Antiquities, Coins, Pictures, and miscellaneous curiosities in the possession of the Society of Antiquaries." At the beginning of the present century the leg bone of an elephant was exhibited and labelled in

Aldrovandi, Musaeum metallicum pp. 515, 869; Museutn IVormi-anum, p. 84; Sibbald, Auctarium Miisaei Balfouriani p. 55; Briick-mann, Epistolae Itincrariae, 11, 36, yj 66, Cent. i.; Catalogue of all the chiefest Rarities. of the University of Leyden.

2 Briickmann, Op. laud., Ep. 66, Cent. i.

Curiosities of London, p. 515. London, 1855, 8vo.

It is the accepted expression, and occurs in the Ashmolean Catalogue of 1836, by Phihp Bury Duncan, A Catalogue of the Ashmolean Museum descriptive of the Zoological Specimens, Antiquities, Coins, and Miscellaneous Curiosities, Oxford, 1836, 8vo.

the Ashmolean Museum as the thigh bone of a giant. Henry the Eighth's hawking glove; King Charles the First's spurs; the hat he used at his execution; Oliver Cromwell's skull, and many other curiosities of this description were to be found in it." The Scottish University Commissioners of 1826 reported, as regards the Hunterian Museum, Glasgow, that the students were allowed to visit it only once a year, and " this visit is regarded rather as an opportunity of witnessing an exhibition of curiosities than as an auxiliary study."

The craving for what w as strange and uncommon led to the fabrication of curiosities. The basilisk was an animal not to be found in nature, but it was exhibited in museums. " The invention is prettily contrivd and has deceivd many; for they take a small Ray, and having turnd it after a certain manner, and rais'd up the fins in the form of wings, they fit a little tongue to it, shapd like a dart, and add claws and eyes of enamel, with other little knacks dexterously piecd together; and this is the whole secrecy 1 Parker, The Ashmolean Museum. A Lecture,1. 31. Oxford, 1870, 8vo; Llewellyn Jewett in The Art Journal, xi., N. S., 1872, p. 177.

Zedler (1739) particularizes Anne Boleyn's straw bonnet. Universal Lexicon, s. v. Museum Ashmoleanum, xxii., 1878; Wendeborn, Der Zustand des Staats, der Religion, der Gelehrsamkeit und der Kunst in Grosbritafinien, iv., p. 287, Berlin, 1788, 8vo; Duncan, Catalogue, supra, pp. 140, 141.

Evelyn mentions the rarities in the Anatomy school at Oxford in 1654. Diary, ii., p. 56. London, 1879. They are also described by Olaf Borrick in 1663, in Bartholin, Epistolae medicinales. Cent, iv., Epist. 92, p. 471. Hag. Com., 1740, i2mo.

Report relative to the University of Glasgow, p. 77. This is not remedied yet. See Finlayson, Plea for a Reform of the University teaching in Scotland, p. 27. Glasgow, 1890.

of making basilisks," There were many similar cheats." The object of showing such things was that they were expected and that the museum should not seem to be incomplete by their not being there. This is how IVIisson explains the presence of the unicorn's horn and of the Remora that stopped the galley of the unfortunate Antony, "another fabulous animal, which for all its fame may be placd in the ranks of unicorns." The presence of mere curiosities, even in the modern museum, has been defended by no less an authority than Mr. John Henry Parker, curator of the Ashmolean Museum: " I do not wish to exclude curiosities from it; they attract people, and when they are brought hither by curiosity, they may stop to learn something better; they may want to know something of the history of the curiosities they have come to see."

Misson, A New Voyage to Italy, i., pp. 134, 135. London, 1699, 8vo.

-Jacob Bobart, the botanist, transformed a dead rat into the feigned figure of a dragon, which imposed upon the learned so far that " several fine copies of verses were wrote on so rare a subject." Pulteney, Sketches of the History of Bo tatty,., p. 313.

In 1822 a mermaid valued at 1000 was brought to London, and was exhibited at the Egyptian Hall, Piccadilly. It was in reality the head and shoulders of a monkey neatly attached to a headless fish. A pretended mermaid was also exhibited in London in 1775; and another in Broad Court, Covent Garden, in 1794. Timbs, Curiosities of London, p. 266. London, 1855, 8vo. "A mermaid from Ceylon" was exhibited in 1835 i the Caledonian Museum of Practical Science, Straiten House, Wemyss Place, Edinburgh. Catalogue of the Works of Art. also of the fohnston Gallery of Pictures. now deposited in the Caledonian Museum of Practical Science, Edinburgh, 1834, 8-o.

The Chinese turn the Remora to account for taking the turtle. Bullen, Idylls of the Sea, p. 170, London, 1899, 8vo.

TJie Ashmolean Museum. the Additions tnade to it in the Season 1870-1871, p. 4. Oxford, 1871.

The defects of the old museums were want of space, insufficient means of displaying the objects, and bad arrangement. There was no proper staff of attendants, so that the collections could neither be kept in good order nor made sufficiently accessible to students. The keepership of the Ashmolean Museum, for instance, was " a mean place." No salary was attached to it, and a scholar of the eminence of Edward Lhuyd had to depend for his subsistence on the fees paid by strangers for seeing the curiosities. The fee for visiting the Green Vaults at Dresden, in 1730, was from four to six gulden, or about nine to fourteen shillings, the greater part of which went to the superintendent. There was thus a great temptation to make museums attractive to the vulgar rather than useful to the learned. Visitors were often hurried through the rooms, and were sometimes allowed to inspect part only of the collection. A traveller, says Montfaucon, can seldom make a

Keysler, Reisen, p. 1299, Hannover, 1751, 4to; English translation, iv., p. 100, London, 1757, 4to.

just advantage of the Musaea or closets of rarities; "for they that preserve them in custody are commonly palld with a task they are obligd so often to repeat, and hurry it over too hastily for the conveniency of the observer." When he visited Bologna he was unable to see the Aldrovandi museum, because the keeper was absent; while in Keysler's time it was so carefully kept that it was never shown except in the presence of a senator.

Then, as now, there were " eyes and no eyes "; and the intelligent sight-seer was recommended in visiting a museum to have his magnifying glass and his note-book with him, that he might examine and record all that was most worthy of observation, advice which is equally pertinent at the present day. The virtue of labels had also been discovered. Everything in the Aldrovandi museum at Bologna was at least in 1688 described on a ticket attached to it; and the same thing was done in the Plater museum at Basle in 1663. Exhibits were, however, often badly placed, and were nearly always arranged in relation to their accidental and not to their dis- 1 The Antiquities of Italy, translated by Henley, p. xvii. London, 1725, fol. See also p. 32. Misson complains of the same thing, A Nczu Voyage to Italy, ii., p. 388. London, 1699, 8vo.

Montfaucon, Op. laud., p. 285.

Reisen,. 950. Hannover, 1751, 4to.

Zedler, "Universal Lexicon," s. v. Raritaten-Cabinet, Raritdten-Kani-mer, xxx. 890.

Misson, A Neto Voyage to Italy, ii., p. 197. London, 1699, 8vo.

8 Ray, Travels through the Low Countries, i., p. 85. London, 1738, Svo,

Friedrich Christian Lesser of Nordhausen followed the same practice Briickmann, Epistola Itineraria, 51, Cent. i. He was also careful to record the provefiance of every object.

tinguishing features. Things were disposed according to size, like pipes in an organ; and the two sides of a room had to balance, so that the most incongruous objects were often placed alongside of each other; an armadillo beside an ostrich egg; a cocoa nut beside a stone swan; a bird of paradise beside a remora. Not that the matter of arrangement was not considered, for the space that a collection should occupy, the uses it should serve, and its proper disposition, the position and size of the rooms, and their decoration, were all questions discussed by the old writers upon museums; but their ideas were too vague and ill-defined to lead to useful results, and they contented themselves with merely reciting what one collector or another had done. Happel considers the arrangement of the Electoral Museum at Dresden to be so perfect as to be in itself a memoria artificialis, but his own account shows how imperfect and confusing it was. It had, however, one department which might well have been

Major, "Bedencken von Kunst-und Naturalien-Kammern," p. 17, in Valentini, Museum Museorum, vol. i.

'Major, Op. laud.,. 16; Moeller, Coinmentaiio de Tecmopkysiotameis, p. 204 sqq.; Neickelius, Museogmphia p. 418 sqq.; David Hultman, Instrucho Musei rerum Jiaturalium, a Thesis supported under the presidency of Linnaeus at Upsala, 14th November, 1753, Upsala, 1753, 4to; and reprinted in Linnaeus, Amoenitates Acadetnicae, iii., p. 446. (Erlangen, 1767); Briickmann, Epistola liineraria, 51, Cent. i.

Happel, Relationes Curiosae, iii., p. 118. The accounts of this famous museum by Martin Zeiller Handbuch von allerley nutzlichen Errinerungen,. 475, Ulm, 1655, i2mo), by Dr. Edward Brown Travels, p. 166, London, 1685, fol.), and in the official Catalogue of Tobias Beutel Cedern-Wald, Dresden, 1671, 4to, and again 1683, 4to, Latin and German) are much more intelligible. In 1755 an official guide to the Natural History department was published, Kmser E? itzuurf der imitated elsewhere. This was a Cabinet d'tgnorance, in which were kept such products of nature as could not be named or classified, such as lapides polyniorphi and other petrifactions.

The object in view was to create surprise rather than to afford instruction. For example, the anatomical collection at Dresden was arranged like a pleasure erarden. Skeletons were interwoven with branches of trees in the form of hedges so as to form vistas. Anatomical subjects were difficult to come by and, when they were got, the most was made of them. At Leyden they had the skeleton of an ass upon which sat a woman that killed her daughter; the skeleton of a man, sitting upon an ox, executed for stealing cattle; a young thief hanged, being the Bridegroom whose Bride stood under the gallows, very curiously set up in his ligaments by P. S. V. Wiel the Younger. Even in Paris at the present day the skeleton of an assassin is exhibited in the museum of natural history.

Kdniglichen Naturalien-Kammer 211 Dresden and also an authorized French translation. The arrangement in this guide is far from perfect, and some objects are placed in curious juxtaposition.

The best of the older accounts of the various Dresden collections is that by Johann Georg Keysler in 1730. Reisen, p. 1299 sqq. Hannover, 1751, 4to. Keysler, Op. laud., p. 1308.

- Beutel, Cedern- Wald, ut supra. Neither edition is paged. This anatomical collection was transferred to the University of Wittenberg in 1732, and a new one commenced at Dresden. Description du Cabinet Roial de Dresden, pp. 3, 34. Dresden, 1755, 4to.

See William Hunter, Two Introductory Lectures. with papers relating to his phot for establishing a Museum iti London, p. 41. London 1784, 4to.

A Catalogue of the cheifest Rarities in the publick Tfieater and Ana-tomie Hall of the University of Leyden. Leyden, 1591 but? i69i 4to. Supra, p. 29. The young thief was not in the edition of 1683.

The great museum of Frederik Ruysch was set off with all the nicety and ornamental taste belonging" to his countrymen. Plants disposed in nosegays, and shells arranged in figures were mixed with skeletons of animals and anatomical preparations, and suitable inscriptions from the Latin poets were placed at proper intervals. Levinus Vincent of the Haoue arranged his corals so as to represent shrubs and trees.

There is a print of 1610 of the Anatomical Hall and Library of the University of Leyden, but it is all library. The anatomical exhibits seem to be arranged round the walls, but they are not prominent in the picture. John Macky, writing in 1714 of the collection of the Royal Society, says, "The Repository of curiosities is a theatrical building resembling that of Leyden in Holland. The rarities are put up into boxes as abroad; and the beasts and birds hang-ino" round the room." The Leyden Catalogue professes that the objects "are so set in order that all may easily be found in their Places." But some of the places were not very accessible. These were the Entrance Hall, the Anatomy Chamber, " about the circle of the theatre," "about the beams and walls of the theatre," in four presses, six cases and three cupboards. These cases, however, seem to have

The skeleton of the young Syrian who assassinated General Kl ber. Guid des Etraiigers dans le Museum dhistoire?7aturelle, p. 62. Paris, 1873.

-See his Thesaurus Anirnalhun priinus, Kmstt. 1710,410.

Elenehus iabularum. in Gazophylacio Levini Vincenti. Harlem, 1719, 4to (Latin and French). A series of plates showing the arrangement of this museum. A library of natural history was attached to it.

A Journey through England, pp. 260, 261, 2nd edition. London, 1722, 8vo. As to this arrangement, see Major, Op. laud., p. 16.

been olazed and the rooms were well lio-hted A print of the Royal Library and Museum at Vienna shows the walls are lined with drawers and numerous objects hanging from the roof or on the walls above the drawers. The principal part of the museum was contained in a long gallery in which were a double row of cabinets, twenty in number, joined by the back and sides and carried up to the roof, but with so little space round them that the visitor could hardly pass; while " an infinite number of things were fastened to the ceiling and walls."

The entrance hall, it was held, ought to present a striking appearance and be set out with crocodiles and tortoises, bears white and grizzly, sword-fish, whales, sharks, Egyptian mummies, and so on. Like the old apothecary's shop:

Here Mummies lay most reverently stale, And there the Tortoise hung her Coat o' Mail; Not far from some huge Shark's devouring Head The Flying-Fish their finny Pinions spread. Aloft in rows large Poppy Heads were strung, And near a scaly Alligator hung. In this place, Drugs in musty heaps decayd, In that dry Bladders and drawn Teeth were laid. Keysler complains of the ineffective arrangement of the Kircherian Museum; and the list of curiosities which he gives shows that its method was very faulty."

yionconys,oitrtial des Voyages, Ft, ii., p. 151. Lyon, 1666.

- Valentini, Museum Museorum, ii., PI. 38.

Misson, A New Voyage to Italy, i., pp. II2, 114. London, 1699, 8vo.

Major, Unvorgreijffliches Bedencken von Kunst- und Naturalien-Kam-iiiern, p. 16 in Valentini, Museum Museorutn, vol. i.

Garth, The Dispensary, Canto ii., p. 17. London, 1726, 8 o. Cf. " The Doctor," in T. E. Brown's " Fo'c's'le Yarns," Collected Poems, London, 1900, 8vo. There is a curious picture of a druggist's shop in Renodaeus, Institutioncs Pharmaceuticce. Paris, 1605, 4to.

Keisen, p. 485. Hannover, 1751, 4to.

Antiquities and artificial rarities suffered most in the old museums. Of the great Medicean Museum at Florence Father Montfaucon says, in 1700, "In another room adjoyning" is amass'd a vast quantity of ancient vessels, the like number I never saw, but in no order because a proper place is providing to range them in. I cursorily took notice of two most ancient tripods, basons for sacrificing, and ladles, a measure calld sextans and vessels for liquids, clasps or buckles, curry-combs, a kettle-drum, and much more of that sort." In the Gaddi Museum at Florence he found "many ancient sacrificing vessels, statues, seals, and other thinors of that sort. There is also a series of medals or coins, but in no order so that we could not examine them."

It is obvious that to lump all archaeological objects in one division under the oreneral title "artificial curiosities" could convey no real idea of their nature, nor was the arrangement helped by subdividing them into articles of wood, of metal, of glass, and so on. Addison, when describing the Florentine Museum, says, "The next two chambers are made up of several artificial curiosities in ivory, amber, crystal, marble and precious stones, which all voyage writers are full of." Amongst them were the Venus de Medici and other pieces of sculpture.

A century later things were little better. " The British Museum," says one who visited it in 1786, " contains many collections in natural history; but, with the

The A niiqiiiiies of Italy, irsinslbXdhy Henley, p.255. London, 1725, fol.

"Op. land., p. 256.

"Remarks on Italy," Works, ii., p. 161. London, 1811, 8vo.

exception of some fishes in a small apartment, which are begun to be classed, nothing is in order, everything is out of its place; and this assemblage appears rather an immense magazine, in which things have been thrown at random, than a scientific collection, destined to instruct and honour a great nation." In addition, the museum was difficult of access."-

When the objects were classified it was of course in accordance with the science of the day, so that classification represented, as it must necessarily do, the contemporaneous state of scientific opinion.

Kentmann, following very much the system of classification proposed by Agricola, arranged his mineralogical collection in twenty-six divisions:

Saint Fond, Travels hi England, Scotland, a? id the Hebrides, i., p. 89. London, 1799, 8vo. He contrasts with the British Museum the better arrangement of the Edinburgh Museum. Supra, p. 157.

- Peale, Discourse on the Science of Nature, p. 20. Philadelphia, 1800, 8vo.

A French traveller (Louis Simond), who visited the Museum in 1810, says, "We had no time allowed to examine any thing; our con-

The first division "Earths" contains "earths" proper of fifty kinds, and eight other sub-divisions, clay, marl, stone marrow (medula), and so on, ending with vessels made from clay. The title "Stones" includes male loadstone magnes) and female theamedes), which repels instead of attracting iron, gypsum, asbestos, brontiae, cerauniae, and glossopetrae; stones which take their names from animals or parts of animals, stones produced from wood, stones that melt with heat.

Mercati arranged his collection under ten heads: (i.) Earths; (ii.) Salts and nitres; (iii.) Clays; (iv.) Sued acres, which included copperas, misy, metallic ink meianteria) (v.) Siicci pingues. Xhdx is, sulphur, bitumen, pit coal, and the like; (vi.) Marine objects, such as alcyonium the Halcyon stone, a stony concretion bred of the waves of the sea, from which the Halcyon was fabled to make its nest; true coral and sponge; (vii.) Earths like stones, sarcophagus, calamine, manganese, and others; (viii.) Stones engendered in ductor pushed on without minding questions, or unable to answer them, but treating the company with double ciitcndres and witticisms on various subjects of natural history, in a style of vulgarity and impudence which I should not have expected to have met in this place, and in this country." Jour? ial of a Tour imd Residence in Great Britain during the Years 1810 and 1811, i., p. 84. Edinburgh, 1815, 8vo.

i. e. green vitriol. See Lesser, Epistola depraecipids Naturae et Artis curiosis speciniinibus Musei vel potius Physiotechnotamei. Friderici Hofffuanfii, p. 7. Nordhausae, 1736, 4to. Hoffmann (1660-1742) was a physician and professor of medicine at Halle, and a F. R. S.

Pliny, Historia Naturalis, xxxii., 28.

Sarcophagus, or the stone of Assos, is described by Pliny, Historia Naturalis, xxxvi., 27. According to De Boodt Gonmarum et lapidum Historia, p. 405) there seem to be included under the term sarcophagus stones of a light and spongy character which contain alum, nitre and salt. See Aldrovandi, Musaeuni metallicum, p. 692.

animals, bezoar, stag's tears, toad-stone, pearls; (ix.) Lapides ISiojixopcpoi; (x.) Marbles.

Elias Brackenhoffer, of Strasburg, followed the fourfold division of Fossil, Vegetable, Animal, and Artificial objects, and all the specimens in his great collection found their place under one or other of these heads. Fossils included stones, mineralia media, and metals. The subdivisions of stones show the uncritical character of the mineralogy of the time. These were, Lapides majores molles; stones taken from animals; meteoric stones, including ceratmiae and bronteae; Lapidesfossiles minores; Silices minores; various stones; petrifactions, amongst which were petrified wood, the petrified molar of an elephant, the stone horn of a cow, an ox tongue petrified, petrified earth showing the mark of a horse's shoe; gems and precious stones, including lapis lazuli, and many others; and corals. The mineralia media included earths and sulphurs. Amongst Animals a crocodile was to be found, as also parts of animals, and zoophytes. Vegetables stood by themselves. The primary division of Artifical objects was into those of wood, of glass, or of ivory. Other artificial objects were pictures, gold and silver work, works of art in marble, wax, and other materials; antiquities and coins.

Ole Worm divided his museum into two sections: Natural Objects and Artificial Objects; the former

Mtisaeuni Brackenhofferianmn, Strasburg, 1683, 8vo.

There was also another catalogue of this Museum, by Johann Joachim Bockenhoffer, Musaeum Brackenhofferia? ium. Strasburg, 1677, 4to, pp. 52. Reprinted in Valentini, Miiseiiin Muscorum, ii., Appendix XX., pp. 69-81. Franckfurt-a-M. 1714, fol.

being subdivided into Fossils, Plants, and Animals. Artificial Rarities were classed according to the substance of which they were made. The subdivisions of fossils were similar to those of Kentmann, but Worm's descriptions are fuller and more exact. The section relating to the animal world included, what would now be treated as, anthropological specimens. The section " Artificial Rarities " deals with coins and with vessels, utensils, tools, weapons and other articles of clay, amber, stone, gold, silver, bronze, iron, glass, and wood. The tabular synopsis of the contents of Worm's museum, by Seger," gives at a glance a view of the whole arrangement and of the system of classification of the animal, vegetable, and mineral kingdom then in use.

A view of the interior of the Museum is prefixed to the Museum Wonnianmn which gives a very good idea of the appearance and arrangement of a seventeenth century museum, n the floor and on two shelves above it were boxes and trays containing the smaller objects, beginning with earths and salts, and proceeding in order through the mineral, vegetable and animal kingdoms, till they ended with parts of animals. Interspersed amongst the trays or hung from the shelves were various freaks and oddities. On a shelf over these there was a miscellaneous assemblage of statuary, antiquities, birds, fish, bones, coral and petrifactions. The upper parts of the walls were covered with tortoises, crocodiles, and lizards, skeletons, spears,

Afuseuin IVoriinafiuin, p. 344. Lugd. Bat., 1655, fol. Synopsis niethodica rarioriini. in Mtisaeo. Ohn Wormii. Hafniae, 1653 and 1658, 4to.

lances, and arrows, paddles and costumes from Greenland. Between the windows hung horns, antlers and heads of deer and other animals: underneath on the floor lay vertebrae of a whale. From the roof were suspended a great polar bear, a shark and other fish, various birds, and an Esquimaux Kayak.

The Copenhagen Museum as arranged by Holger Jacobaeus was divided into two parts. The first part had seven sections: (i.) Man commencing with an Egyptian mummy and what was called a Danish mummy- and other animals, quadrupeds; (ii.) birds; (iii.) fish; (iv.) shells; (v.) reptiles and insects; (vi.) plants; (vii.) metals, minerals, stones, and earths. In the second part there were five sections: (i.) Artificial objects of metal, wood, bone, horn, and amber amongst which was the ivory ship navis bellica ex ebore) which had attracted the attention of the Earl of Carlisle's secretary-; (ii.) weapons, clothes, implements and utensils from India, China, and elsewhere; (iii.) antiquities; (iv.) scientific and mechanical apparatus amongst which is included a magic Lantern; and (v.) coins, medals, and seals. Nehemiah Grew, in his Catalogue of the Royal Society's Museum, followed the same general classification as Worm, but arranged the classes in a different order, Animals, Plants, Minerals, and Artificial Curiosities. He places " Humane Rarities " at the head of the division "Animals," beginning with an Egyptian mummy; and then proceeds to others "according to

This was a favourite arrangement. It was adopted by Legati in his account of the Cospi Museum. Museo Cospia? io, p. i. Bologna, 1677, fol. i. e. a desiccated body. Bartholin wrote considerably on this subject.

the degrees of their approximation to human shape and with one another "; a classification which is approved of in Zedler's Lexicon He finds fauh with Aldrovandi who commenced with the horse because of its use to man. His whole volume is full of curious information. Rings made of the teeth of the hippopotamus are believed to be very effectual against the cramp. In Scandinavia the otter is tamed and "will bring the fishes into the very kitchen to the cook." " The squirrel, when he hath a mind to cross any water for a good nut-tree, picks out and sits on some light piece of barque for a boat, and erecting his tail for sail he makes his voyage."

Sir Robert Sibbald adopted the old fourfold arrangement of Fossil, Vegetable, and Animal substances, and Artificial rarities, "Fossils" are divided into Minerals media mineralia), Stones, and Metals. " Minerals " include earths, salts, sulphur, and bituminous substances, amongst which he reckons petroleum,- asphalt pissaphalhiin), jet, cannel coal or bastard jet, as well as mummy, amber and ambergris. " Stones"

Zedler, "Universal Lexicon," s. v. Naturalien-Cabiiiet.

Sibbald's specimen of petroleum was " the oyl found floating in Saint Catherine's Well, near the Church of Liberton" supra, p. 197, n. 2). His asphalt was found in a stone quarry belonging to the laird of Roughsols, now Rochsoles, and was presented to him by Alexander Monteith, Deacon of the Surgeons of Edinburgh. Auctarium Musaei Balfoiiriani, pp. 31, 32.

Amber was for a long time classed with the bitumens. Zacharia-Pillingen, Bitujnen et lignum fossile Mtumittosum, pp. 32, 40. Altenb., 1674, 8vo; Parkinson, Organic remains of a former World, i., p. 224.

Bog butter was known as " mineral tallow," was also treated as a bitumen, although it was questioned whether it might not be of animal origin. Parkinson, Op. laud., i., p. 214 sqq.; Jameson, Mineralogy of the Scottish Isles, ii., p. 129. Edinburgh, 1800, 4to.

include slate, flint, marble, alabaster, loadstone, crystals and gems, pearls, corals, and petrifactions. Amongst human rarities he includes, "a piece of human skull, that was never buried, with a moss growing upon it, commended for peculiar virtues in medicine." Artificial curiosities embrace various philosophical instruments; and such things as "cochleare Hirtense a spoon of an odd shape made in Hirta of the horn of one of their sheep"; nine portraits; Slezer s views; and drawings of many antiquities; maps; inscribed stones from the Roman wall, coins, books, and manuscripts.

The arrangement of the Cabinet de la Bibliotheque de Sainte Genevieve, adopted by Father Claude du Molinet (1620-1687)," was much more orderly, and has been commended as a model. The collection was divided into two main sections, Antiquities and Natural History. In the first came Antiquities (a) relating to the Christian religion, (d) to the religion of the Egyptians and Romans, and (c) to the rites of burial, (d) Roman weights and measures. Then followed coins and medals, arranged according to countries and periods, and engraved gems and talismans in stone and metal, and lamps. The Natural History section was divided into birds, animals, fish, fruits and plants, shells, stones and minerals.

Siip7a, p. 56.

-Paris, 1692, fol. See also Lister, A Journey to Paris in i68g p. loo. London, 1823, 8vo; p. 115, Paris, 1887, 8vo.

Northleigh mentions that Father Molinet had " a curious collection of Rarities of his own."

"Encyclopedic incthodiqtiej A? itiquities T. i., p. 549, s. v. Cabinet. Paris, 1786, 4to.

Jakob von Melle 1659-1743), pastor at Lubeck, otnni nostra laiide viajor, arranged his extensive museum on a scheme similar to that of Sibbald. There were two main divisions, Natural and Artificial. The former comprehended Fossils, Vegetables, and Animals, at the end of which he places homo sapiens. Artificial curiosities he subdivided into ei ht classes: (i.) Things pertaining to religion and superstition; (ii.) coins; (iii.) engraved gems; (iv.) sepulchral urns and the like; (v.) arms and utensils; (vi.) costume and personal ornaments; (vii.) books, charters, and manuscripts; (viii.) miscellaneous,-

Professor Baier of Altdorf (1677-1735) arranged his natural collection, or Physiotameion, in seven overlapping divisions (i.) minerals and metals; (ii.) earths and stones; (iii.) figured stones, which he regards as liis2is natnrae but which evidently took shape largely according to the observer's imagination; (iv.) petrifications, animal and vegetable; (v.) petrified shells; y.) exangtiia, shell fish, sea urchins, etc.; (vii.) litho-phytes, corals and the like. He had also a collection of Artificial objects, including antiquities, gems and coins and works in marble, wood and amber.

Friedrich Christian Lesser (1692-1754), a Lutheran

Briickmann, Epistola itineraria, 31, Cent. i.

"Festschrift zur xxviii. Versamvilung dcr deiitschen anthropologischen Gesellschaft. Lubeck, August, 1897, p. 16. A contemporary collection at Lubeck was that of Hermann Eeckhoff, which was sold by auction in 1732. Musetan Eeckhoffianum, Lub., 1732, 8vo.

Sciagraphia museisiii. Norimb., 1730, 4to, three plates supra, p. 117).

Amongst the friends to whom he was indebted for specimens were (pp. 20, 21) John Woodward, F. R. S., Johann Georg Kesner of Frankfurt supra, p. 146), Johann Craft Hiegel supra, p. 23), and Jacob von Melle.

clergyman of Nordhausen and a well-known naturalist and museographer, took the Mosaic account of the creation as the basis for arranging the contents of his museum He accordingly placed the mineral kingdom first, then the vegetable, and next the animal; and, in each division, the more perfect object followed the less perfect. In the first division he began with casts, followed by salts, sulphur, stones and metals. Amongst vegetables, funguses were placed first, then came mosses, plants aquatic and terrestrial and parts of plants, the roots, wood, bark, sap, leaves, fruit and seeds. In the animal kingdom he put insects first, then soft-shelled and hard-shelled animals, creeping things, fish, birds, animals void of reason, and lastly reasoning man. Artificial objects were arranged in the same order, that is, according as the substance from which they were formed belonoed to the mineral, the vegfetable, or the animal kingdom. Paper and books thus fell into the division of artificial objects made from vegetable substances. Lesser held views similar to those of It was visited and described by Briickmann, Epistolae Itinerariae, 50, 51, Cent. i.; 33 Cent. ii.

He gave a detailed account of the museum (Naturalien-und-Kunst-cabinet), the size and disposition of the cabinets and cases, the labelling and arranging of the objects, and his system of classification in the Hainburgischcs Magaziii iii. (1748), p. 549 sqq. This is followed, p. 559 sqq., by an account of the Naturalien-Cabinet of Professor Carl Clusius of Leyden. See also Briickmann, Op. laud.

Lesser had previously described the collection of Friedrich Hoffmann (1660-1742), professor of medicine at Halle and F. R. S. Epistola de praecipius naturae et arils curlosls speclnilnlbus Miisei vel poll us Physlo-technotainel. Friderlcl Hoffmann. Nordhusae, 1736, 4to. Supra PP- 35. 213.

Derham in reference to the works of creation, as evidence of the beino- and attributes of God, and advocated them in a series of works.– Thoresby, like Grew, set out with human rarities, and includes "a pugill of the dust (unmixd with earth) of a noble Countess, not easily distinguishd from common dust and ashes," and the hand and arm of the great Montrose. The division "Artificial Curiosities" is subdivided into a great number of heads which, although not altogether logical, made it comparatively easy to trace a particular object.

Johann David Koehler (1684-1755), historian and numismatist, and the editor of Moeller's book on museums, prepared a Travellers' Guide to libraries, coin-cabinets innnophylacia), picture-galleries i pinac-othecae), museums of antiquities inusea antiquarid), of natural history gazopkylacia naturae), and of artificial curiosities, or industrial art rerzwi ai tijicium thesauri which was published after his death in 1762, and again in 1788 and i8io. His views

Lithotheologia, Nord., 1732, 8vo; Hamb., 1735 " I75i- I" French, La Haye, 1742, 8vo: Insecto-Theologia, Franckf., 1738, 8vo, and later editions. Originally published in 1735 under a different title. In French, La Haye, 1742, 8vo; Italian, Venezia, 1751, 8vo; English, Edinburgh, 1799, 8vo; Testaceo-Theologia, Leipzig, 1744, 8vo, which passed through several editions, and was also translated into French.

"A Catalogue and Description of the Rarities in this Museum," p. 36 sqq., in Ducat us Leodicnsis, vol. ii., 1816, fol.

"Aiiiieisung fiir Reisende gelctric, Bidlioiieken, Miinzkabinette,. Naturalien- tind Ku7istknmi)icr7i init Nutzen zu besehen. Leipzig, 1762, 8vo. Magdeb., 1788 and 1810, 8vo.

There was an earlier work of the same kind by Johann Reiske, Dissertatio qua pinacoihecas, ciineliothecas, et societates doctoruin ifi Europapraecipuas breviter explicare. voluit. Guelferb., 1685, 4to.

as to the scope and object of a museum were definite and decided.

A museum of antiquities, he holds, consists of three parts; statues, inscriptions, and vessels or utensils in-st7u)nenta sacred, military and domestic of metal or clay. Cabinets of natural history are to be regarded as the treasure-house of God; and embrace objects from the animal, the vegetable, and the mineral kingdoms. He places man at the head of the animals, and begins the list with mummies Egyptian and others, including desiccated bodies foetuses, monsters, skeletons, giants' bones, which he points out are really bones of beasts, and calculi. Then follow in order quadrupeds, reptiles, birds, insects, fish, and shells. Herbariums are included amongst exhibits of the vegetable kingdom, but he explains that botanical specimens generally form special collections. The mineral kinofdom is divided into metals, semi-metals, inflammable matter, salts and stones. The metals he takes in detail. Inflammable matter includes sulphur, bitumen, pit-coal the best of which, he says, is found in Scotland. Salts include vitriol and alum. The earths he enumerates in order. Stones he classifies as common and precious. Alternatively they may be arranged according to some special quality, e. g. porosity or sweet scent. Amongst the more remarkable common stones are marble, porphyry, and alabaster. He then takes up precious stones, beginninor with the as ate and endingr with the diamond, the king of gems. Then follow the figured stones gebildete Steine, lapides Jigurati, lapides

Ed. 1762, p. 234.- Cf. supra, p. 159.

petrifacti). He mentions that two opinions had been advanced as to their origin; the one that they were due to diluvial forces, the other that they were produced by the plastic power of nature. Of fiofured stones belonoino- to the animal kingfdom he deals first with man. As yet, that is in 1755, he says, no part of a human body has been found petrified, although in mines bodies have been met with encrusted in stone. He next takes up figured stones of quadrupeds, birds, and fish, glossopetrae and shells; then those of the vegetable kingdom, wood, fruit, and leaves.

A museum of Industrial Art iykimst-Kannnci) he defines' - as a collection of objects which man has produced by untiring industry and the imitation of nature, and consists of objects which indicate great intelligence and industry. Art and nature must be distinguished.

Linnaeus has remarked that those who visit museums of natural productions, generally pass them over with a careless eye, and immediately take the liberty of expressing a dogmatic opinion upon their merits. "The indefatigable collectors of such objects," he adds, " sometimes have the fate of beingf reckoned monsters; many people wonder at their great but useless labours, and those who judge most tenderly, exclaim that such things serve to amuse persons of great leisure, but are of no real service to the

Ed. 1762, p. 251. As to such bodies see Mercati, Metallotheca pp. 6, 227, note by Lancisi, 2 Ed. 1762, p. 256, In the ed. of i8ro, p. 832 technotheca or techno-thylacium is given as an equivalent.

community." To correct such views he proceeds to examine the design and end of such collections. The globe, he says, may be regarded as a museum furnished with the works of the Supreme Creator, disposed in three grand classes, fossils, vegetables, and animals. The world is destined to the celebration of the Creator's glory, and man has been placed in it as the herald and interpreter of the wisdom of God. Hence a collection of natural productions is, as it were, an offering from all the inhabitants of the earth, in which the spectator may behold the works of creation and the Divine order of the universe. "He who views only the produce of his own country may be said to inhabit a single world; while those who see and consider the productions of other climes bring many worlds in review before them. We are but on the borderland of knowledge; much remains hidden, reserved for far-off generations, who will prosecute the examination of their Creator's works in remote countries, and make many discoveries for the pleasure and convenience of life. Posterity will see its increasing museums and the knowledge of divine wisdom flourish together; and at the same time antiquities and history, the natural sciences, the practical sciences of the manual arts will be enriched."

King Adolf Friedrich of Sweden (b. 1710, d. 1771) formed a museum in the palace of Ulricsdahl, and

Museum Adolphi Friderici Regis, Swedish and Latin, 33 plates, Hobiiiae, 1754, fol. Preface.

The Preface was translated by James Edward Smith under the title. Reflections on the Study of Nature, London, 1785, 8vo, reprinted in his Tracts, London, 1798, 8vo. It was his first publication.

Queen Louisa Ulrique (b. 1720, d. 1782, sister of Friedrich the Great) had another at Drottningholm, which were arranged by Linnaeus according to his own system. The king's collection consisted mainly of quadrupeds, birds, insects, and shells, with a valuable herbarium; the queen's of insects, shells, corals, and crystals.

In a thesis propounded by David Hultman. a pupil of Linnaeus, at Upsala in 1753, similar views are expressed;"" and reference is made to the museums of the king and queen, of Count Tessin (1695-1771), and of the University of Upsala as examples of well-ordered collections. The museum building, he states, should be of brick, longer than it is broad, with windows facing the north. He gives practical directions as to the best methods of preparing, preserving, protecting, and setting out the specimens, many of which are still of value and are interesting as no doubt embodying the methods of Linnaeus.

Musemn Ludovicae Ulricae Reginae, Holmiae, 1764, 8vo. To this is added a Supplement to the king's collection in which various animals acquired since the date of the earlier catalogue are described.

"Instructio Musei rerum naturaiuiu, in Linnaei, Ainoenitates Academicae, vol. iii., p. 446, Erlangae, 1787, Svo.

Museum Tessimanu7n, Holmiae, 1753, fol. Edited by Linnaeus. Latin and Swedish, with 12 plates.

As to the Upsala Museum see Thunberg, Museum naturaliutn Academiae Upsaliensis, Upsaliae, 1787-98, 4to, 2 vols.; Peale, Discourse on the Science of Nature p. 23. Philadelphia, 1800, 8vo.

The library, herbarium, and museum of Linnaeus were purchased in 1784 for a thousand guineas by James, afterwards Sir James, Edward Smith, and after his death were presented to the Linnaean Society of London, Gentleman s Magazine, liv. (1784), pp. 393, 488, 869; Lady Smith, Memoir and Correspondence of the late Sir fames Edward Smith., London, 1832, Svo.

Lonor and minute directions are s iven in the Encyclopaedia Pertheiisis for the formation of a museum of Natural History, the construction and furnishinor of the buildino- and the arrangement of the contents. The windows ought to be placed in the two longest sides of the building, that it may be equally lighted during the whole day. On one wing must be placed eleven presses with shelves, supported on wooden brackets. These presses were intended to contain the eleven classes of the mineral kingdom, viz., i. Waters. 2. Earths. 3. Sands. 4. Stones. 5. Salts. 6. Pyrites. 7. Semi-metals. 8. Metals. 9. Bitumens and sulphurs. 10. Volcanic productions. II. Petrifactions, fossils, and lusus naturae. On the second wing of the cabinet ten presses were to be placed for specimens from the vegetable kingdom, i. Roots. 2. Barks. 3. Woods and stalks. 4. Leaves. 5. Flowers. 6. Fossils and seeds. 7. Parasite plants, agarics and mushrooms. 8. The juices of vegetables; as balsams and solid resins, resinous gums and gums properly so called. 9. Extracted juices, sugars, and dregs. 10. Marine plants, and plants growing on the shores of the sea. The third wino- was also to have three presses for objects from the animal kingdom. I. Lithophytes. 2. Zoophytes. 3. Testaceous animals. 4. Crustaceous animals. 5. Insects. 6. Fishes. 7. Amphibious animals, reptiles, and oviparous quadrupeds. 8. Birds w4th their nests and eggs. 9. Viviparous quadrupeds. 10. Man. Like the older museums the last-mentioned section was to include embryos and monsters, an Egyptian mummy, and stony concretions.

Vol. XV., pp. 593-597. Edinburgh, 1816, 8vo, second edition.

The so-called decoration of a cabinet was still deemed a matter of importance. " For this purpose the tops of the presses are commonly ornamented with shells of a very great size, foreign wasps' hives, the horn of a rhinoceros, an elephant's trunk, the horn of an unicorn, urns and busts of alabaster, jasper, marble, porphyry, or serpentine stone. Here likewise are placed figures of antique bronze, large lithophytes, animals made of shells, bouquets made of the wings of Scarabaeus, gourds cut into two, painted and made into bowls, plates, vases, etc., as they are used by savages; little trunks of bark, books made of the leaves of the palm tree, globes, spheres, etc. The floor of the cabinet may likewise be paved with different kinds of common stones, which are susceptible of a polish." The ceiling was to be painted white, divided into three spaces and furnished with hooks and brass wires on which were to be hung all sorts of things, sugar canes, palm leaves, knotted sticks, stuffed animals, lizards, crocodiles, caimans, sharks and sword fish, large serpents, deer and other horns; Indian and Chinese dresses, arms, weapons, and utensils; " in short, various curiosities from nations ancient and modern, if they can be found; and various furniture and utensils of different nations ancient and modern." The piers of the windows were to be furnished with presses to hold mathematical and philosophical instruments. " On the semi-circular shelves below are placed stones formerly used by savages for hatchets, some curious pieces of lacker-work, Indian pagodas, trinkets belonging to the savages of the north and to the Chinese, which are made of ivory or yellow amber, or of coral mounted with gold, silver, porcelain-clay, kriacks of Siam, and Turkish cangiars, which are a kind of pogniards, Indian curiosities of silver, and the galians which the Turks and Persians use in smoking tobacco and aloes. The drawers under the press contain a collection of medals, china-ink, lachrymatory phials, and the most beautiful engraved stones of Europe, or an impression of them in wax or sulphur, counters, cameos, antiques, talismans, ancient weights and measures, idols, urns, lamps, instruments of sacrifice and false jewels."

This idea of a museum was, thus, in 1816 practically what it had been two centuries earlier, a collection

Of unicorns and alligators,
Elks, mermaids, mummies, witches, satyrs,
And twenty other stranger matters.

The subdivisions of the three kingdoms of nature are different, but otherwise the museum was set out as in the days of Aldrovandi or Worm. The only modern idea is that the museum should contain a library, that the rarer objects should be figured and the drawings placed on the wall, and that there should be a section of comparative osteology, including those animals which most nearly approach to man.2 In 1823 Mr. John Shute Duncan was appointed Curator of the Ashmolean Museum. Finding that it was in a very neglected state he applied for and

Prior, Epistle to Fleetwood Shepherd Esq.

2 The directions in the Encyclopaedia Perthensis are, however, translated without acknowledgment from Valmont de Bomare's Dictionnaire dhistoire naiurelle, iv., p. 384, Paris, 1775, 8vo; iv., p. 128, Lyon, 1791, 4to.

obtained authority to have the specimens cared for, rearransi ed. and added to. It consisted, he savs, of: I. Ancient Rehcs. 2. Arms of different nations.

3. Dresses and implements of half-civilized nations.

4. Rarities (a) Royal gifts.) Memorials of remarkable persons, (r) Amulets, ( ) Curious works of Art. 5. Pictures. 6. Books, MS. and printed. 7. Specimens illustrative of zoological arrangement " collected with a hope of continually exciting a remembrance of the pious works of Derham and of Paley." A taste for the study of natural history had been excited at Oxford at this time, by Paley's A atnral Theology and other popular works, in which Duncan participated.- He rearranged the specimens in three divisions according to Paley's plan, and so gave "an exalted interest to the collection, such as no exhibition of the kind had hitherto displayed."

"The first division proposes to familiarize the eye to those relations of all natural objects, which form the basis of argument in Dr. Paley's Natural Theology; to induce a mental habit of associatinof the view of natural phenomena with the conviction that they are the media of Divine manifestation; and by such association to give proper dignity to every branch f natural science."

Introduction to the Catalogue of the Ashmolean Museum Oxford, 1826, 8vo; apparently not published and not followed by a catalogue. There is a copy in the British Museum, 7206, h 5. (i).

-He published Botano-Theology, 1825, 8vo; and Analogies of Organized Beings. Oxford, 1831, 8vo.

Philip Bury Duncan, A Catalogue of the Ashmolean Museum, Oxford, 1836, p. vi. Mr. P. B. Duncan succeeded his brother as Keeper of the Museum in 1829, and held office until 1854.

"The second division exhibits relics of antiquity, arranged according to the order of time, with some specimens of curious art of uncivihzed as well as of refined nations."

"In the exhibition of animals the order of Cuvier has been generally adopted. The name of every specimen is conspicuously affixed, and hand-catalogues explain the general principle of the arrangement, and the contents of each cabinet to which they refer."

The view of the interior of the Museum on the title-page of Mr. P. B. Duncan's Catalogue shows an arrangement similar to that of a seventeenth century collection.

In recent years the books, coins, and medals were transferred to the Bodleian Library, and the natural history department separated from the antiquarian, and transferred to the New Museum. The collections have been largely increased by the liberality of Mr. Parker and Dr. Hortnum, and by the acquisition of a long series of Egyptian, Roman, British, Anglo-Saxon, and English objects; and the Ashmolean is now strictly an Archaeological and Ethnological Museum of great value and excellently arranged.

P. B. Duncan, Op. laud., p. vii.

Arthur John Evans, The Ashmolean Museum as a Home of Archaeology in Oxford. Oxford, 1884, 8vo.

Sir William Flower thinks, and probably with justice, that John Hunter is to be regarded as the founder of the modern museum, the distinguishing features of which are speciahzation and classification. A museum has been described by Huxley as "a consultative library of objects"; and just as special libraries are required, so special museums have become a necessary aid in scientific research. Instead of one museum embracing every subject, or at least many subjects, we have museums which are limited to one or to a few special subjects, as, for instance, museums of Natural History, museums of Geology and Mineralogy, Industrial, Commercial, Agricultural, Chemical, Educational and Military museums, museums of Archaeology,

An excellent exposition of a systematic classification of natural history objects will be found in Fritsch, Principien der Organisation der natur-historischen Abtheilung des neuen Museums zu Prag. Prag, 1888, 8vo; Koch, Die Aufstellung der Tiere im neuen Museum zu Darmstadt, Leipzig, 1899, 8vo. As to the classification of archaeological museums see Schwartz, Grundsdtze fiir die Ordnung von Sammlungen vorge-schichtlicher Altertiimer, 1898, 8vo.

museums of Art and of Antiquities Christian and secular and sundry others.

Archaeology furnishes a good example of what is gained by careful and accurate classification, and the bringing together of objects for comparison. Archaeology has been called 'the science of sepulchres." This is true, in a sense, for it is from the resting-places of the dead that we have recovered the greater portion of the material remains of prehistoric peoples which we now possess; and the recognition of the fact that interments afforded valuable aid in the elucidation of the past was one of the great steps in archaeological science. But while this is so, it is the museum which has made them intelligible. Whoever it may be that first spoke of the "three-age system," it was Christian Thomsen who first turned it to practical account, and it was the arrangement of the great museum of Copenhagen, according to this system, that created the science of Archaeology. Prior to his time the museum was but a valley of dry bones; in his hands and by his genius these were made to live and to tell the story of the past. The co-relation of the various 1 Johann Daniel Major and Christian Stieff were amongst the earliest to recognize the value of interments for archaeological purposes. See Stieff, De Urnis in Silesia. Epistola Wratislav., 1704, 4to; Major, Bevol-ckertes Cimbrien, Plon, 1692, fol. The latter observes (p. 44) that in many sepulchral urns one or more stone axes have been found, and therefore he concluded they must have been the work of man.

James Douglas (1753-1819) clearly distinguished three periods about 1790, Nctiia Britannica pp. 150, I54n. London, 1793, fol., but published 1786-93. It was present to the mind of William Cunnington of Heyles-bury in 1802, Archaeologia, xv., p. 126; and was adopted by Sir Richard Hoare in 1812, Ancient Wiltshire, i., p. 76.

monuments of antiquity to one another and to the present time was sketched out by him in broad outline, and soon a host of observers all over the world arose to fill in the details. Immense progress has been made since the publication, in 1836, of Thomsen's classification; and the history of the past, the growth of culture and the progress of civilization are now being investigated and recorded in every country on sound scientific lines. " Archaeology," says M. de Quatrefages, "which formerly was regarded as a matter of curiosity, having interest only for a few privileged persons, has become a science well nigh positive in its character."

Every museum of archaeology is now arranged more or less in accordance with Thomsen's principles, with such modifications as circumstances require. German museums generally follow this classification; the Stone Age is divided into Older and Younger, that is Palaeolithic and Neolithic; the Bronze age is similarly divided, the latest portion of that age being known as the Hallstatt period; the transitional period leading to the Iron Age is known as the La Tene or pre-Roman period, then comes the period of Roman domination, followed by the period of the great migrations (Volks-wanderungszeit), the Franko-Merovingian period and the Wendish period. The Musee de Saint Germain is arranged according to epochs suitable to France: In most German museums sheets are hung up, on which are figured in colour the characteristic objects of each period. Those prepared by the West Prussian museum and pubushed at Dantsic, six in number, are perhaps the most useful. Others are published at Hanover by the Provincial Museum; at Halle for Saxony; at Stuttgart for the Rhine and the German Danube districts; and at Vienna for Austria-

Gaul prior to the use of metals; Gaul after the introduction of metals; the Gaulish, the Roman, and the Gallo-Roman epochs. This system is practically that of M. Gabriel de Mortillet by whom the museum was organized and who classified the great collection in the Paris Exhibition of 1867. His classification is, however, merely a modification of that of Thomsen. Starting with the three x ges of Stone, of Bronze, and of Iron, he divides them into six periods, Eolithic, Palaeolithic, Neolithic, Tsiganian, Galatian, Roman and INIerovingian, and these periods again he divides into Epochs named from the places where the objects characteristic of each have been found

The names given to ages, periods, or epochs, are immaterial. What is of value and what is aimed at in every properly organized museum of archaeology is to discriminate and illustrate the stages of human culture, in other words to trace the growth and development of civilization.

A most useful feature of modern museums is the separation of objects into national and foreign, the latter being reserved as objects with which to compare, and by which to illustrate the former. Nothing has done more than this to place archaeological science upon a sound basis; and yet fifty years ago so little had this principle been thought of, that there was not a single room in the British Museum specially appropriated to British Antiquities,

Hungary. See Von Hauer, Allgemeiner Fiihrer durch das K. K. natur-historische Homuseum, p. 137. Wien, 1898, 8vo.

G. de Mortillet, For? nation de la nation Francaiseyp-p. 192, 193. Paris, 1897, 8vo. Musee Prehistorique, Introduction. Paris, 1881, fol.

and even gifts of national antiquities were reluctantly received and sparingly acknowledged. The few that were preserved were mostly unclassed and practically unavailable for reference and comparison.

As we approach recent times archaeology shades into antiquities, and the archaeological collection grows into the historical. In every considerable museum therefore, the archaeolograical section is followed by an historical and is supplemented by an ethnographical, and in some cases by an anthropological, section.

One of the greatest museums of the day is the Germanic National Museum at Nurembercr, estab-lished in 1852 for the illustration of German historical research.- It contains an enormous amount of material, much of it of the kind that was to be found in the museums of the seventeenth and eighteenth centuries;-stone implements and clay urns, Roman and other antiquities, carvings, glass and porcelain, ecclesiastical vessels and vestments, scien-

Roach Smith, Collectanea Antigua, i., p. 171; iii., p. 183. London, 1848.

- Hektor, Geschichte des Germanisches National museums von seinem Ursprunge bis sum Jahre 1862, Nuremberg, 1863; Das Gerjnanische Nationalmuseum und seine Sainmlungen. Wegweiser fiir die Besu-chenden. Niirnberg, 1861, 8vo, and other editions; Essenwein, Das Germanische Nationalmuseum, Nuremberg, 1884; Leitschuh, Das Ger-manische Nationalmuseum in Niirnberg, Bamberg, 1870; Die Kunst-und Kultur-geschichtlichen Sammlungen des Germanischen Museums, Niirnberg, 1899; Stegmann, Das Germanische National-Museum zu Niirnberg in seinen Rdumen und Gebaulichkeiten, fol., Niirnberg, 1896; Anzeiger des Germanischen National-Museums, Leipzig, 1884-94, 8vo. This was a continuation of Anzeiger fiir Kunde der deutschen Vorzeit, 1832-39, and N. S. 1853-83, 8vo.

tific apparatus, and all that used to pass under the name of artificial curiosities. These have, however, been arranged so as to tell the history of the German land and the German people, chapter by chapter, and subject by subject, from the earliest period down to the present; prehistoric, Roman and German. Objects illustrative of civil life and ecclesiastical life, war, agriculture, handicrafts and trade, art and science, are set out in order, so that the student has everything grouped before him and the mere passer-by can read and understand their import. The I lesson of the museum is the importance of order and method. These are what orive scientific value to the collection. It was the want of these that made the old museums comparatively worthless.

The recognition of the fact that the products of the lower forms of civilization of the present time materially assist in understanding the life, the thought and culture of prehistoric peoples, and of many of the manners and customs of our own day, was a great help to the progress of archaeology. The importance of this comparison seems to us to be obvious, but it was not grasped, or at least, was not acted upon until comparatively recent times. Aldrovandi, as we have seen, did not recos nize that the ancient stone weapons dug out of the soil of Italy were identical with the stone knives and stone axes in use in India in his own day, examples of which he had in his own museum. So little was comparison thought

Chiocci, in his description of the Musaeian Calceolari, mentions (p. 308) when treating oi cerminiae, that in the New World stones were found of so sharp an edge as to equal iron, and were fashioned into axes, shovels, and other tools and weapons which in Italy were made of iron.

of that Anselm de Boodt, after describing ccrauniae, adds that because all these stones resemble a hammer, a wedge, an axe, a plough-share or some such other implement pierced for a handle, some persons thought that they are not thunderbolts, but tools of iron which have been petrified. In the Imperial library of Vienna amongst other curiosities was shown an Arabian sacrificial knife or axe shaped like a ceraunia and hafted in wood. The ceraunm itself was apparently not recognized as an artificial object. Ole W orm describes a flint exactly like the point of a hunting spear, which was found in a low hill in Ripen along with an urn containing ashes and bones. He had in his collection an arrow point of Lydian stone sent to him from Iceland in 1643, which had been found in the blubber of a whale, but this did not enable him to decide as to the character of the Ripen object. But for the assumed impossibility of working flint he would probably have come to the conclusion that it was artificial. As it was he remained in doubt, and refers to Paracelsus who styled such things Gamahu. Of these there were two varieties the one found in sand and streams, fashioned exactly as if made by man, but in fact created by God, and endowed with miraculous powers. The artificial Gamahu were stones on which

Gemmariim et Lapidii n Historia, ii., c. 260.

2 Briickmann, Epistola Ithieraria, i Cent, i., p. 6. Wolfenb., 1728.

Museum IVormianutn, p. 85.

0p. laud., p. 350.

"Gamachies," says Sibbald, " are found near to Marlsfield, the Laird of Grubbet's house. The young laird, a worthy gentleman, gave me this account of them. There is a steep precipice of clay on the side of the Cttle river that passeth by Marlsfield House; towards the middle of this pre- by a peculiar constellation images of man and animals have been impressed Nehemiah Grew following Worm includes these objects amongst regularly shaped stones under the name anchorites, from their resemblance to an anchor, or "flat bolt-head," or " to the head of a bearded dart from whence I have named it." As proof of their origin, he quotes a story told of Terzago " That the corps of one struck dead with thunder, being inspected in the presence of Septalius and several others, and a black wound observed about the hip, and searched to the bone, they found therein a round and edged stone, which being broken had a very strong sulphurious stink. With this author," he adds, "I scarce think anything of this nature incredible to those that read the relation given at large by Wormius of the Norwegick mouse." Sir Robert Sibbald adopted Grew's opinions. Worm, Grew, and Sibbald were all physicians of large experience and cipice there boileth out a red shining clay, as tough as melted wax, with a blue sliminess on the top; when any of this clay falleth in the stream, 'tis rolled down by the current, and is moulded into an hundred dififerent shapes, of birds and beasts and other things; and groweth to the consistence of a stone in a few days, although at first very soft and malleable." Auciariudi Musaei Balfouria? ii, p. 57.

Supra, p. 3, Paracelsus, "De Imaginibus," c. 7. Opera, ii., pp. 499, 502, Genevae, 1658, fol. Jacques Gaffarel collects all the learning on Gamahes in his Curiositez inouyes sur la sculphire talistnaniques des Persons, chap. v. (Paris, 1629, 8vo). In English, by Edmund Chilmead, Grecian and musician, p. 96 sqq. (London, 1650); in Latin, ed. J. A. Fabricus, p. 74 sqq. (Hamburg, 1706); Valentini, Museum Museorutn, i., p. 52.

2 Op. laud., pp. 303, 304.

"Auctarium Musaei Balfouriani, pp. 58, 67; Miscellanea eruditae Antiquitatis, p. 36. d men of undoubted ability, and although it may seem surprising that, with all the facts before them, they went so far astray, it is not difficult to understand their position. To arrive at a different opinion would have required almost a complete break with the whole science of the day. Errors of a similar kind have been committed in our day. The bone objects found in prehistoric cave deposits, which were long known as batons de commandemeiit, have, by comparing them with similar objects used by the Eskimo, been shown to be arrow-stretchers; and it is probable that many of the opinions which we now think beyond question will be shown by future inquirers to be erroneous.

In the Catalogue of the Copenhagen Museum, of 1710, lapides ceratmiae and glossopetrae appear as in older collections, but they are not looked upon as in any way explaining the true nature of cerauniae. Stone hammers and flint daggers are described by name, and reference is made to Louis Hennepin's account of Louisiana and the use of stone weapons by the Indians," and also to their use by the Greenlanders. Attention is directed to bronze weapons, and although the author cannot understand why the early inhabitants of the country preferred bronze to iron, he admits that such was the case and cites the well-known passage in Hesiod, and refers to Homer and the figures on Trajan's column. He quotes Claude Du Molinet's suggestion, that the reason why bronze objects only of early date were found is that iron more readily decayed.

Museum regiutn, i., 7, Nos. 64 and 67 (ed. 1710).- Op. laud., ii. 3, Nos. 24, 25, 26. 3., ii. 2, No. 80.

The fact that the use of stone had preceded the use of bronze, and the use of bronze that of iron, had long been vaguely suspected. Sir William Dugdale, being perhaps ignorant of the speculations of the learned world regarding gamahus and other cognate subjects, recognized flint implements as artificial objects made by the ancient Britons, " inasmuch as thev had not then attained to the knowledge of workino- iron or brass to such uses." This inference was not, however, arrived at from a consideration of what was to be seen amongst uncivilized tribes, but by reasoning on the finds in ancient graves. Professor Johann Christoph Iselin, of Basle (1681-1737), writing to Father Mont-faucon in 1718, points out that the earliest weapons were of stone, followed by those of bronze, and then by those of iron. This, he says, is proved by the sepulchres of the Germans. The oldest have most frequently arms of brass and those of a later age have commonlv iron." A laroe number of stone axes and bone objects were found in an interment at Cockerel in Normandy in 1685, which satisfied Montfaucon that they belonged to a people who were ignorant of the use of metals. Plot seems to have been the first to appeal to modern examples to illustrate the old.

When Edward Lhuyd was in the Highlands of

The Antiquities of Warwickshire Illustrated, p. 765 (1656, fol.), where a flint celt in the collection of Elias Ashmole is figured. See Wood, Atjienae Oxonienses, iv. 358.

Montfaucon, Antiquity Explained, translated by Humphreys, v., p. 135. London, 1722, fol.

Op. laud., p. 132.

Supra, p. no.

Scotland in 1699 he was shown many stone arrow heads which the people ascribed to the fairies, and remarks, "They are just the same chippd flints the natives of New Engrland head their arrows with at this day; and there are several stone hatchets found in this kinodom not unlike those of the Americans."

He adds that Elf-arrow heads had not been used as amulets above thirty or forty years, from which he concluded that they were not invented for charms, but were once used in shooting here, as they are still in America.

In his arrangement of the Copenhagen Museum Thomsen sorted out and arranged the ethnographical objects as a separate and independent collection, and took steps to provide material for this part of the museum from every available source. After his death it was taken in hand by Worsaae, who modified and improved the system of arrangement, and the museum is still one of the foremost of its kind in Europe. Similar collections have been organized at Christiania and Stockholm. In Eno land we have the g-reat collec-tions of the British Museum; of the India Museum, and of the Ashmolean at Oxford; in Paris there is one in the Louvre and another in the Musee du Trocadero;" besides the Musee Guimet founded at Lyons in 1879 by M. Emile Guimet, presented to the State and transferred to Paris in 1885, the leading object of which is to illustrate the history and practice

The Philosophical Tra? tsaciiof2s, xxviii. (1713), p. 99.

Hamy, "Les origines du Musee dethnographie" x Revue cpEthno graphic, viii., p. 305.

of religion. There is a magnificent ethnographical museum in Berlin,- and others in Leipsic, Hamburg", Dresden, Darmstadt, and various other German towns. There are two in Vienna, one in Rome," and others in Florence, Modena, Venice, Madrid, Lisbon, Leyden, and Moscow. The Asiatic Museum of St. Petersburg is one of great importance, and is founded on the old collections of Paludanus and others, acquired by Peter the Great. The anthropological and ethnological collections in the National Museum at Washington are amongst the finest in the world, and the ethnographical and ethnological publications of the Smithsonian Institution, founded upon the collections in the museum and upon personal observation of the agents of the

Milloue, Catalogue du Musee Guimct. Lyon, 18S3, and later editions.

- Fiihrer durch das Mitseiim fur Volkerkufide, Berlin, 1895, O! Bahnson in Mittheilungen der ajithropologischen Gesellschaft in Wien xviii. (1888), p. 115.

There is also in Berlin an excellent museum of German National costumes Museum fiir deutsche Volkstrachten und Erzeugnisse des Hausgewerbes described in Fiihrer durch die Sammlung des Museums. Berlin, 1895, 8vo. Second and enlarged edition.

Q? olini, Cronaca del Museo Prcistorico ed ettiograjico di Roma. 3 parts. Roma, 1884-87, 8ao. There is likewise the Museo Borgiano,? j, p. 247.

Gaddi, museo etnografico-ajitropologico dclla R. Universita di Modena, Modena, 1870, 4to.

There is an account, translated from the Danish, of the Ethnographical museums of Europe particularly in Germany, Austria, and Italy, by Dr. Kristian Bahnson of Copenhagen, in Mittheilungen der anthropologischen Gesellschaft in Wien., vol. xviii., pp. 109-164. Wien, 1888. Translated from the Danish into Enghsh, The Archaeological Review., ii. (1889), pp. i, 73, 145, 217, 289.

Supra, pp. 96, 115, 116, 182. The Catalogue of 1741 contains a large quantity of Oriental objects, well arranged. Museum Imperiale Petro-politanum, ii., Pt. i., p. 94 sqq. See also Dorn, Das asiatische Museum der kaiserlichen Akademie der Wissenschaften zu St. Petersburg. St. Petersburg, 1846, 8vo.

institution, have been of the greatest value to science. 7here is a fine collection of ethnographical objects in the New York Museum, another at Chicago (the Field Columbian Museum), and there are similar collections in many other of the museums of the United States and a good one in the Australian Museum at Sydney.

The objects to be served by an Ethnological Museum are well stated by General Pitt-Rivers in a memorandum reoardins: the collection which he presented to the University of Oxford:

"The specimens, Ethnological and Prehistoric, are arranged with a view to demonstrate, either actually or hypothetically, the development and continuity of the material arts from the simpler to the more complex forms.

"To explain the Conservatism of savage and barbarous Races, and the pertinacity nth which they retain their ancient types of art.

"To show the Variations by means of which progress has been affected, and the application of Varieties to distinct uses.

"To exhibit Survivals or the vestiges of ancient forms, which have been retained through Natural Selection in the more advanced stages of the arts, and Reversions to ancient types.

"To illustrate the arts of Prehistoric times, as far as practicable, by those of Existing Savages in corresponding stages of civilization.

"To assist the question as to the Monogenesis or Poly- 1 The Academy of Natural Sciences of Philadelphia, Pa., has a good collection of human crania. Catalogices by J. A. Meigs, Philadelphia, 1857, 8vo.

- Bennett, A Catalogue of the specimens of Natural History and miscellaneous curiosities belonging to the Australian Museunt, Sydney, 1837, 8vo; Guide to the Australian Museum, Sydney, Sydney, 1890, 8vo.

genesis of certain arts; whether they are exotic or indigenous in the countries in which they are now found; and, finally:

"To aid in the solution of the problem whether Man has arisen from a condition resembling the brutes, or fallen from! a high state of perfection.

"To these ends objects of the same Class from different countries have been brought together, but in each Class the

Varieties from the same localities are usually placed side by I side, and the geographical distribution of various arts is shown in distribution maps.

"Special Finds, ser-ing to illustrate the correlation of the arts, or of forms, have been kept together."

See also Introduction to Catalogue of the Anthropological Collection lent by Colonel Lane Fox for exjiibition in the Bethnal Green Museum. London, 1874, 8vo. This was the collection subsequently presented by the author to the University of Oxford.

Of an earlier date we have Jomard, "Caractere et essai de classification dune Collection ethnographique" appended to Lettre a M. Fr, de Siebold sur les Collectiom Ethnographiqucs, Paris, 1845, Bvo; and on Siebold, Lettre sur Vutilite des musees ethnographigues, Paris, 1843, 8vo.

In Glasgow we have considerable collections, both archaeological and ethnographical, in the Hunterian and Kelvingrove Museums. In the former there is an extensive and varied collection of South Sea weapons, paddles, carvings and manufactured articles brought home by Captain Cook. The Kelvingrove Museum is primarily a museum of the Industrial and Economic Arts, but has likewise a natural history and an ethnographical department; and contains the Livingstone collection of implements, utensils, and other articles from Central Africa,

See Paton, Sketch Guide to the City Indiist ial Museum of Glasgow, Glasgow 1877, 8vo; and Report on the Kelvingrove Museum, published annually since 1877; P. S. A. Sco., xxii. (1888), p. 351.

The origin of this museum dates back to 1846. In the winter of 1846-47 the Glasgow Philosophical Society, with the assistance of the Town Council, had an Exhibition of Industrial Art, which proved very attractive and financially successful. There was a surplus of 1000, which was set aside for purposes of a similar kind, and it was hoped that the exhibition "may thus have laid the foundation of a museum which may become gigantic in extent." Statistical Account and Catalogue of the Glasgow Philosophical Society's Exhibition of Models of Works of Art, etc., Glasgow, 1847, 8vo. The Daily Exhibitor, Glasgow, 1847, 8vo; Eleven numbers issued (24th December, 1846 9th January, 1847) during the exhibition.

a collection of tools and weapons from New Guinea, and smaller collections from Australia and New Zealand. There is, however, no organized system of collection, and yet no place is more favourably situated than Glasgow for obtaining the necessary specimens. Glaso'ow has a magnificent mercantile fleet and commercial relations with every country under the sun, and especially with the islands of the Indian Archipelago and of the Pacific, but practically no advantage has been taken of this for obtaining material for her museums. Hull has been more fortunate. The large ethnographical collection in the museum of that town owes much to the merchants of Hull, and to the commanders of vessels sailing from the port of Hull.

It is not to be expected that a shipmaster can turn himself into a museum-agent, but the commanders of vessels, trading to out-of-the-way places, have many opportunities of obtaining objects illustrative of the life of the people, their religion, their warfare, their arts and industries. They often do not know that such things are of scientific value. If they do know-that they are appreciated by scientific men, they are generally ignorant of what to get, and what inquiries they are to make and what to record concerning the objects they secure. It would be of immense advantage to our museums if a short memorandum were prepared, stating what sort of objects are wanted and the particulars to be recorded regarding them, and a copy given to each officer of a ship going foreign. Along with the note it would be desirable to issue a book of blank schedules, in which each article as obtained would be described in a systematic and uniform manner.

The British Museum invites the co-operation of all persons interested in Natural History in collecting-specimens for the Natural History collection, and has issued a series of short manuals for their cruidance Other institutions might follow this example. The Natural History section of the Edinburgh Museum was, as we have seen,- built up from the collections of officers in the Royal Navy.

In these days of missionary enthusiasm more advantage might be taken of the presence of cultured and experienced men, in uncivilized countries, to obtain systematic collections of the arts and industries of the people amongst whom they reside. Livingstone was one of the noblest of missionaries, but he was at the same time a most accurate and careful observer, and did much towards our knowledge of the anthropology of Africa. The Jesuit missionaries of the seventeenth century made large collections in the countries to which they were sent, which they forwarded to Paris. The Museo Borgiano in the college of the Propaganda

The following notice has been issued by Dr. Ray Lankester, the Director of the Natural History Department of the British Museum: " Notice. Persons going abroad, who are willing to help the Natural Museum by collecting Specimens, are invited to apply for information regarding Specimens wanted, and the method of their preservation at the Secretary's Office on the first floor. There is no part of the world from which Specimens of scientific value may not be obtained."

The Museum publishes nine small tracts, "Hints for collecting and preserving Specimens of Natural History."

-Supra, p. 158.

2 See Evelyn, Diary, ii., p. 165. London, 1879. These collections are still continued. See, for example, Milne-Edwards Rapports sur diverses collections envoyees au Museum par le P. Armand David, Missionaire de la congregation des Lazaristes a Pekin in Nouvelles Archives du Museum dhistoire naturelle, i. (1865). Bulletin i.

Fide at Rome is filled with the contributions of Roman Catholic missionaries of the present day Although a large number of its objects have been deposited in the British Museum, the museum of the London Missionary Society still contains a considerable amount of valuable material collected by their missionaries in the lands in which they labour. The Evangelical Missionary Museum at Basle is of a similar character. There is a missionary museum at Canterbury; and another at Utrecht supplied with objects sent home by the Dutch missionaries in New Guinea and other parts of the East. The American missionaries have a museum in their college at Ooroomia in Persia. The Moravian missionaries have done much for the increase of our knowledge of the lands in which they labour, both by their writings and by the collections which they have formed.

G. A. Colini, Couezioiii etnografiche del Museo Borgiano in Bollettino della Societa Gcografica Italiana, vol. xxii. (1885), pp. 316, 914; Schmeltz, Ethnographische Musea in Midde7i-Eiiropa p. 49, Leiden, 1896, 410.

"British Micseum Report 1891, p. 62.

Several of the illustrations in Professor Ratzel's History of Mankind (London, 1896, 8vo, 3 vols.) are from objects in this collection. The collection of the Church Missionary Society has also provided a number of the illustrations.

Katalog der Ethnographisclien Sammhmg iin Miiseiivi des Missions' hauses zii Basel, Basel, 1882, 1883, and 1888, 8vo; Schmeltz, Op. laud., p. 40.

There is another and larger ethnographical collection belonging to the University of Basle.

The Archaeological Review, ii., p. 311.

' Bossart, Kiirze Aniueisiuig Natitralicn zit sanimlen. Barby, 1774, 8-o. The author was Superintendent of the Museum of the United Brethren's Seminary, and gives some account of its origin and progress. This volume was intended for the use of the missionaries.

Glitsch, Versiich einer Geschichic der tistorischen Sajmnhing der

Temporary museums of ethnographical objects arranged by the various missionary organizations with a view of promoting interest in their work are common, and are often very attractive. Glasgow contributes largely to the support of foreign missions, and, if the attention of missionaries were directed to the subject, there is no doubt they would give valuable assistance in providing additions to our museums. One requisite, however, is that a scheme be prepared, and distinct instructions given of what is wanted. At present whatever comes into the museum is by chance and in a haphazard way. A museum cannot be built up in this fashion. Objects must be sought for systematically, and unfortunately must often nowadays be paid for, as there are many competitors in the market. In addition to money, time and trouble and skill must be expended in making a collection, and an agent must know what he wants, and be able to distinguish what is valuable from what is useless.

Compare the position of Glasgow with that of any of the three great trading towns of Northern Germany, Lubeck, Hamburg, and Bremen ocelli Germaniae.- Bremen has a population of somewhat less than 200,000 persons. Its Cathedral and Rathaus

Briider-Unitdi Herrnhut, 1891, 8vo; Fiihrer diirch das ethnographisches. Museum. lb., 1891, Svo.

A manual on the subject, edited by C. J. Fison and H. G. Malaher, has been published by the Church Missionary- Society. A Manual for Stewards at Missionary Loan Exhibitions. London, 1899, 8-o. There was a temporary exhibition in Glasgow of this kind, 5-14 March, 1899, which was visited by many thousands of interested visitors.

Heineccius, Scriptorcs de Jure nautico, Dedication. Hal. Mag., 1730.

and quaint street architecture bear witness to its greatness and artistic taste in times long past; while its parks, its library, and museum mark the scientific spirit and culture of the present and the generosity of its citizens, A recent deputation sent to inspect the parks of continental cities reported that Glasgow had nothing to learn. The deputation evidently did not visit Bremen or its park. The town library is a collection of over 100,000 volumes, beautifully kept and housed in a spacious building of purple brick, with a reading-room which the British Museum might envy. The museum (Stadtisches Museum flir Natur-Yolker- und Handelskunde) occupies another large and well-planned building near by. It contains a small collection of archaeological objects, mostly from the neighbourhood, and a special collection from northwestern Germany presented by Mr. P. I. Sparkuhle; a good botanical museum and a large natural history collection. The latter cannot, of course, vie with a national collection, such as that in Cromwell Road, London, but it is very comprehensive and is most methodically arranged and labelled, and includes anatomical and other preparations and microscope exhibits. In London they have recently set up a new whale-house, but the specimens in Bremen are just as interesting, and are even better shown. The orround flat of the new buildinor contains a large ethnographical collection gathered from all the uncivilized portions of the globe, arranged according to countries, with models of dwellings, costume, and illustrations of the domestic life of various peoples. Alongside this are specimens of the raw and manu- factured products of these and of other countries, mostly non-European; tobacco from every place where it is grown, and in every state of preparation; all sorts of fibres, grains, and wood; models of cotton plantations and cotton preparation, of indigo fields and indigo manufacture, of Chinese tea gardens, of saltpetre works and petroleum works. Great numbers of the exhibits and many of the most valuable are gifts from citizens of Bremen. Bremen has also an Industrial museum (Gewerbemuseum), and proposes to set up an Historical museum

Georg Blohm, a merchant of Liibeck, on his death in March, 1878, bequeathed 150,000 marks for the good of the town, and, after consideration of how it might be best applied, it was resolved to expend it in the erection of a museum building. The municipality granted a site; the building was proceeded with and was opened on i6th May, 1893. It is a handsome structure of red and black glazed brick in the old Liibeck style; and contains a splendid collection of objects illustrative of the history and life of Liibeck, a museum of industrial art (Gewerbemuseum), a commercial museum (Handelsmuseum), and excellent ethnographical and natural history collections. The Liibeck collection extends from prehistoric to comparatively recent times, so as to present a continuous picture of the life of the old Hanse city. Amongst the objects illustrative of Liibeck in the medieval and historical periods are models of ships and boats, houses

There is a short account of the B: emen Museum in Schmeltz, Ethno-graphische Miisea in Midden-Europa, p. 92. Leiden, 1896, 4to. The stipend of the museum is 2 00 per annum.

and workshops, domestic furniture, tools and implements, instruments of punishment and of torture, dress and costume, books and bookbindings, manuscripts, coins, medals and seals, maps, plans and views of the town and its buildings. Ecclesiastical life is shown, in a separate section, in clerical vestments and altar furniture, pictures, plate, carvings, and the like. The natural history collection was commenced about the beginning of the present century and is of considerable extent, well arranged and well shown. The ethnographical collection is large and valuable, and dates from the end of the seventeenth century, when Jakob von Melle commenced the formation of his museum, which subsequently passed to Dr. J. C. Lindenberg, burgomaster of Liibeck, by whose son it was bequeathed to the Society for the encouragement of popular Industry (Gesellschaft zur Beforderung gemeinniitziger Thatigkeit). It was then combined with other collections, and the ethnographical side was enriched from time to time with gifts from Liibeckers sojourning in Brazil, Australia, Eastern and Western Africa, and other distant lands. In 1897 the German Anthropological Society held its congress at Liibeck so as to have the advantage of the rich stores of the museum for illustration and discussion at its meetino s. The whole museum is under the management of a joint committee appointed by the Senate of Liibeck and the Gesellschaft zur Beforderung gemeinniitziger Thatigkeit. In addition 1 Filhrer diircji. das Mtisetiin zii Liibeck, Liibeck, 1896, 8vo; Festschrift zur xxviii. Versaiiinlitfjg dcr deutscken atitjiropologischen Gesellschaft, Liibeck, August, 1897. Liibeck, 1897, 8vo.

to the museum the town possesses a large and valuable library of nearly 100,000 volumes. Hamburg is a great seaport, an industrial and manufacturing centre, somewhat resembling Glasgow. In the fifties a small collection of objects illustrative of archaeology and ethnography, prehistoric antiquities, and Hamburg antiquities, was established in the rooms of the Natural History Society of Hamburg. These were embraced under the general title of Historical-Culture Museum (Culturhistorisches Museum), and placed under the management of a Commission. In 1878 the ethnographical department was transferred to the hall in the museum-building in the Steinthorplatz, and took the name of " Museum fiir Volkerkunde." A new Commission was appointed, and at the same time Herr C. W. Luders gave his valuable collection to the city, and, later, parts of the ethnographical and anthropological sections of the rich museum brought together by the untiring efforts of the great mercantile firm of Godeffroy were acquired. When the new Natural History Museum was built, the collections were transferred to it and arranged in 1891. The ethnographical and archaeological

There is an excellent catalogue of these sections, by Schmaltz and Krause, Die Ethnoi raphisch-Aiithropologische Abtheiliing dcs Museum Godeffroy in Ha7 ilmrg. Hamburg, 1881, 8vo. See also Schmeltz, Filhrer durch das Museum Godeffroy. Hamburg, 1882, 8vo. Schmeltz is now keeper of the Ethnographical Museum at Leyden.

As to Johann Cesar Godeffroy himself (1813-1885), see Meyers, Konver-sations-Lexikon, s. v.; and " Museum Godeffroy " in The Popttlar Science Monthly, viii., p. 699. New York, 1876.

The principal part of the ethnographical collection went to Leipzig. The remainder of the museum was purchased by Mr. Damon, of Weymouth.

objects occupy the upper floor in the new building; they are very numerous and representative, and are admirably arranged.

Besides its museum of natural history and archaeology, ethnography and anthropology, Hamburg has a museum of Arts and Industries, a botanical museum and laboratory, excellent chemical, physical and metallurgical laboratories, and a great town library of 600,000 printed and 5000 manuscript volumes. The population of Hamburg is considerably less than that of Glasgow, but its appliances for scientific research are far superior to ours.

What is required in Glasgow as in Hamburg is a Special Commission to take charge of and enlarge the museums of Archaeology, Ethnography, and the Applied Arts. It is not questioned that the intentions of the Town Council have been o-ood; but in order fully to develop the collections, it is necessary that there should be added to the administration a certain number of citizens who have special knowledge of the subject. The plan of a hybrid Commission composed partly of citizens and partly of members of the municipal body, is universal in France, Germany, and the United States, and has been found to work to

Brinckinann, Das Hanibiifgiscjie Museum fiir Kunst und Gewerbe, Hamburg, 1894, 8vo; Mittheilungen der anthropologischen Gesellschaft in Wicn xviii. (1888), p. 143.

Petersen, Geschichte der Hamburger Stadtbibliothek. Hamburg, 1838, 8vo.

2 The Hamburg Observatory is maintained by the town, and does excellent service in the interests of the port. The Town Council of Glasgow recently withdrew a small annual grant to the Glasgow Observatory for transmitting correct time, and it was with great difficulty that it could be induced to restore it.

the greatest advantaofe. It is also the rule in this country where the Library Acts are in operation, and this would be one of the advantages that would have been gained if these Acts had been adopted in Glasgow.

Instead of adopting the Acts the Corporation obtained, in 1899, special powers, under a Tramways Act, for taxing the city for the maintenance of public libraries. Their object was to get rid of a Commission, as required by the general law,- and to secure to the Town Council the sole and uncontrolled administration. Unfortunately, no body less fitted than the Town Council to create and administer libraries could have been selected. The administration must necessarily be that of officials, which may be good or may be bad, but can never be independent, while the Council can thwart good or accentuate bad management. The town museums ars in the same plight. A more vigorous and enlightened administration, and a more liberal expenditure of money are required in order to place the municipal museums of Glasgow in anything like the position which they ought to occupy.

When Professor Bastian was put in charge of the great Ethnographical Museum of Berlin, one of the first steps that he took was to bring together a Committee of Assistance of prominent citizens, which has

"An Act to authorise the Corporation of the City of Glasgow to construct new tramways, to establish libraries, to extend the boundaries of the city, to raise further moneys, and for other purposes " (62 and 63 Vict, c. clxvi.) 29-41.

2 " The Pubhc Libraries Act (Scotland) 1867 " (30 and 31 Vict. c. 37) 14.

3 This was so stated by the Lord Provost at a meeting of the Council on 20th September, 1897. The Glasgow Herald, 21st September, 1897.

been of the orreatest use in obtaininof funds, enllstinor sympathy, and in organising collecting expeditions and other work.

Glasgow has an ancient history extending back to the period of the Roman domination, with many evidences of a much earlier occupation. A museum of Old Glasgow, similar to the museum of the City of Vienna, to the Provincial Museum of Berlin or the Musee Carnavalet of Paris, could still be formed, but the lapse of each succeeding year adds to the difficulty. Alongside of such a museum would appropriately be placed a collection illustrating, chronologically and topographically, the domestic life, home industries and costumes of the people of Scotland, such as we find in every town of any importance on the Continent and in many in America. If there be much further delay in commencing; the formation of a Museum of Scottish History and Civilization, every trace of Scotland as it was will have vanished.

Considering the limited funds at the disposal of the authorities the collections in the University museum are good and are well shown. A large sum of money is, however, necessary to bring the museum and the University library up to present-day requirements and to maintain them in an efficient state. The late 1 The Museum fiir osterreichische Volkskunde, in Vienna, is an excellent example of this kind. of museum. Another is the Museum flir deutsche olkstrachten und Erzeugnisse des Hausgewerbes, in Berlin.

One of the features of the National Museum at Wellington, N. Z., is a beautiful Maori house. The house, besides being a perfect specimen of Maori art, contains a large collection of weapons, household appliances, and other objects illustrative of Maori life and culture.

Maori art is well described by Hamilton, Tie Art Workmanship of the Maori Race iii Neiv Zealand. Dunedin, 1896, 410.

University Commission made no provision for either. They disposed of the whole of the additional grant made by Parliament for University purposes without reference either to library or museum, and left the income of both much as it had been half a century before, althousfh the number of students and of the teachino- staff is doubled, and the need of a well-equipped library and museum has been becoming more pressing every year. The only step which the Commission took in reference to the museum was to issue a draft ordinance for the sale of the Hunterian coins, which they were, with some difficulty, induced to cancel. To bring" the Universitv abreast of the times a further grant is urgently needed for the library and museum as well as for laboratories, apparatus and additional staff. This provision is required not only for medicine and science, but also for philology and history. L The anatomical collections in the University museum and the collections of natural history and geology are used as aids in the teaching of certain subjects, but no practical use is made of the other collections, as no means exist at present for doing so. The recently published catalogue the first of an intended series of the coins in Dr. Hunter's collection shows the rich store of material that the University possesses in this department,- and yet it has

General Report of the Commissioners under the Universities Scotland) Act; 1889, pp. xlii., 237. Edinburgh, 1900. fol.

2 Since the above was written a Lectureship of Classical Archaeology has been established in the University of Glasgow. New rooms for the botanical, anatomical and surgical museums have been provided and a museum of materia medica has been organized.

A grant by the Carnegie Trustees has also done something towards filling up blanks in the library.

to lie dormant for lack of a professor of classical archaeology. In most Continental Universities ample provision is made for subjects such as this, and for takino- full advantaoe of museum collections. In the University of Berlin there is not only a professor but also five privat-docents of classical archaeology whose lectures are based on the collections in the museum, and several of the numerous professors and lecturers on classical philology use the same collections for illustrating their expositions of the classics. In some German Universities there is likewise a Chair of Christian Archaeology, with a special collection of objects and a library of reference for the use of the department. This subject is not confined to Roman Catholic institutions, but is thoroughly and systematically studied in several of the Protestant Universities, and one of the leading German text-books is by the pastor of a rural parish. In Germany museums are made the basis of instruction, and every subject which can be made intelligible by means of a museum is provided with a teacher. With us museums are regarded too much as mere exhibitions, and are too little employed for practical teaching.

Handbuch der kirklichen Kwist-Archdologie des deiitscjien Mitt el-alters by Dr. Henrich Otte, pastor of Frohden. Leipzig, 1883-84. Fifth edition. See as to museums of Christian Archaeology. Op. laud., i., p. 7.

In Berhn there is a "Verein fiir religiose Kunst in der evangelischen Kirche " with a membership of between 300 and 40c.

The faculty which is the least trained, under our present system of education, is that of observation, and yet none is of greater value and none is deserving- of more careful cultivation. While accurate observation is the foundation of all original scientific work, we do comparatively little to develop the habit in the young. Their eyes are holden that they can see nothing save book-print. The museum ought to be an adjunct of the schoolroom, as it now is of the University lecture-room, and children should be trained to observe just as they are taught to cypher or to swim.

In a general sense a museum is a popular educator. It provides recreation and instruction for all classes and for all ages. Its doors are open to all alike, and each visitor gets profit or pleasure by viewing its objects just as he does from a visit to a picture gallery. The modern museum has, however, more definite aims. A museum has now become a recognised and necessary instrument of research; it plays an important part in university and technical instruc- tion, and it should be adopted as an aid in elementary and secondary education.

The majority of our museums are general museums open to the public and intended for the preservation of suitable objects of various kinds, and for rendering these useful for instruction and amusement. In some cases, general museums have been established or extended with the special object of assisting in education, and in others provision is made for carrying on research work. But taking museums as a whole, far too little use is made of them as ordinary instruments of education.

It is the practice in Denmark and Sweden for schoolmasters to conduct their pupils through a department of their town-museum, and to explain to them the more important and typical objects of some section of it. This familiarises the children with the objects, it teaches them what to observe and how to distinguish points of difference, and to recognise points of resemblance. It compels them to employ their own eyes and not to depend upon those of others. Black-board illustrations, photographs, coloured drawings, lantern demonstrations, are all excellent in their way, but, as a rule, a lesson from the object itself is superior to one from a picture of the object. Size, in particular, is a characteristic which is very imperfectly, and often inaccurately, learnt from a drawing. Book illustrations are not made to any particular scale. Each draughtsman pleases himself, and objects in the same set of illustrations are frequently drawn to different scales. The result is that one often forms a wrong conception of an object, which he knows only from a drawing or a photograph. Museum lessons to school children are not unknown in this country, but they are not carried on systematically as part of our educational methods, and are intended rather for amusement than for serious instruction.

Some of our museums are designed for educational purposes; and others prepare specimens, which are lent to schools in their neighbourhood. Some schools are furnished with type specimens of certain classes of objects, just as some are provided with casts of works of ancient art or models of modern machines. All these are excellent in their way, but do not supersede the necessity for larger and more general collections. A school cannot be turned into a scientific academy, and a school museum can seldom be of such extent as to make it independent of other collections. There is too much of so-called science taught in schools at present, and to add to this anything like technical instruction in a museum would ruin elementary education. But children ought to understand something of the ordinary things mentioned in their lessons. These are explained nowadays by woodcuts in school books, or in books of reference, or by diagrams or plates on the walls of the schoolroom, but this should be supplemented by an inspection of the actual objects. The canoes, weapons, implements and house-goods of primitive times, the arms and armour, horse trappings and banners of the

When the Glasgow Normal School was founded in 1836 it was arranged to provide it with a museum and a library. Third Report of the Glasgozu Educational Society's Norinal Seminary, p. 22. Glasgow, 1837, 8vo.

middle ages, as seen in a museum, and explained by a competent teacher, will make a far more vivid impression on the pupil, and will give far more accurate ideas than a library of illustrated books. The same applies to the natural productions of our own and of foreign countries; to the ordinary beasts, birds, and fishes. The sight of even a poorly set up whale in a museum will tell more to a learner than an accurate drawing to scale.

The usefulness of a town or general museum should not, however, be dependent upon the services of a guide. As far as possible it should be self-interpreting; it should explain itself. Museum lectures and demonstrations, in which certain objects or sections are explained by an expert, are of the greatest value and are a happy means, in some cases, of popularising science, and in others of assisting scientific students. The success of such lectures and demonstrations is, nevertheless, dependent, to a large extent, upon the arrangement and display of the exhibits, and the better the work of the curator is done the more does the museum become an instrument of education in the hands of the lecturer.

The majority of the visitors to museums are not classes or societies, but units. Some are students who come for a definite purpose, and to obtain certain information. Others are beginners groping their way, and seeking to grasp more clearly what they have been learnino; from text-books. The laroer number of all visitors have probably no very distinct aim before them, but all wish to know what the object is they are looking at, and to have some general information about it.

For all visitors, methodical and scientific arrangement, easy and unobstructed means of observing, and proper labelling are essential. The objects must be arranged according to the best accepted system. They must be placed so as to be seen. One must not interfere with the other. The cases must not be overcrowded, and every object must be shortly and systematically described. There was something to be said for the scheme of the old museums which brought a number of large and striking objects into view as the visitor entered the museum. The modern method of setting out natural history specimens impresses the imagination of the ordinary visitor, and gives him in a concrete form the result of years of patient observation of many trained naturalists. The display and grouping of the objects are, as far as possible, an exact reproduction of nature itself, and the sight of birds, or other wild creatures in their native haunts, is a source of much pleasure to the least instructed visitor, while it enables the student to see with ease what he probably may never have an opportunity of observing for himself. Better methods of taxidermy, improved methods of arrangement have done much to make the zoological departments of our museums most valuable educational aids. He must be a dull man who does not derive pleasure or instruction from a natural history museum arranged on modern lines. Jv good guide book with a clue-plan should be found

Since the above was written an interesting account of Sir William Flowers work in museum arrangement and the preparation and exhibition of specimens has appeared in Charles J. Cornish's Sir William Hetiry Flower: A personal I Ie? noir. London, 1904, 8vo.

in every museum, but in many museums no catalogue of any kind is to be had. The Trustees of the British Museum have pubhshed, for the use of students, elaborate catalogues of every department and collection. They have also issued a series of short popular handbooks, prepared by the ablest officers of the staff, which have been of immense service in making known the contents of this vast storehouse, and in helping intelligent visitors to understand and appreciate the objects placed on view. The handbook to the Miner-alogical Department in Cromwell Road, for instance, is admirably adapted for enabling any person of ordinary intelligence to view the collection with pleasure and profit. Directions are placed in the gallery informing: the visitor how to examine the exhibits in the most profitable manner, and each exhibit is fully described on its own ticket. Of a similar character is the handbook, by Dr. W. D. Matthew, to the remarkable collection of fossil horses in the American Museum of Natural History in New York.

The full and systematic labelling of specimens is a matter which has of late received much attention and is carefully carried out in the best museums. The provenance of the object is not, however, always recorded upon the ticket, which in many cases is a serious omission. As a rule it is of importance that the exact locality from which each specimen has been obtained should be recorded, and also in many cases the geological position of the spot. If it came from any particular collection this should be specified. This does not apply to archaeological objects alone; it is equally necessary as respects zoological, geological, and other similar specimens. The date of finding or of acquisition is often Hkewise of importance. All these particulars and various others, such as the name and address of the donor, or of the vendor, should be recorded in the accession register, so that as far as possible the history of each specimen may be traced. The price paid should be recorded in the case of purchases. Every entry should be drafted and revised before being inserted in the register, and every ticket should be checked with the reoister before beinor issued.

Every museum should, as far as possible, have a predominant character. This goes without saying in the case of a technical museum; its special character must necessarily predominate. But even in the case of a general museum it should have some distinctive feature. Local museums are necessarily general museums, and should aim at illustrating the town or district in which they are established. Such museums are often crowded with what are popularly-known as curiosities; odds and ends connected with the town, furniture and utensils presented to the museum simply because they are old and out of date, gifts by friends in foreign lands, birds, beasts, eggs, and fossils. When huddled together in cabinets or on shelves such objects are useless for scientific purposes, and curators are far too ready to consign to the dust cart what they do not like, and much valuable material has in this way been destroyed. What is wanted in such cases is patience and method. Antique furniture and utensils, old-fashioned clothes, old prints and the like, when properly arranged, become an historical museum, one of the most instructive and attractive sections of any collection. The materials of the great Northern Museum at Stockholm, of the Historical Museums at Berne and Basle, of the Carnavalet Museum in Paris, are mostly of a common-place character when taken individually, but when grouped together so as to bring before the eye the life of former days, they become of the greatest interest and value.

Neither a local nor any other museum is to be filled with whatever comes handiest, without regard to its fitness. Every object acquired for the museum should be selected with a definite end in view, and should be placed in its appropriate position in relation to the other objects which it is intended to supplement or explain. As a rule, a poor specimen is better than a blank; when a better one turns up the other will be removed. Every museum should aim at having the best available specimens. But while this is so, there is too great a tendency to get rid of exhibits merely because they are not in fashion, or because they represent some exploded doctrine. Obsolete specimens and old arrangements ought in many cases to be retained, for the very reason that they embody forgotten ideas, and are to be shown as illustrating these.

A museum should illustrate the growth and development of civilisation and the arts. Early printed books are of great interest and of considerable value; and in many museums the progress of the art of printing is illustrated by examples. The first forms of machines are often highly prized, and museums of early inventions and old machines are not unknown. The

Specimens which ilhistrated the geology and natural history of two hundred years ago would be just as instructive, in their own way, if we could get hold of them, but many of them have been swept away by modern curators, who forget that at the end of fifty years much of what they now value will, in its turn, have become obsolete, and will be useful only for illustrating the science of the nineteenth century.

Free libraries supported by the rates have spread, and are spreading all over the country. The opportunity of consulting the best books is a boon to all classes of the community. The results have not, however, corresponded with the expectations that were formed by the advocates of free libraries. These libraries have no doubt afforded amusement to large numbers of the population, and the free library is a comfortable lounge for idlers on a rainy day and during strikes, but the solid advantages of the scheme have been confined, almost wholly, to those who are students. Free museums were in the field before free libraries, but have not been so vigorously pushed. In 1845 an Act (8 and 9 Victoria, c. 43) 1 One of the survivals is the fine chipped flint, " coup de pong," found near Gray's Inn Lane about 1690, and now in the British Museum. It is the earliest recorded find of a flint implement in the Quaternary gravels, whether in Britain or in any other country. See Evans, Ancient Stone Implements, p. 581, second edition, London, 1897; Boyd Davvkins, Early Man in Britain, p. 158, London, 1880.

It seems to have been acquired by John Conyers supra, p. 134); from whose collection it passed into that of John Kemp supra, p. 124) then to Sir Hans Sloane, and with his collection to the British Museum supra, p. 139). If all the old collections had been preserved, it may be that other equally interesting finds would have been disclosed.

was passed, enabling Town Councils of boroughs having a population exceeding 10,000 persons to levy a small rate for the establishment of museums of Art and Science for the instruction and amusement of the inhabitants. This was followed in 1850 by the Public Libraries Act of that year (13 and 14 Victoria, c. 65), which recited "that it is expedient to promote the establishment and extension of Public Libraries, and to give greater facilities than now exist for establishing and extending Public Museums of Art and Science in Municipal Boroughs, for the instruction and recreation of the people," and made provision accordingly. Various amending Acts have been passed enlarging the scope of both statutes, and free museums are now commonly joined with free libraries, but there are many such libraries without corresponding museums.

Town Museums, whether supported by the rates or otherwise, are necessarily local museums, and should have a local character. The history of the town, the flora and fauna, the geology and archaeology of the In the same year the Act for the better preservation of Works of Art and Scientific and Literary Collections (8 and 9 Victoria, c. 44) was passed.

2 Lord Bacon recommended that for the proper pursuit of natural science histories should be written, or at least exact catalogues prepared, of the metals, minerals, plants, and animals of each district. Acting upon the suggestion, Joshua Childrey (1623-70) prepared and published: Britannia Baco7iica; or the 7iattiral rarities of Enxiajid, Scotland and Wales, according as they are to be found in every Shire, historically related accordini to the precepts of the Lord Bacon. London, 1660, 8vo, and again 1661 and 1662. It was translated into French, Paris, 1667, 8vo.

Sibbald's Scotia lllustrata, Edinburgh, 1684, fol. was another attempt in the same direction.

district ought to be represented as fully as practicable, so that the townsfolk may have the opportunity of becoming- acquainted with their own town and neighbourhood from the point of view of history and science. A town museum should have as its aims amusement, culture, scientific study and research, and technical instruction. If you join any knot of labouring men, or some family party as they go round a good museum on a holiday, you will be surprised to find what intense enjoyment they have in looking at well-known natural objects, the larger animals, the brilliant plumage of birds from far-off lands. They go for amusement and they get it, but in addition they carry away a certain amount of information which is useful in itself and gives pleasure when recalled. A museum is the easiest means of self-instruction. It is one of the surest means of producing enlightenment and of raising the people above the depressing influence of dull and common-place surroundings, Ingenuas didicisse fideliter artes Emollit mores, nee sinit esse feros.

To the more thoughtful visitor the museum is an instrument of culture and education. In it he has presented to him the results of science in an easily intelligible form. A museum has inspired many a youthful visitor with a love of nature, and is the means by which the amateur naturalist can most readily and most certainly enlarge his knowledge and test the correctness of his own observations. Schoolboys and young men are always to be seen comparing their specimens with those in the museum cases, identifying species, or checking their own identifications. To the man of science a crood museum is essential. Its collections are a fair index of what has been ascertained on any particular subject, and give him a definite basis from which to w ork., A local museum may be made conducive to the development and improvement of the trade and industries of the place. Commercial, economic, and technical museums, to which reference has already been made, have been of the greatest benefit to the towns in which they exist. Several of our town museums have added to their collections a special section to illustrate the industries of the place. This is as it should be, but the system might be greatly extended. A handicraftsman may be no great reader, and may not be able to follow detailed accounts, such as are given in technical handbooks, of machinery, designs, or manufacturing processes, but every workman understands and is interested in his own craft, and can appreciate and profit by actual examples illustrating the development and improvement of some pattern or movement, some tool or process. The eye of the artificer is trained and his taste cultivated by the study of form and colour as displayed in the productions of the most skilful workmen. Chantry often mentioned the inconvenience he had experienced in his early days from the want of opportunity of training his eye by the inspection of the best models. Familiarity with such models insensibly cultivates the taste and trains the eye of the artist. It is said that the Romans only besfan to esteem art after the collection of statues in the city had increased to such an extent as to make them common. Having become accustomed to look upon beautiful objects, they gradually came to understand and to appreciate them. " Where a people have free access to the means of instruction afforded in the memorials of their past success, in the arts of civilization, and can glory in the names which have made their country renowned by genius, and skill, there is hope of a new birth to greatness; nd however free and powerful, where our people ar6 systematically excluded from the sight and enjoyment of the proofs of our present refinement and progress in the arts, and never by the remotest chance see such testimonies of the national growth to greatness of our progress from early times in art and science, or learn to be proud of our national history by its monuments of its heroes by the memorials of them which art can alone provide, there is an element of decay,"- The establishment of science and art museums has been of great service in improving the artistic side of our manufactures, and has in this way been of substantial advantage to the manufacturing industries of the country, and if these museums were more systematically used they would be of still greater advantage. Technical schools and colleges are springing up on all hands, but a technical museum is a necessary adjunct; and every town that has a technical school or college should endeavour to supplement the teaching of lecturers by the town museum,

C. H. Wilson, On the Formation of Provincial Museujhs and Collections of Works of Art, in Transactions of the Architectural htstitute of Scotland, 1854-55, P- 56.

just as they provide technical books in the town library. In Glasgow we have an admirable School of Weaving, Dyeing and Printing, with a small but appropriate museum. As a complement to technical instruction in the construction of the loom, in the arts of weaving, calico printing and dyeing and in designing, a series of carefully selected examples of different kinds of looms, of woven and printed fabrics of various descriptions, of the materials used and the designs employed, such a museum is essential. But in a manufacturinq town in which weavino- and calico printing are amongst its leading industries, the public museums should make special provision for assisting these industries. To a certain extent it is now done, but the scheme could with advantage be much extended. Glasgow is one of the great centres of shipbuilding, and its museums ought to represent much more fully than they do models of the hulls of vessels of all types arranged in sequence of development, the scheme of rigging and sails of sailing vessels, the machinery of steamboats, and the various apparatus required on shipboard.

Writing nearly fifty years ago, an eminent Glasgow citizen, Mr. Charles Heath Wilson, pointed out how municipal museums might be utilised in connection with local architecture: "To take one item of a municipal museum architectural designs let us think for a moment what London might have possessed, had the municipality but entertained the idea which I now present to you, had the plans, elevations, perspective views, and models of all the buildings, which, since the time of Sir Christopher Wren, have been successively laid before that great corporation been preserved in one place. Consider for one moment the priceless value, the indescribable interest of such a collection. When in London with my colleagues of the Council, we visited dusty depositories in search of such municipal treasures, we found one sketch by Wren, the sketches by Thornhill for his Chiaroscuri in the Cupola of St. Paul's, and very little sketches they were, and besides these, thickly coated with dust, some half-dozen models of city improvements. Our municipalities pay for drawings and models, it is only necessary, to frame, glaze, register, and preserve them. I think that I need hardly speak of the value of such collections, for reference, for instruction, and for a variety of purposes which must present themselves to your minds."

The arts and crafts a. re not the only things that can be advanced by a museum. It can do much for a trading community. Articles of commerce, the raw materials, the processes by which these are obtained, the manufactured goods, the style in which they are made up, the boxes and bales and wrappers most suitable for each market can all be shown with advantage in a commercial and economic museum, and the town museum of a commercial community should as far as possible serve the purpose of such a museum. We are being constantly reminded that trade is lost to this country because British manufacturers and merchants will not provide the

On the Formation of Provincial Museums and Collections of Works of Art, in Transactions of the Architectural htstitute of Scotland, 1854-55, p. 59.

class of goods wanted by particular countries or will not make them up as foreign buyers desire. This, to a certain extent, is true, and insular conservatism is blamed, but it is not the only reason why our manufacturers do not meet the requirements of foreign customers. Ignorance has more to do with the matter. Whenever the British manufacturer knows precisely what is wanted, and is satisfied that it will pay him to make the necessary alterations on his machinery, designs or methods he will make it. If he could examine the article required, ascertain by inspection how it is to be used, and what form, size, or design is more suitable for one market than another, he would have reliable data on which to act. Without this the reason for the change proposed may not be obvious.

The museum of a county town ought to have an agricultural section. Many County Councils provide lectures on agricultural subjects; but there is much that the farmer and the husbandman can learn by the eye in an appropriate museum, and it is far easier and pleasanter to learn by observation than by the ear. Information so obtained is more firmly grasped and retained than if got from a book or a lecture. Hence the necessity and the importance of methodical arrangement, of concise and accurate labelling in every museum.

As an instrument of scientific research a well-equipped museum is nowadays indispensable A museum is once again, as in the days of the Ptolemies, a place for study; and one of the features of a great museum such as those of W ashington, and Harvard, of the Natural History Museums of London or of Paris, is the provision made for systematic study and for following out special lines of research. A working library, a laboratory, and a workshop are the essential adjuncts of the modern museum, just as a lantern, with screen and slides, and an electro-motor are part of the apparatus of every scientific lecture room. Every Professor of a branch of science requires a museum and a laboratory for his department; and accordingly in all our great universities and other teaching institutions we have independent museums of botany, palaeontology, geology, mineralogy, and zoology, of anatomy, physiology, pathology, and materia medica, of archaeology prehistoric and historic, classical and Christian each subject taught having its own appropriate collection. The provision and maintenance of these collections, and of the apparatus needed for turning them to account, add largely to the cost of scientific education as compared with even a few years ago, but it is impossible to teach any branch of science or to carry out any scientific investigation without such appliances. The subdivision of labour, the specialisation on small sections of a great subject demand special collections and apparatus to meet their needs, so that the cost of scientific museums and their accessories is ever expanding. One general museum used to be thought enough for a well-equipped University. This is now supplemented by a score of departmental collections, and these are found insufficient. Such collections, however, are for teaching and working purposes merely, and do not supersede the general collection, which requires to be far more extensive and representative than was formerly deemed necessary, even in a strictly scientific museum. Each branch of science is dependent upon its neighbour, and each shades into the other. It is impossible, for instance, to study living forms of plants or animals without reference to extinct forms, and a palaeontological collection must supplement the botanical and zoological departments. The palaeontological shades into the geological and the geological into the mineral-ogical department, and so on. If we seek to illustrate human progress, we enter upon a vast and ever-widening field. Anthropologists and archaeologists are slowly reconstructing in visible form the history of the past. Each part is being fitted into its place like the articulations of some ancient animal, and the skeleton is being clothed with muscle and tissue and skin as it was in life. It is in the museum that this is being done, and to enable it to be accomplished the museum-authority must aim at full and extensive collections, and these must be arranged with the greatest care and fulness of knowledge.

The laboratory and the work-room make considerable demands upon the resources of a museum. Large quantities of material for research must be provided, a thing which was hardly thought of until recently. The note books of a student in his laboratory work are now considered a better test of his training and progress than a sheaf of certificates of attendance upon lectures. Observation, reflection and resource are developed in the laboratory.

Skilled assistance is required in a museum to an extent which, a generation since, was unknown. It is impossible, however, without such assistance to utilise the collections for the purposes of research or to employ them as means of instruction and for the training of observers and investio-ators. The relation between collection and apparatus, teachers and workers must balance. Material is useless without apparatus for treating it, research cannot be pursued without workers, teaching without demonstrators and students. The salary account has consequently increased and will continue to increase. Printing is an additional item of expense which a good museum must incur. The work in the museum to become useful must be communicated to the world and bulletins containing information as to the results of research, the preparation and mounting of specimens and the accessions to the collection should be issued. Several of the American museums publish such bulletins and collect them into volumes at intervals. The Novitates Zoologicae of the Hon. Mr. Rothschild's museum at Trin are well known.

A oreneral museum cannot be turned into a school of research, and it would cease to be a means of general instruction and information if it were. But by means of type specimens and judicious arrangement it can at once satisfy the wants of the scientific visitor, of the student, and of the ordinary visitor. From lack of space very few museums are able to display all their specimens in such a subject as natural history, and even if they could it would not be wise to do so, as many objects are injured by exposure to light and also by dust which invades the best constructed cases. It is sufficient for ordinary purposes to exhibit merely the typical objects, but a notice placed beside the examples shown should state that the other members of the series can be seen upon application to the curator. It is also desirable, in some instances, to change the exhibits from time to time, so that all the more important should be shown in turn. Most museums have duplicates. These should not be shown, as this only leads to confusion: duplicates are, however, always useful for special examination or experiment, or for exchange.

A picture gallery and a library are regarded as essential in every well-regulated town. Why should a museum not be considered equally necessary? A museum is a library of illustrations, bibliotheca sine libris, as it has been termed by Schelhammer, and it is just as important to provide objects for study as to provide books which tell about them. A library of classical archaeology is of little use without a museum of ancient sculpture or of casts to illustrate it. No one can become a palaeontologist or a miner-aloq: ist without a cabinet of fossils or of minerals. History, as now pursued, is founded upon the study not only of original documents, but of all the objects of public and private life that are accessible. The novelist is not satisfied unless he portrays the times he describes with the accuracy of an archaeologist, and the stage depicts the scene it presents as faithfully as possible. The material for such study and equipment are to be found principally in museums. The descriptions in books, and even the delineations of artists, can be made thoroughly intelligible only by an examination of the object described or represented. To study archaeology without a museum is like studying art without a gallery, or anatomy without a subject. Many of the best modern works on archaeology, such as those of Sir John Evans, Joseph Anderson, and Dr. Robert Munro, of Bertrand and Reinach, Montelius, and Sophus Miiller, Linden-schmidt and Von Sacken, are practically museum studies, systematic expositions of museum exhibits.

An objection often urged against rate-supported libraries is the excessive quantity of poor fiction that is provided and read. But go beyond this and note the books in the hands of the readers in the Reading Room of any free, rate-supported library, and which figure in the official returns as "history," "biography," "travels," "science," or under some other imposing title, and it will be seen that they are mostly books of ephemeral interest, of no real value, and not possessing the merit which many works of fiction have, of being literature. The proportion of standard works either of literature or science that is consulted is very small, and of those that are read still smaller. The readers who call for such books are mostly university or technical college students, who sometimes find the public reference library a convenient place for working up a subject. Comparatively few general readers, and it is they who chiefly use such libraries, consult anything but the class of books that are supplied by the ordinary circulating library.

In the museum there are no "penny dreadfuls, no "pot-boilers." The exhibits placed on view are the best that can be obtained and are the same to every visitor. The casual observer looks upon the same objects as the man of science. The one may derive more instruction from his inspection than the other does, but this is the result of training. The one has learned to use his eyes, the other has not. The museum, however, does not, like the library, require to provide material for the idler as well as for the man of science. Its collections are all of the highest class and of permanent value. The specimens do not grow out of date, nor are they superseded by newer ones. On the contrary, each addition generally enhances the value of those on hand. It helps to complete a group; it illustrates some feature in the former exhibits, and will probably be itself in turn illustrated by some later addition. Another advantage a museum has, as compared with a library, is that the objects are not depreciated in value by being passed through the hands of casual visitors or made vehicles of disease, as often happens with books. It is sad to see in the rate-supported libraries a so-called reader with foul clothes and filthy hands vacantly turning over the plates of some handsome volume, and another burying his face in the outspread pages of a stately folio, and going to sleep.

In no way can time or money be more profitably employed than in providing and maintaining museums. Much requires to be done, and the work should be pressed on without delay. Exhibits of many kinds are becoming scarcer and more difficult to obtain. This applies even in the case of some Natural History specimens, and it is especially so as regards j ethnographical objects. Material is rapidly disappearing. It would be more difficult to furnish an historical museum now than it would have been fifty years ago, but it would be easier to do so now than it will be even a generation hence. Objects of archaeological value are constantly being found, but as a rule they are more suitable for supplementing the collections of existing museums than of setting out new ones. Every year increases the difficulty, for there are certain classes of objects which turn up only occasionally, and when they do they generally pass into some existing collection. On the other hand there is a considerable amount of material that is lost because there is no museum to receive it. This would not be so if there was a local museum. (Objects which would be of comparatively small interest in a general museum acquire a value, when preserved in the place where they are found. This is the function of local museums. A museum is wanted in every county to bring together the objects of interest found in the district, particularly such as illustrate its antiquities and history, its people and their surroundings, their industries and trade.

A large expenditure is requisite for maintaining the older and well-established museums. A general museum must endeavour to keep all its sections abreast of the times, and this requires constant watchfulness, sound learning, great labour, and considerable expenditure of money. The weakest part of a museum is gener-

A notable example of what can be done in this way is the collection made by James Smith, "the Whitechapel antiquary," a working man in London, whose collections have found a place in the Guildhall Museum, and add materially to its interest and value. As to James Smith see the Bibliography Vol. III., s. v. Smith (James).

ally the financial, but as a rule it is the part which can most easily be strengthened.

Money is grudged for museum purposes by the Imperial Exchequer as well as by the finance committees of towns and counties. This arises, to a large extent, from ignorance. Funds are voted readily for the purchase of pictures, but very sparingly for museum exhibits. Town councillors and county councillors are slow to appreciate the value of museums and the necessity of keeping them up-to-date. There is a general impression amongst those who have the control of public money that any collection will answer the purposes of a museum, that once a museum is established it requires little or no attention, and that any person can take charge of it. The truth is, that considerable and increasing expenditure is essential. Large, well-designed, well-equipped, well-heated, and well-lighted buildings are required. A sufficient and competent staff is necessary, and must be liberally remunerated. A museum curator ought to be a man of culture and resource; his assistants must have a thorough knowledge of several branches of science, and must possess much manual dexterity. Specimens niust be got and paid for, and in many cases carefully prepared for exhibition. A museum cannot depend for its supply upon the generosity of friends or the resources of the dealer. Collection in the field is often necessary and a scientific expedition of the most modest character is apt to be costly. Provision must be made for the staff and for a certain number of students carrying on research work, and for the provision of scientific apparatus. For these, and many other purposes, liberal orants are required. The money can in most cases be provided if the authorities see fit to vote it; the material to be collected, the men to carry on ythe work are more difficult to find.

Some museums are under the management of universities and scientific institutions. Others are controlled by town councils and other local bodies. It is essential to transfer the management of the latter to specially selected commissions, composed of persons possessed of knowledo e of the needs and aims of a modern museum. It is sheer waste of public money to entrust to town councils the administration of the funds raised by assessment for libraries and museums. Institutions in the hands of such bodies are no doubt managed, after a fashion, but they are managed not by the councillors but by the officials they appoint, and just to the extent that these gentlemen possess the art of handlingf and humourinor a committee. A museum is the best exponent of science. It tells more than the best text-book. It can give lessons which the professor cannot teach. No one would venture to entrust the preparation of a treatise on archaeology or zoology to a town council, but it is not seen to be quite as ridiculous to entrust the same body with the organization of a museum of archaeology or zoology. Complete devolution is in this case absolutely essential for the well-beingr of museums and for enablinor them to afford the aid that is required for the advancement of trade, of the arts, of science, and of culture.

Prior to 1858 the University of Edinburgh was controlled and managed by the Town Council of Edin- burgh, but the arrangement was inconvenient and inadequate, and adverse to the best interests of the institution, and was abohshed in that year, and the administration committed to a body acquainted with university work, a change which has been of the greatest advantage to the university. The management of a university by a municipal corporation is no more anomalous than the administration of a museum by a similar body, and it is as much in the interests of museums, as it was of the University of Edinburgh, that municipal control should cease. y The formation and administration of museums, their adaptation to changing circumstances and to the requirements of the time are of supreme importance for the well-being of the State, for the instruction and advancement of the people, and should be entrusted, in every case, to a governing body of a stable and non-fluctuating character, independent of party and of the ballot-box, and composed of persons of scientific training, who understand and sympathize with the ends which the museum is intended to serve, and who are able to assist the administration by their skill and experience.

The principal museums of other countries issue bulletins, memoirs, and other periodical and occasional publications founded upon and explanatory of the museum collections, and the results of the work in their laboratories. To some extent this is carried out in Eng-land, but it is on a much more limited scale than is done abroad. Many of our museums do nothing but exhibit specimens; they make no provision for research, and give no encouragement to systematic study. Our municipalities receive large sums of money from the State for educational purposes, but no municipality, so far as I am aware, has devoted any part of its funds for utilizing its museums and publishing the results of research.

The country is slowly awakening to the necessity there is for an adequate and regulated training in every field of culture and every department of industry. One of the most potent engines by which this is to be secured is the museum. Some of our museums are amongst the finest in the world; many are lending valuable assistance to the advancement and appreciation of art and science. A large number, however, are still content to be mere holiday resorts. All, even the best, must advance, and for this end enlightened and sympathetic administration and a liberal income are required. The museum of 1897 is far in advance of the museum of 1847! but it in turn will be old-fashioned by the end of twenty years and when the coming century is half-way through its methods and arrangements will probably be wholly superseded by something better. We are ever moving onwards, but we do not reach the goal.

And men through novel spheres of thought, Still moving after truth long sought, Will learn new things, when I am not.

Thou hast not gained a real height, Nor art thou nearer to the light, Because the scale is infinite.

THE LEYDEN CATALOGUE OF 1591. Supra p. 29.

There can be no doubt that the date, 1591, on one edition of the Leyden Catalogue, is a mistake for 1691. The University was only founded in 1575 after the great siege, and there is no evidence that a museum of any kind existed in 1591. The first collections seem to have been made by Peter Pauw or Pavius, who became professor of botany and anatomy in 1589-

The title-page of the edition of 1683 is practically identical with that of 1591: "In Leiden a. cid ioc Lxxxiii." The 1591 edition is dated in the same way except having Leyden for Leiden and apparently c has dropped out after id. The edition of 1683 was printed by Jacobus Voorn, that of 1591 by J. Voorn, presumably the same person, as the Address to the Reader is in both cases by Jacobus Voorn. If so he could not print both in 1591 and 1683.

There are two copies of the 1683 edition in the British Museum, entered in the catalogue under Voorn (Jacobus); the one is marked b. 482 (3) and belonged to Sir Joseph Banks; the other 1044, c. 34 (i).

Adam, Vitae Medicoruvi Cerinajiorutn, p. 434, Heidelb. 1620, 8vo

The Catalogue of 1591 is identical with that of 1683, except that it contains some additional articles. In the second British Museum copy, 1044, c. 34 (i) there is a contemporary slip inserted as follows " After that these books were printed, these following rarities were brought into the Anatomy Chamber." They are six in number and all appear in the 1591 edition. One of them 'Two blue coat soldiers in their skins" is entered as No. 32 at the foot of page 2 and is preceded and followed by two other specimens numbered respectively 31 and T, T,. Page 2 of the 1683 edition ends with No. 30. Page 3 of both editions begins with No. 31, and the numbers run on consecutively, clearly showing that Nos. 31, 32 and 7 2) of the 1591 edition were an insertion. The second object mentioned in the slip is "a Saw-fish." This is entered in the 1591 edition as No. 104', there being already a No. 104 as in the 1683 edition. It is needless to deal with the other numbers.

The last page of the 1683 catalogue ends with No. 53. There are six additional articles in that of 1591. One of them is "a curious sceleton set up by Professor Nuck."

The oreat anatomist, Professor Anton Nuck of Leyden, was born about 1660 and died prematurely in 1692. He could have made a preparation in 1691 but not in 1591. Many of the objects in both catalogues are gifts from " Dr. de Bils." There can be no doubt that this is Lodewijk or Louis de Bils, the anatomist who died about 1672. There are also various gifts by " Pr. Carpenter, Governor in the East Indies." Pieter de Carpenter, from whom the Gulf of Carpentaria takes its name.

was born in 1616 and died in 1659, which proves, if more were required, that the apparent date 1591 is wrong.

There is an edition in Latin, also printed by Jacobus Voorn at Leyden in 1690 (Br. Mus. b. 482 (3)) which inspection shows was subsequent to the edition of 1683 but corresponds with that of 1591. The Latin equivalent of "two blue-coat soldiers in their skins," is " Sceletus duorum militum qui sua signa deseruerant."

This is a reprint of a list, prepared by a Committee of the British Association which the Association has been good enough to allow me to use. As that list was limited to Provincial Museums, I have prefixed a list of London Museums. I have omitted the columns containing the name and address of the curator, principal officer or owner; the number of visitors weekly; the duplicates for exchange; and terms of admission, as also a considerable portion of the "Remarks" column. In some cases other remarks have been substituted.

In the British Association list "the collections are named in the order of their numerical importance in each Museum; that is according to the numbers of specimens in each department." Where two dates are given, the second refers to removal to the premises occupied in 1887.

M. stands for Museum.

The figures 1, 2, 3, 4 in the " Class" column denote the four classes, in which the Committee arranged the museums in their schedule, founded upon the superficial area of the rooms, the size and character of the collections, the annual cost, the staff, and the number of visitors.

Report. of the British Association. Manchester. 1887, p. 97. London, 1888, 8vo. lb. Bath, 1888, p. 124. London, 1889, 8vo.

-':- 7 i; w"

ii,.- c =" P rt73 . JUSca- -TT–T i J"- J" 2 S c,9"o J" J-n be J xi = "2 s . fe fel?-SS 5-2 o. S o b- S."

1j Sig si U–2-jj-j- I gb (S–S= Srt,-

"5 Ous jiu 53 c; ti h ni- rr-o ri t; rt h; i o g H r o-g5 II 8 J-2 12 U go 2 5-=-S2– = h go 2 St;-PH gc: S ts So o-3 5;-,0 r,0,055 IUi, a j=-o a "J.2 5–C . rt oi-a offl

D CJ-!

4-:. Srt

"rt- C3 r N "-rt N- J d d I "H dc-g. S o".1 dc

CO u b c3—. U.:=- = .0-s o S c: i:. Is o tf r; M.—- p-bc St: i-5!-S-r =? Si" "- "-u-JJ- i) o'Tjs or; o 0.5 o. S 2 K-a xj= x.-c. js r; o't!

3fc-; t re 3 rt–

LIST OF MUSEUMS IN THE UNITED KINGDOM .2-3 (u

C5. aj 4J o Xt3 iz;.

LIST OF MUSEUMS IN THE UNITED KINGDOM 0-i; O ,0-o; fco i-gl M S

Lightning Source UK Ltd.
Milton Keynes UK
UKOW05f2214080813

215098UK00001B/268/P

9 781153 040952